changing welfare changing states

new directions in social policy

changing welfare
changing states

new directions in social policy

John Clarke

SAGE Publications
Los Angeles • London • New Delhi • Singapore

SAGE Publications Ltd
1 Oliver's Yard
55 City Road
London EC1Y 1SP

SAGE Publications Inc
2455 Teller Road
Thousand Oaks, California 91320

SAGE Publications India Pvt Ltd
B1/I 1 Mohan Cooperative Industrial Area
Mathura Road, New Delhi 110 044
India

SAGE Publications Asia-Pacific Pte Ltd
33 Pekin Street #02-01
Far East Square
Singapore 048763

British Library Cataloguing in Publication data

A catalogue record for this book is available from the British Library

ISBN 978-0-7619-4202-3 (hbk)
ISBN 978-0-7619-4203-0 (pbk)

Library of Congress control number: 2003115335

Printed and bound in Great Britain by Athenaeum Press Ltd., Gateshead, Tyne & Wear

Contents

Preface   vii

Introduction   1

1   Standing on shaky ground:
the problem of welfare states   11

2   Taking a cultural turn   31

3   Putting people in their place: the
contested social in social policy   52

4   Unstable states: globalization
and destabilization   72

5   Living with/in and
against neo-liberalism   88

6   Governing welfare: systems,
subjects and states   106

7   Performing for the public   126

8   Unsettling thoughts,
unfinished business   147

References   160

Index   175

Preface

No book springs fully blown and complete from the head of its author. It emerges from determinate conditions and social relations of production. Neither the conception nor the execution of this book would have been possible without the distinctive intellectual environment and working practices of the Open University. It is one of the few places where forms of collaborative intellectual work are valued – and I am fortunate to work in a faculty and a department where the challenges and rewards of collective work are taken seriously. I could not have written this book without the Social Policy Group at the OU or without the encounters with friends and colleagues elsewhere in the faculty – economists, sociologists, psychologists, political scientists and geographers who pursue vital academic and political questions across disciplinary boundaries.

I have also benefited enormously from taking the concerns and arguments of this book out for the occasional trip in the form of seminar and conference papers. I am grateful for both the invitations to, and conversations at, the universities of Bielefeld; Birmingham (before it took the step of closing Cultural Studies); the Graduate Center of the City University of New York; Loughborough; University College, Nene; Newcastle; North Carolina, Chapel Hill; Stanford; and Texas, Austin. Conference papers that got revised and reworked into what follows were presented at conferences of the American Anthropological Association; the Canadian Anthropological Society/Société Canadienne Anthropologique and the Society for the Anthropology of North America; Crossroads in Cultural Studies; the European Social Policy Research Network; the Social Policy Association; and the 'Spacing Social Work' conference at Bielefeld. I feel especially fortunate to have 'discovered' anthropology and anthropologists in this process – especially the CASCA/SANA axis and its commitment to doing hard work in hard times.

Much of the formative work got done while I was a visiting scholar at UNC Chapel Hill. The Open University's study leave arrangements made the visit possible – and Larry Grossberg made it come true. The School of Communications generously accommodated me and I have been fortunate to have friends at Chapel Hill who enable me to think hard, especially Judy Farquhar, Dottie Holland, Bill Lachicotte, Cathy Lutz, Don Nonini and John

Pickles. The conversations ranged from formal talks through sitting in on graduate seminars to relaxed sociability – but were constantly engaging and always thought provoking.

The book has been constantly reshaped by such conversations – at home and away. The following people have influenced me more than they know, even if I fail to make the best of what they teach me. Locally, OU colleagues who have helped to keep me moving include John Allen, Simon Blackburn, Jean Carabine, Allan Cochrane, Celia Davies, Paul du Gay, Janet Fink, Gordon Hughes, Maureen Mackintosh, Doreen Massey, Eugene McLaughlin, John Muncie, Rob Paton and Margi Wetherell. In the many elsewheres, I am very grateful to Davina Cooper, Hilary Cunningham, Ann Davis, Dana Davis, Hartley Dean, Sharon Gewirtz, Akhil Gupta, James Hay, Sue Hyatt, Bob Jessop, Anu Kantola, Cindy Katz, Fabian Kessler, Catherine Kingfisher, Belinda Leach, Winnie Lem, Tania Li, Ruth Lister, Jeff Maskovsky, Wim van Oorschot, Hans Uwe Otto, Christopher Pollitt, Ali Rattansi, Melanie Rock, Sasha Roseneil, Neil Smith, Ida Susser, Fiona Williams, Ann Withorn, Nicola Yeates, Holger Ziegler and the Widersprüche collective.

Finally, a few people have seen me though the whole project. Karen Phillips at Sage has managed to be a friend as well as an editor – and has been patient and supportive in both roles. Gail Lewis continues to be a constant inspiration – insisting on the importance of thinking again, and helping me to do it. Larry Grossberg remains my alter ego – friend, comrade, critic. Our conversations are interrupted by time and distance – but always get picked up again. Janet Newman has taken the trouble, time and again, to make sure that both the book and I came out in good shape. I have lost count of the 'reinventing' conversations, the sharp editing and the thought-provoking suggestions that she has provided. Despite all this support, what remains is my responsibility and reflects my limitations.

Introduction

The idea of the welfare state has served as a political and social touchstone. Once, welfare states were used as a measure of social development – marking the extent to which societies were ready to temper inequalities and ill-fortune, or were prepared to deal with the problems of market failure by making collective provision for their citizens. More recently, political attacks on their value and viability have been taken as evidence of the failure of collectivism, the rise of neo-liberalism or the destructive impact of globalization. Rather than embodying the long march of progress, welfare states are now discussed in terms of their decline, end, retrenchment or transformation. This book is about what has been happening to welfare states. More accurately, it is centrally concerned with how we *think about* welfare states and their changing fortunes.

This is an important distinction. This book is not a comparative or international survey of welfare states. There is a rich field of such studies, and I will make much use of them during the course of this book. But I see no reason to add to them, since they are also part of the problem that this book addresses. They typically use impoverished and unreflective conceptions of welfare states – most often as systems of income distribution or redistribution. These welfare states also seem to operate in 'thin' social landscapes – peopled only by economic forces, socio-economic groups ('classes') and political parties. I will be arguing that a much richer scholarship has been developing over the last twenty years about welfare states and their contexts. This work enables us to think of welfare states as more than income distribution systems – and to grasp their relationship to social landscapes in much more dynamic, contested and complex ways. For example, a whole variety of studies have suggested that welfare states have something to do with the formation of social divisions other than class – shaping gendered and racialized positions (and the forms of inequality associated with them). Welfare states have something to do with the construction of citizenship and the questions of who is included as a member of a nation, and under what conditions. Welfare states have something to do with the management or regulation of 'problem' populations. They may indeed involve the exercise of power, control and authority over subordinated social groups, rather than the benevolent provision of benefits and services. All these suggest that reducing them to 'distribution systems' misses important dimensions and dynamics of welfare states.

The book argues that we should 'think again' about welfare states – and that we should think better. Studying welfare states should engage us in thinking difficult thoughts: how welfare states might be more than one thing at once; how they may be experiencing multiple and contradictory pressures for change; and how the dominant tendencies and trends might be being resisted, deflected or refused by other social forces. Such a view might also enable us to escape from the oppressive requirement to make binary choices: choosing between the 'end' and the 'survival' of the welfare state, or between the state and the market. Such binary structuring of theoretical choices induces an intense sense of frustration that what we might know about welfare states and their transformation is constantly being squeezed into analytical straitjackets that inhibit our capacity to think productively.

In part, this book is a product of my marginal relationship to the study of welfare states and those academic disciplines that usually lay claim to the term: political science, sociology and social policy. Within such disciplines, the dominant tendencies have been objectivist (the welfare state is an object of study whose features may be discovered through investigation) and structuralist (both welfare states and their social, economic and political contexts take the form of distinct and identifiable structures – institutions, classes, parties, states etc.). My own intellectual formation took shape largely in tension with such orientations. I encountered sociology as it messed with phenomenological, interactionist and hermeneutic approaches that foregrounded the construction of meaning and the 'social construction of reality' (Berger and Luckmann, 1966). The link between sociology and cultural studies for me came primarily through the 'new' sociology of deviance and its concern with forms of social control. I met cultural studies as it developed an approach to the contested and conflictual production of meaning as a terrain in which social groups struggled to create and maintain forms of domination and subordination. I am a product – and a part – of what has been described as 'the cultural turn' in the humanities and social sciences (Chaney, 1994; Clarke, 1996; 2000a; 2002b; Steinmetz, 1999). So, in this book, I have tried to bring the perspectives of the 'cultural turn' into a productive engagement with the problems of studying welfare states. This is not a matter of theoretical overthrow of one perspective by another, but a view that working in and through the dynamic tensions between these different approaches might better illuminate welfare states and what has been happening to them.

It is, therefore, a rather idiosyncratic approach to thinking about welfare states. It draws on a strange array of analytical, empirical and theoretical resources garnered from diverse sources. Both my own intellectual development and the institutional settings in which I work predispose me to a 'border crossing' practice – discovering useful, valuable and exciting things elsewhere, beyond the conventional disciplinary habitat of social policy. Before noting some of these 'elsewheres', though, I want to stress that even 'at home', social policy has been a fertile and productive ground for rethinking and critical engagement with welfare and welfare states. Too much of this gets lost, repressed or forgotten when analysts move to 'the big picture'. Such big pictures tend to feature 'the usual suspects': the big battalions of globalization, neo-liberalism, modernity (or postmodernity), post-Fordism, or the needs/interests of capital. In the process, questions about contradictory, complex and uneven processes get written out of history while 'welfare states' are made to testify to the power of whatever motor of change is being discussed (see also Mann, 1998). My border crossings have taken me to a variety of other disciplinary places – cultural studies, social history, geography and anthropology. Each of these offers resources to enrich our grasp of welfare states (what they do and mean); the shifting landscapes in which they operate; the processes of change and realignment they undergo; and how they intersect with people's lives in complex ways. Each of these other disciplines feeds my concerns partly because they have experienced or been part of the 'cultural turn' that has arrived in social policy, political science and political economy much later than elsewhere (but has been fiercely resisted in the same manner). Such refusals take a grimly familiar form: the assertion of the 'real', 'material' or 'fundamental' knowledge produced by 'proper' social sciences, rather than the (unproductive) fascination with the ephemeral, epiphenomenal and 'merely cultural'. Despite this, I remain committed to (obsessed with) the view that this tension might be productively explored, rather than left as a dispiritingly barren opposition.

This is also a difficult book because it is about arguments and analyses that do not proceed in a simple logical sequence. Nor is it disciplined by the systematic display and exposition of 'evidence'. I am not apologetic about this, but social policy is an odd academic setting for such an approach. It is often understood as a 'junior' subject – an 'applied' subject, indeed – that exists below the high table of 'real' disciplines and receives their wisdom gratefully. This position is the result of processes of feminization and infantilization through which social policy is subordinated. Its 'applied' character predisposes it towards a 'feminized' identity: the useful rather than the academic; the 'handmaiden' of the state or government rather than an actor in the realm of pure knowledge (where the big boys play). But its subordinate status is also infantilized: the 'knowledge' provided for it needs to be 'predigested' and turned into simplified but usable gobbets, rather than the 'difficult' knowledges of real disciplines. I think of this as the 'Heinz baby food' model: the creation of puréed and reduced knowledge that can be easily consumed and digested. Big conceptual shifts, and the big arguments around them, tend to arrive late and simplified in the field of social policy. They appear as new truths that we can 'apply' – but shouldn't mess with. As elsewhere, I think that subordinations exist to be contested and resisted.

So what follows is an attempt to generate useful knowledge by forcing different approaches into difficult conversations. This, I think, defines my 'method': the construction of creative encounters between different and contending perspectives in a way that refuses to settle, or to think that it is a matter of coming down on one side or the other. These are often perspectives (and people) who would rather not talk to one another, so the 'conversations' are occasionally a little strained and uncomfortable. But since my experience is one of being frustrated by the non-existence of these conversations, I think it is worth trying to make them happen. Too often, claims are made in one place that are challenged or undercut by knowledge generated elsewhere. For example, the much asserted 'end of the welfare state' has to confront evidence of sustained high levels of spending on 'social protection'. Alternatively, claims about citizens having become 'consumers' might need to distinguish between modes of address (or interpellation) and identification. People might be hailed as consumers – but this does not guarantee that they act, or think of themselves, as consumers. And, of course, there is a further problem that even consumers do not necessarily behave like the 'consumers' imagined in economic or marketing models (Gabriel and Lang, 1995). So, I think we may learn things – analytically and politically – from forcing some of these conversations around welfare states. My view of such encounters rests on a view of 'rethinking' as a continuing process – rather than a one-off event. Part of the pleasure of writing this book has been discovering the challenge to 'think again' on a regular basis. I hope that some of the liberating sense of that challenge has survived the writing process.

My interest in this sense of 'dynamic tension' derives from a conviction that there are always things being forgotten, repressed or ejected whenever we offer accounts and analyses – and that keeping such things in play, or bringing them back into view, may make a difference. The book engages with several forms of premature closure feature that need to be challenged. Let me just note their presence here. One is the disconcerting insistence that narratives are linear and unidirectional – the trajectory that leads unerringly to the 'end of' something (welfare states, nation-states, collectivism, for example). A second is the strange form of pseudo-history perpetrated by many social scientists where we move *from* the (overunified, simplified and rather tedious) past *to* the (overunified, simplified, but much more exciting) present. Such accounts also tend to tell us that the process is over: we have arrived at the new condition and there is no 'unfinished business'. A third closure is the slippery claim that some forms of analysis are more 'real', 'material' or 'basic' than others – a 'truth claim' that should be treated as sceptically as all others, whether founded in biology, genetics, human nature or economics. Finally, there is the perverse exclusion of questions of contradiction, resistance, contestation and instability from accounts of welfare state transformation. Such exclusions allow for the telling of compelling, linear and inevitabilist narratives – but only at the expense of not seeing struggles to transform welfare states as uneven and unfinished. They also lead us to ignore the different directions envisioned or imagined in such struggles.

I will have much more to say about all of these stumbling blocks in the course of the book, but highlighting them here signposts the sort of analytic thinking that I want to develop. This book does not deliver a new 'theory of the welfare state'; indeed it has no ambition to do so. We have enough theories that turn up to tell us what we will find. I have an interest in a more mobile and unfinished sort of 'theorizing' that orients us towards the problems of trying to understand the present – as a conjuncture of the complex and multiple routes that brought us to this point. It might also help us to see the different ways out of the present that there might be (rather than following the carefully constructed motorway that dominant forces direct us to use to get to their future). This, I think, is part of the 'good sense' of cultural studies as an intellectual project. It is described in a wonderfully suggestive metaphor by Stuart Hall:

> I want to suggest a different metaphor for theoretical work: the metaphor of struggle, of wrestling with the angels. The only theory worth having is that which you have to fight off, not that which you speak with profound fluency. (in Grossberg, 1996: 265–6)

I think this is a vivid – and vital – view of theorizing, one in which advances are made through engaged argumentation, rather than through the application of a fixed and stable theory to an empirical phenomenon. Hall has consistently promoted a view of conjunctural analysis as the most challenging, and most politically important, intellectual task. It is the most challenging because it involves such careful attention to the multifaceted, 'overdetermined', complexity of the conjuncture – the particular situation that is the result of 'many determinations', rather than the latest example of a major force of change. It is politically important because it speaks to the relations of force that shape the present – and its characteristic instabilities and possibilities (more extensively discussed in Hall, 1996). This orientation leads me to write this book with a series of concerns in mind. I have tried to develop:

- a view of social institutions, arrangements and relationships as 'constructed' (and therefore both challengeable and changeable – though not necessarily easily);
- linked to a view of them as contested – the focus of multiple and potentially divergent or opposed projects or designs for their future (even if there are dominant forces and voices); and
- an approach to institutions, arrangements and relationships as contradictory – containing antagonistic pressures, forces, interests and potentials (that may be contained, but may also overflow their containment).

This more 'contingent' view of social formations challenges their apparent naturalness, solidity and inevitability. This is an urgent analytical and political consideration when we are confronted by more insistent views about the inevitability, necessity and inescapability of the dominant forces and tendencies of the age (the irresistible rise of globalization, neo-liberalism, the new capitalism, individualism, consumerism etc.). In practice such irresistible forces are resisted (though not always successfully) and it matters that our analyses recognize and register such interruptions of the march of power. It matters because we should not tell stories that reproduce or reinforce the illusions that dominant forces try to construct. They want us to believe in the inevitability of their rule – so we should not describe their rule as inevitable. They want us to accede to their vision of how the world should be – so we should not close out the possibility of other imaginings of how the world might be. They want us to succumb to the 'natural' conditions of competitive capitalism – so we should not reinforce its authority by attributing to it more reach, potency and effect than it has.

We are pressed upon by the weight of these stories of power. They testify to power's all-embracing, all-pervading and inescapable achievements. They squeeze – in material and symbolic ways – the spaces that we inhabit. The point of an orientation towards the constructed, contested and contradictory composition of the world is to create breathing and thinking space: to lift the pressure, to find the 'leaky' parts of the system and the weak points of its embrace. Such an orientation – the stress on the constructed, contested and contradictory – leads to a different view of change and transformation. It invites narratives that are about the uneven, unfinished and unstable character of change. In particular, it is a claim that we have not yet arrived 'at the end' and that being unfinished matters analytically and politically.

This is not a view that everything is 'in flux', constantly contested and immediately changeable. Such romantic celebrations of fluidity and resistance produce only the mirror image of structuralism's obsession with solidity, power and closure. In the process, postmodernist claims about flux and fluidity tend to conflate different levels of analysis. It may be true that, abstractly, everything is contingent, polyvalent, contestable and changeable. In concrete situations, however, social arrangements have differing densities, proving more or less resistant to change. They are also more or less contested: some pass themselves off as natural features of the social world for generations. Similarly, everything may have different potential meanings, but this is empirically only significant in the process of contestation: the struggle to articulate alternatives to the dominant, established and heavily sedimented meanings. It is, as I argued above, the tension here that is potentially productive: the problem of understanding *both* how some arrangements get produced, stabilized and settled as 'structures', *and* how they may come to be unsettled, contested and changed.

The scope of the book

I have already noted that this is not a systematic comparative study of welfare states or welfare systems. The comparative literature on welfare states is extensive and growing (e.g. Alcock and Craig, 2001; Cochrane, Clarke and Gewirtz, 2001; Huber and Stephens, 2001; Kingfisher, 2002; Sykes, Palier and Prior, 2001; Taylor-Gooby, 2001a). Much of this is overshadowed by the work of Esping-Andersen and his analysis of welfare regimes and transitions (1990; 1996). The growth of comparative studies reflects two core issues about welfare states at the beginning of the twenty-first century. First, there is a growing concern with 'dynamics' rather than static comparison – an interest in transition, trends and trajectories in place of the classification of settled states, systems or regimes. Secondly, it reflects a greater interest in the forces beyond the nation-state that may be influential in reshaping welfare states – forces or pressures that are international and global. Although, as I will argue later, these questions are often oddly theorized, the rapid growth of comparative analysis speaks to the 'unsettled' character of welfare states and their changing contexts.

In contrast, this book engages in extremely unsystematic comparison – using examples and illustrations from diverse national and regional settings to raise questions about the transformations of welfare states and how they are being theorized. My interest in comparison, then, is more about what questions are posed by the juxtaposition of examples than about what is revealed by typologies or case by case analysis. What, for example, do we gain from contrasting the 'end of welfare' in the USA with the dismantling of state welfare in the former Soviet Union, or with the demand for basic public welfare in Africa? In particular, what are their implications for how we think about globalization and welfare states? This is an approach that, I am sure, will frustrate and irritate those who do engage in systematic comparison. It is, so to speak, 'all over the place'. There is little I can do to avoid such criticism since I am deeply committed to the practice of using divergent examples and illustrations to develop analysis and argument. Being 'all over the place' has other implications: one is that places matter, and that more careful attention to the shifting arrangements of spatial relationships and political-cultural formations may be important.

Despite drawing on diverse examples, there is an implicit spatial structure to the book. It has a predominant focus on the United States and the United Kingdom. Behind this is a rather less developed interest in European welfare states (allowing for the fact that 'Europe' is itself an unsettled and shifting space: Fink, Lewis and Clarke, 2001; Hudson and Williams, 1999b). Beyond them are regions and nations that are used more suggestively – and tentatively – to pursue analytical and political problems (for example, about the spread and limits of 'neo-liberalism'). I am conscious that I am not an 'expert' in relation to any of these places, or their welfare systems, policies and politics. My knowledge is partial, fragmentary and uneven – but I can live with that, since I have no ambition to be that sort of expert. The geopolitical structuring of the book is shaped by the combination of two processes. First, it reflects the dominant structure of attention in comparative social policy. The 'European' welfare states of Northern and Western Europe have been the predominant foci for comparative studies – extended intermittently to other Anglophone settings – Australia, Canada, New Zealand and the USA. The USA, in particular, has exercised a long-standing fascination over comparative studies – such that explaining 'American exceptionalism' has been a major preoccupation. Comparative social policy extends unevenly to Central and Eastern Europe (itself a reinvented political and cultural 'space' with changing boundaries) and sometimes to 'Mediterranean' welfare states. Rather less is written about welfare states, systems or policies outside the West/North axis. This layered structure of attention reflects particular configurations of politics and power.

Secondly, the UK/USA axis has always exercised a particular fascination over me – and speaks to questions about the political and cultural formations of neo-liberalism (e.g. Clarke, 1991; 2001c). European welfare states – and the shifting shape of 'Europe' – form a second focus of comparative work with my colleagues at the Open University (e.g. Cochrane, Clarke and Gewirtz, 2001; Fink, Lewis and Clarke, 2001). Such work has pressed precisely upon questions of changing relations between nation, state and welfare – and about the construction of a 'European' model of welfare that exists in tension with the Anglo-Saxon or neo-liberal model (Leibfried, 2000). But one of the shocking discoveries to be gained from encounters with geography, history or anthropology is that these places – 'the West' – do not exist in isolation from 'the rest'. This is, as Akhil Gupta (2000) reminds us, not just the effect of contemporary globalization. It implies the shifting field of relationships created and recreated in different historical orderings of the global. The transition from colonial relations to postcolonial ones marks not just the colonized – but also the colonizers. The dismantling of the 'Second World' of the former Soviet bloc is intimately connected to changes in the West – not least the problem of rethinking where the West begins and ends. Somewhere here is a spatially, politically and culturally more differentiated, and more productive, set of approaches to the 'global' than the argument about globalization and welfare states usually allows.

At one level, I know that I do not know enough about any of these places – or the relationships between them – to do them justice. On the other hand, what little I know tells me that attention to them 'makes a difference'. It makes a difference to how we think about welfare states, and about what has been happening to them. So, unsystematic and undisciplined comparison – the sense of being all over the place – is a critical part of the approach taken here, and contributes to the 'unsettling' of taken for granted notions of welfare states (and their nation-states).

The structure of the book

Just as the approach of the book draws on examples and resources from diverse contexts, so the structure of the book reflects a movement across a diverse set of topics and analytic focal points – the construction of the social, globalization, neo-liberalism, governance, and performance management, for example. I think there are compelling reasons for the exploration of each of the issues in the book – and why they appear in the order that they do.

The first chapter starts with the deconstruction of 'welfare states', reflecting the efforts of political projects during the last twenty years to deconstruct or dismantle welfare states in practice. Such efforts have aimed to break up the institutional, political and cultural arrangements that linked welfare and the state together in the distinctive formations that we learned to call 'welfare states'. The chapter also looks behind welfare states to their institutional and conceptual shadow – nation-states, which have also been subjected to unsettling pressures. The unsettling of these familiar combinations of nation, state and welfare provides the political and analytical springboard for the book.

Chapter 2 takes a cultural turn to see what this might mean for social policy and the study of welfare states. It draws out a set of orientations to thinking about culture – and about thinking culturally. The cultural turn provides the intellectual leverage for my concerns with the constructed, contradictory and contested nature of social formations and the subsequent chapters try to put these into practice.

Chapter 3 pursues questions of the meaning of welfare into an examination of the 'social', exploring the changing content of what counts as 'social' in social policy. Western welfare state development in the 1960s and 1970s – what some have referred to as 'the Golden Age' (Huber and Stephens, 2001) – is not simply the enlargement and enhancement of a pre-given field of benefits and services. It was also marked by a series of intersecting and overlapping struggles to make differences, divisions and forms of inequality recognized as a basis for social claims on welfare states. Such struggles – around gendered and racialized divisions, and around disability/ablebodiedness, for example – changed welfare states in unanticipated ways. Shifting meanings of the social contribute to the conflicts over welfare – and unsettle the ways in which it is articulated to the formation of nations and peoples.

Chapter 4 moves our attention to the much debated issue of globalization and its impacts upon welfare states and nation-states. I argue that the debate about globalization and welfare states has been unhelpfully dominated by the binary formulation of the 'end/survival' of the welfare state. Instead, I suggest that we need to address the different forms and trajectories of globalization more carefully. This can provide a basis for assessing the ways in which they have 'unsettled' or 'destabilized' aspects of national welfare state formations. The chapter concludes that the dominant tendency in globalization is the 'neo-liberal' project of making the world conform to a distinctive vision of freedoms (those of capital, markets, and consumerism) sustained by 'flexibilities' (of labour, of regulation and of states).

Chapter 5 takes up the issue of neo-liberalism and its central role in the politics of anti-welfarism and anti-statism. Neo-liberalism has been the dominant force in thirty years of assaults on taxation, public spending and collective provision as inhibitions to enterprise and freedom (understood as the freedoms of the market). But the chapter is also concerned with the limitations of 'neo-liberalism' as an explanation of welfare state change: not all changes can be satisfactorily accounted for as meeting the aims and ambitions of a neo-liberal project. This also raises questions about the geopolitical and cultural limits of neo-liberalism in practice. Its advance has been partial, deflected by the challenges of building alliances and making accommodations, and encountering diverse forms of resistance and refusals to 'go with the flow'. Even its successful installation as the conventional wisdom of supranational agencies is not the same thing as 'ruling the world'.

Chapter 6 brings the question of the state back into sharper focus. I suggest that we have seen the 'remaking' of states, rather than their abolition. There are substantial variations in how states are being remade, but common trends include the blurring of the boundaries of public–private; the shift from direct rule to dispersed coordination through processes of decentralization, devolution, contracting and partnership; and the influence of the 'new public management' on governance processes and relationships. This chapter explores some current analyses of shifting forms of governance and governmentality as a basis for reflecting on the forms of instability inherent in governing welfare in the twenty-first century.

Chapter 7 examines one distinctive feature of the new governance in more detail. In the context of a variety of economic and political pressures, there is a new obsession with managing the 'performance' of public services. This chapter examines some of the contradictions inherent in 'performing for the public'. Taking the idea of performance seriously, it asks how different parts of a dispersed state manage their performances, and for what audiences. I am particularly interested in the instabilities that are put into play by the scepticism and cynicism of audiences: the problem of public doubt.

Chapter 8 draws together some of the main arguments from across the book about how to think about welfare states and what has been happening to them. It argues that the diverse struggles to transform welfare states – to abolish them, to create them anew, to preserve them and to remake them in the image of new needs – are continuing, rather than concluded. Welfare states have been profoundly unsettled, and remain deeply contested for both material and symbolic reasons. Welfare states (in their various forms) make a difference to how lives are lived. They shape the conditions in which people make a living: the material conditions that they support (and deny); the forms of relationship and practices that they make possible, sustain or repress; and the forms of imagined solidarity between people that they represent. The chapter reasserts the importance of thinking of these processes as constructed, contradictory and contested – and of thinking of their results as uneven, unfinished and unstable.

one

Standing on shaky ground: the problem of welfare states

What's been happening to welfare states? During the last twenty years, welfare states have been the focus of campaigns to transform, reform, abolish and modernize them. Political movements, governments and other agents sought to change their core features and sought to persuade us – as taxpayers, citizens and consumers – of the urgent need for change. The terms used were diverse – and are a tribute to the flexibility of language within contemporary political discourse. 'Reform', for example, was made to mean a variety of things from dismantling existing programmes of welfare provision to creating new ones. Established expectations about the relationships between welfare, the state and social progress were disrupted. Since the mid 1970s, welfare states were rarely far from the centre of the political action in the advanced capitalist societies of the North and West.

Not surprisingly, the changing fortunes of welfare states have also been the centre of considerable, and concerned, academic attention. In part, this atten-tion reflects a mixture of uncertainty and anxiety. Up to the end of the 1970s, mainstream and critical studies of welfare states tended to share an assumption about the central and necessary role that the collective provision of welfare played in advanced capitalist societies. Critical challenges were focused on transcending the limits, constraints and failures of existing welfare states. From diverse, though overlapping, standpoints – feminism, anti-racism, user move-ments and Marxism – analytical and practical challenges emerged that sought to expand the possibilities of collective welfare. The rise of the New Right shat-tered the assumption of the necessary link between advanced capitalism and the welfare state – as 'rollback', 'retrenchment', 'retreat' and even the 'end of welfare' came to dominate the politics of welfare. In a peculiar way, 'progres-sive' criticisms of welfare states were simultaneously appropriated, outflanked and outbid by new, and powerful, political forces.

The debate about what has been happening to welfare states is wide rang-ing. It draws on many perspectives, theories, disciplinary legacies and political orientations. This chapter begins with an overview of conceptions of welfare state change. However, my purpose is not to summarize and comment on the whole field of arguments. Rather, I argue that this disjunctured field of argu-ments suggests some analytic problems in the ways in which we think about welfare states. As a result I argue that some critical reflection on the key terms of the field would be useful – in particular, the ways in which 'welfare', 'nation' and 'state' are combined. This critical reflection has to take account of the way in which those terms – and their institutionalization – have become destabilized and unsettled in practice. What happens when taken for granted terms become problematic? Such shifting meanings (and their social consequences) pose the problem identified in the chapter title: how do we go about 'standing on shaky ground'? Finally, I argue that these concerns – with shifting and contested meanings – point to the importance of the 'cultural turn' in the social sciences, and its value for social policy and for the study of welfare states in particular.

What's going on?

Welfare states and their changing fortunes have been the focus for a rapidly growing academic literature – not just from social policy scholars but from economists, political scientists, anthropologists and sociologists. There are many reasons why welfare states should be such an object of fascination. State involvement in welfare has been a significant, if not defining, feature of modern (or late twentieth century) industrialized and/or capitalist societies. Welfare states mark a distinctive site of connection between people, politics and policies, constructing relationships, practices and identities of 'citizenship'. In the last three decades the state's involvement in welfare has been one of the most fiercely contested focal points of national and international politics – particularly those associated with the rise of neo-liberal views about the proper relationships between economy, society and government. Changing forms of national and international economies, shifting domestic pressures and demands, new forms of governing, have all been identified as intersecting with welfare states. So, what has been going on? Figure 1.1 summarizes some of the main conceptions of welfare state change. I have tried to capture some of the main directions and dimensions of change identified by social scientists looking at welfare states. I don't claim that this survey is exhaustive, but it indicates something of the range of views at stake in studying welfare state change.

The list in Figure 1.1 might not be exhaustive but it is puzzling. Don't we know what has been happening to welfare states? What we see here are different analyses of change and the highlighting of different dimensions of change. This is not a situation that is going to be settled by a classical social policy retreat to empiricism: 'just give us the facts'. Each transformation here is driven by a conceptualization of welfare states that foregrounds particular features, relationships, or institutional forms. So, attention to the structure of welfare provision provides accounts of the transformation of structures and systems – from state to market, or from state monopoly to welfare pluralism. Others identify the shifts in the dominant political ethos or orientation – from welfare state to enabling or disciplinary state. Still others focus on the changing forms of 'welfare capitalism' – from Fordism to post-Fordism, or welfare to workfare. Attention to different features gives rise to different accounts of the trajectory or tendency of welfare state change.

From		To
Fordist	——————▶	Post-Fordist welfare state (Burrows and Loader, 1994)
Welfare state	——————▶	Workfare state (Peck, 2001)
Welfare state	——————▶	Enabling state (Gilbert, 2002)
Bureaucracy	——————▶	Markets (or quasi-markets) (Bartlett, Le Grand and Roberts, 1998)
State monopoly	——————▶	Welfare pluralism (Rao, 1996)
State	——————▶	Market (Loney et al., 1987)
Welfare state	——————▶	Disciplinary state (Jones and Novak, 1999)
Modern welfare	——————▶	Postmodern welfare (Leonard, 1997)
Welfarism	——————▶	Post-welfarism (Gewirtz, 2002)
The social	——————▶	The death of the social (Rose, 1996a)
Male breadwinner system	——————▶	Dual breadwinner system (J. Lewis, 2000)
Keynesian welfare state	——————▶	Schumpeterian workfare regime (Jessop, 2000a)
Public administration	——————▶	New public management (Butcher, 1995)
Hierarchy	——————▶	Networks (Rhodes, 1997)

Figure 1.1 *Transforming welfare states*

This list raises two problems for me. The first concerns the process of telling history as a unilinear shift from one thing to another. In the process, both the past and the present/future tend to be simplified – and sometimes grotesquely oversimplified. For example, accounts of the 'state monopoly' of welfare provision omit the roles played by private and voluntary sector agencies in the old welfare system. Similarly, accounts of the old welfare state as embodying 'universalism' (Giddens, 1994) repress evidence of a whole variety of exclusions and subordinations that were the focus of challenges, around gender, age, able-bodiedness and more (see also Mann, 1998). But the same point may be made about conceptions of the present/future which 'over-read' the depth and scale of change. To what extent do politics, policies and practices persist from the 'old'? If they do persist, how do we make sense of their coexistence with the 'new'? The temptation in telling definitive stories is to treat such persistence, or other troubling deviations, as merely 'residual', doomed to wither away. I will be arguing that looking carefully at such coexistent trends and their contradictions is politically and analytically important. Simplifying histories (the account of From–To) tend to squeeze out the most interesting and important dynamics.

Some analysts are attentive to this problem, recognizing that tendencies are both dynamic and unfinished. There may also be other trends and tendencies. Jamie Peck's study of 'workfare states' is exemplary in his insistence that:

> The political economy of workfare cannot be reduced to a unidirectional process of enacting a grand vision of 'post-welfare' but instead finds its expression in the messy histories and uneven geographies of institutional change. For all the simplicity of the workfare narrative, the realities of workfarist policy-making are inevitably more complex, more provisional. It is for this reason that workfare is conceived here as a regulatory *project*, as a set of political and institutional strategies, rather than as some kind of stabilized, post-welfare *state*. (2001: 19, emphasis in original)

This emphasis on strategies and projects that attempt to dominate is helpful. Rather than assuming their success or coherence, Peck opens up questions of unevenness – political and geographical. This feels more like the 'messy' realm of politics and policy in which unfinished and contested attempts are made to transform welfare states. Despite this, Peck's study illustrates a second problem about the analysis of welfare state change – the tendency to isolate and focus on a limited conception of welfare. Partly because his attention is focused on the welfare–workfare nexus, Peck's view of both welfare and workfare is addressed specifically to policies directly engaged with the regulation of labour markets and labour forces. In the process, other elements of welfare provision are ignored. Does the shift to post-Fordism associated with workfarist regulation also have consequences for pensions, family policies, health care, social care, and the national conditions of welfare citizenship? It could certainly be claimed that they do – but my point is that Peck leaves these other dimensions of welfare out of the story. He shrinks 'welfare states' to their labour market policies and connections. I will argue later in this chapter that this focus reflects a long-standing bias in political economy analyses (which leave out much of what welfare states do). But it also derives from Peck's starting point of US meanings of welfare and workfare – and I will return to these meanings of welfare later in this chapter.

Such selective focusing on welfare states explains part of the puzzling and paradoxical list of changes that I summarized above. Different conceptions of change draw attention to particular aspects of welfare states and their transformation. For example, welfare states may have experienced the introduction of markets in a variety of forms: exposure to competition, internal markets and forms of quasi-consumer choice (Clarke, 1999a). But what do we make of those areas of policy and practice where 'markets' have not been the dominant principle of change? The temptation, of course, is to leave them out of account in favour of a clear analysis. We might want instead to argue for a richer analysis that is attentive to the complexity and contradictoriness of a social phenomenon like a welfare state.

The end of the welfare state?

Many of the analyses summarized above claim or imply a shift from the welfare state to something else: the workfare state, the disciplinary state, the enabling state or welfare pluralism, for example. The temptation to announce the 'end of the welfare state' is clearly a significant one. It both makes for a good story and (in some cases) sounds a political alarm, signifying a loss of political and social values, resources and forms of solidarity. Nevertheless, an increasing number of studies have argued against such 'epochal' views of change. Instead, they have argued that it is more accurate to talk of the 'persistence', 'resilience' and 'survival' of welfare states, even in the face of intensifying pressures (Kuhnle, 2000; Kvist and Jaeger, forthcoming; Taylor-Gooby, 2001a). For example, Keesbergen has argued that successive theories of the crisis of the welfare state have, since the 1970s, consistently overestimated its imminent collapse:

> Empirical and historical research necessarily lags behind sweeping theories. But whenever empirical evidence is presented, there seems to be little confirmation of radical changes induced by the dramatic crises that the theories so forcefully prophesied. No doubt, the empirical studies record extensively the immense pressures on, as well as the massive challenges to, the welfare state. Moreover, they provide evidence for incremental adjustment in the major programmes, decreasing growth of social expenditures and retrenchment. But they also demonstrate the substantial gap between the crisis theories and the conservative or neo-liberal political rhetoric of retrenchment on the one hand and the actual resistance against change of most of the welfare state's core programmes on the other hand. (2000: 20)

Much of the available empirical evidence supports Keesbergen's argument that the more extravagant claims might be tempered a little. For example, Table 1.1 summarizes European (EU) states' spending on 'social protection' between 1980 and 2000.[1] This is the period of the sustained attack on welfare states, if not the end of welfare. Although there is a small downward trend in most states during the last five years, this is a decline from a high point in 1993, not the start of the period (Abramovici, 2003: 1). Patterns of growth and decline vary substantially between countries.

Table 1.1 *Percentage of GDP spent on social protection by European states, 1980–2000*

	1980	1986	1995	2000
Belgium	28.0	29.5	29.7	26.7
Denmark	28.7	27.5	34.3	28.8
Greece		15.5	20.7	26.4
Germany	28.6	28.0	29.4	29.5
Spain		17.5	21.9	20.1
France	25.5	28.5	30.6	29.7
Ireland	20.6	24.3	19.9	14.1
Italy	19.8	22.5	24.6	25.2
Luxembourg	26.4	24.8	25.3	21.0
Netherlands	30.4	30.9	31.6	27.4
Portugal	13.0	16.4	20.7	22.7
UK	21.6	24.4	27.7	26.8
Austria		26.7	29.7	28.7
Finland		25.5	32.8	25.2
Sweden		33.7	35.6	32.3
EC12/EU15		25.8	28.4	27.3

Source: Eurostat (1999); Abramovici (2003)

However, gross spending patterns may not be the best available indicator of welfare state resilience, since they may conceal other sorts of changes. Changes in policy, purpose, access conditions, forms of delivery and social-demographic makeup may all be taking place below the level of the data on public spending. An endemic problem of social policy analysis is that the gross data on spending and welfare/social protection programmes say little about many of the issues that ought to be interesting. There are important questions about who gets the money, for what purposes, under what conditions (see, for example, Daly, 1997). The Eurostat data in Table 1.1 tell us nothing about what social protection (or 'welfare') has meant in terms of policy and practice, or about the institutional and governmental arrangements through which it is organized.

1 Social protection denotes social benefits (and the costs of their administration) around eight functions: sickness and health care; disability; old age; survivors; family and children; unemployment; housing; social exclusion (where not classified elsewhere). See Abramovici (2003).

Questions about the *why* and *who* of public spending on social policies are about what welfare means in practice. By contrast, questions about the *how* of spending point to issues of system, structure, process and the governance of welfare: they are about the 'state' part of the welfare state. Many of the transformations summarized in Figure 1.1 address these organizational issues about the welfare state – pointing to markets, welfare pluralism, the new public management and so on. The multiple movements towards expanded roles for the private sector, the third or voluntary sector and the domestic/familial realm raise important questions about the relationships between the state and welfare. What does the state have to do for it to be a welfare state: make direct provision; fund provision; regulate provision; or coordinate multiple providers? Despite the economic arguments from neo-liberalism, competing providers are not simple functional alternatives. Their sectoral location may have consequences for the services they deliver, and for the experiences of working in and using such services. For example, the growth of the welfare state in the 1960s and 1970s had significant employment effects, creating new jobs with (relatively) good conditions of employment – especially for women and, in some countries, minority women in particular (see, for example, Malveaux, 1987). Huber and Stephens argue that the growth of welfare state services was part of a larger social, economic and political expansion:

> Expansion of welfare state services in turn has a positive feedback effect in that it enables more women to enter the labor force and creates demand for labor in these services, a demand that is predominantly met by women. Where welfare services are publicly provided, this leads to an increase of the female public-sector labor force. Increased female labor force participation, particularly in the typically well-organized public sector, increases the level of organization of women through unionization and thus the potential for women's political mobilization.
>
> This process of economic and social mobilization of women also leads to increased political mobilization of women, in existing parties, in women's organizations, in new social movements, and so on. The combined effect of mobilization and of the expansion of the public sector also makes women stronger supporters of the welfare state and the public sector in general and of the political left, reversing the traditional direction of the gender gap. (2001: 47)

This view of the social and political implications of state employment raises questions about how we think about changing sectoral balances and the work associated with them. But it also signals a problem about how we think about the welfare state as an employer and a site of labour, as well as an agency of social policy and practice. Such questions will reappear later in the book, but for now I want to return to the argument about the 'end of the welfare state'. Despite its undoubted limitations, the evidence in Table 1.1 suggests one rather mundane conclusion. Despite the small decline in the later 1990s, welfare spending in EU countries persisted at relatively high levels throughout the period of the assault on welfare. Such data suggest we might not have arrived at the end of welfare – or the end of the welfare state. It is counterfactual evidence in relation to such claims – but it is not very helpful in dealing with the more widespread sense that 'something has been going on' in welfare states.

So, how might we think about 'what's been going on' in a different way? We have problems of establishing the form, tendency and weight of change in part because there is no simple, singular object of study – the welfare state. It is important to learn some of the lessons of comparative study: there are, at the very least, different welfare states. Their histories, structures and trajectories are not identical. Comparative social policy has demonstrated patterns of difference – usually against claims that we are witnessing convergence between nations. Differences exist between national welfare states, between different welfare regimes or types of state, and between different regional tendencies, such as the distinction between European and US models (see, for example, Alcock and Craig, 2001; Cochrane, Clarke and Gewirtz, 2001; Esping-Andersen, 1990; 1996; Huber and Stephens, 2001; Leibfried, 2000; Sykes, Palier and Prior, 2001; Taylor-Gooby 2001a).

But the diversity of welfare state forms is only one aspect of this argument. Equally importantly, welfare states are both compound institutional formations and social 'myths'. They are made up of multiple elements. At the most basic level, 'welfare' is only part of what states do. On the other hand, it is widely understood that welfare states do not exist as coherent singular entities. The competences, capacities and responsibilities involved in providing welfare are differently distributed – functionally, hierarchically and spatially. They also involve diverse relationships with other organizations and actors beyond the state. Just as 'welfare' is historically and comparatively variable, so are states when they are 'doing welfare'. These elements may have their own dynamics, may be subject to divergent pressures and may even be internally contradictory. The banal point, widely understood in social policy, is that 'welfare state' is a convenient shorthand; the more serious point is that it may be an inconvenient shorthand that conceals or obscures critical issues.

Let me return to the different transformations of welfare states summarized in Figure 1.1. One very obvious – and usually irritating – conclusion to be drawn about these different conceptions of welfare state change is that 'it depends what you mean by welfare state'. Indeed, it does. But the meaning of the welfare state is not a simple matter of definition. If it was, we could short-circuit all these difficult arguments merely by imposing the superior – most rigorous, most consensual, most scientific – definition, and then get on with the business of counting. But the problem of meaning is that meanings are not fixed. They cannot be settled by the authoritative imposition of a particular definition. On the contrary, they are changeable and contested. This is the profound sense of 'it depends what you mean by welfare states' – since the meaning of the phrase 'welfare state' is neither stable nor uncontested. This is the point of entry to the cultural turn. Cultural analysis – or cultural studies – works on and through this sense of meanings being contested, changeable and constructed. In the rest of this chapter, I will pursue the destabilization and deconstruction of the welfare state – and examine how its key terms *welfare, state* and *nation* (since welfare states are usually nation-states) have become unsettled.

Destabilization and deconstruction

The welfare state is too readily taken as an obvious and self-evident object of analysis in social policy and related subjects. I am not the first to make this point: as long ago as 1963, Richard Titmuss raged against the elusive and ill-defined character of the phrase, arguing that it should be bracketed in quotation marks (see Veit-Wilson, 2000). Whether this marks Titmuss as an early poststructuralist will not detain us here, but his recognition that the phrase moved – and was given meaning – in the realm of popular consciousness is important. Despite this, most studies of welfare states avoid defining 'welfare state', treating its meaning as self-evident. Typically, such studies tend to treat welfare states as equivalent to a limited operational or functional arrangement (social insurance programmes, for example), or to given and comparable patterns of social expenditure (e.g. Kunhle and Alestalo, 2000).

We may do better to pursue the issue in a different way. The prolific and elusive usage of 'welfare state' is, I would argue, testimony to its political and cultural currency. It is a marker or a symbol of something important in popular understandings and political discourse. At the same time, the fluidity of its use and the absence of rigorous definition mark it out as a *contingent* symbol whose meanings are variable and contested. 'Welfare state' marks the site of major political and cultural conflicts. The phrase is used to define ideals: it is deployed as a normative statement of what could and should be. It has also been used as a negative image. The welfare state can be identified as the cause of, rather than the solution to, social problems, as in the assertion by Milton and Rose Friedman that 'The Soviet Union is the immediate danger perceived by Americans. Yet it is not the real threat to our national security. The real threat is the welfare state' (1984: 73). 'Welfare state' has been a potent mobilizing symbol for a variety of political projects. It is precisely this murkiness of the term – its political, cultural and normative capacities – that makes it interesting. Rather than refining the definition of the phrase, I want to treat its instability, flexibility and mobility as significant features worthy of attention.

My starting point, then, is to recognize the welfare state as a variable social construction (historically and nationally). Then we can deconstruct the phrase 'welfare state' – *and its conceptual shadow, the nation-state* – in order to see why it might be hard to categorize and conceptualize welfare state change or transformation (see also Wincott, 2003). In these terms, we need to think about the welfare state as an invention – a political fiction – an *imaginary* (Lewis, 2000a). What it *represents*, rather than describes, is a set of arrangements in which the state does things that are understood as providing or promoting the social welfare and wellbeing of its citizens. The phrase expresses conceptions of the relationship between politics and policy, between people and government, and between state and society. In the past, it implied a collective orientation to forms of social improvement, progress and betterment (for current citizens and future generations). Its British political-cultural origins lie in the post-war development of collectivist or 'Beveridgean' social policies in the UK – publicly and popularly grasped as the *building* of a welfare state (Briggs, 1961), despite the existence of divergent sources of criticism and challenge (see Clarke, Cochrane and Smart, 1987: 85–123). The wide public and academic circulation of the phrase since then suggests that it functions as what Raymond Williams (1988) called a 'keyword': a focus of political and cultural investment (see also Bennett, Grossberg and Morris, forthcoming). Williams suggested that uncovering the shifting usages rather than the 'proper' meaning of 'keywords' was instructive:

> We find a history and complexity of meanings; conscious changes, or consciously different uses; innovation, obsolescence, specialization, extension, overlap, transfer; or changes which are masked by a nominal continuity so that words which seem to have been there for centuries, with continuous general meanings, have in fact come to express radically different or radically variable, yet sometimes hardly noticed, meanings and implications of meaning. (1988: 17)

Here, I want to decompose the phrase into its two terms – welfare and state – to reflect on the problems of their meaning as well as how they have been brought together into such a potent combination. Welfare is both abstractly elusive and concretely difficult to specify. Sykes (1998: 14) has rightly argued, in relation to comparative studies of welfare state divergence and convergence, that there are important questions of what policies should be considered and why. I have already suggested that comparative studies have tended to ignore this question, preferring to treat welfare states as if they were income transfer programmes. They also tend to treat these income transfer programmes as working on a limited number of axes, typically, socio-economic strata and age groupings (or 'class' and life cycle distributions). However, there are a range of social policies, programmes and relationships that are not always understood – or studied – as part of the welfare state. These include welfare practices and relationships formed at the intersection of the state and the family (the private/domestic realm). Such policies and practices are harder to observe and quantify than the income transfer programmes and have typically been ignored by male-centred scholarship (see, for example, the discussions in Langan and Ostner, 1991; J. Lewis, 1992; Orloff, 1993). As Daly has argued:

> The neglect of gender has also left its mark on which welfare state programs are studied ... Social policies targeted on women specifically, whether as mothers and/or workers, and the dependant-relevant aspects of social provision have tended to be obscured in a scholarship that has mainly been preoccupied with the search for the state's imprint on relations between collective interests, conceived in class, and to a lesser extent, generational terms. (2000: 30)

There are also other state policies and practices with significant social dimensions – criminal justice and leisure provision, for example – that are rarely
included as elements of welfare states, or thought worthy of inclusion in
social policy (see, for example, A. Clarke, 1994; 2000; Muncie, 2000; Stenson,
2000). These might be thought of as welfare-related things that states do in
different ways. For example, some studies have argued that the very high levels of incarceration in the US prison system can be seen as a functional alternative to male unemployment programmes and as a means of managing a
'problem population' (Christie, 1996; Morley and Petras, 1998). However,
penal policies are not conventionally counted as welfare or included in studies of social policy or welfare states. Welfare normally, and normatively,
excludes other state policies and practices that might be understood as elements of social regulation, social reproduction and the management of a
complex social population.

Consequently, explorations of a wider range of state practices involved in
'managing the social' have tended to emerge from critical standpoints – for
example, feminist, Marxist, poststructuralist and postcolonial studies (see, *inter
alia*, Jones and Novak, 1999; G. Lewis, 2000c; Petersen et al., 1999; Stenson,
2000). In such studies, we can glimpse questions of social differentiation and
inequality that go beyond the conventional focus on class. We can catch sight
of the role of the state in shaping, defining and managing the field of social
groups who make up the 'nation' served by welfare (and those who are
excluded from it). Such approaches also call into question the assumption that
'welfare' is benevolent, and that its provision is desired by its recipients (as
users, clients, customers). Questions of control, regulation, surveillance, and
the norms embedded in such processes require us to think of the relationships
between welfare, states and citizens in a more difficult way. Such approaches
also suggest that these processes have a long history, rather than simply being
an effect of the move away from a benevolent welfare state to something
harsher.

The end of welfare as we know it?

These questions about the meanings of welfare are not just academic issues.
There are political, social and cultural contexts in which the meanings of welfare have been contested, challenged and changed. Welfare remains the subject
of conflicting political orientations and pressures. Let me explore one critical
example here: the recent politics of welfare in the United States – particularly
the developments evoked by President Clinton's promise to 'end welfare as we
know it'. The culmination of that commitment was the passing of the Personal
Responsibility and Work Opportunity Reconciliation Act (PRWORA) of 1996
(see, inter alia, Abdela and Withorn, 2002; Mink, 1998; Clarke and Piven,
2001).

Since the 1970s the New Right in the USA has attacked 'welfare' as a key
cause in the economic, political, moral and social decline of the USA

(Clarke, 1991: ch. 5).[2] In the process, it concentrated intense discursive effort on making the term 'welfare' refer to a specific public assistance programme – Aid to Families with Dependent Children (AFDC). This built on a political and institutional separation in the US between 'social security' (based on social insurance) and (means-tested and conditional) 'assistance'. Although the programme distinction is to be found in many welfare states, a distinctive feature of the USA is the close identification of 'welfare' with assistance. The initial distinction – in the New Deal reforms of the 1930s – was both institutional and social. The social security versus assistance structure differentiated social groups in terms of eligibility, accessibility and the conditionality of benefits; such differences were both gendered and racialized (see, inter alia, Gordon, 1994; Mink, 1990; Quadagno, 1994).

In the 1980s and 1990s a whole gallery of associated phrases ('being on welfare', 'welfare dependency', 'welfare mothers', 'welfare queens' and so on) was used to designate AFDC and its (supposed) disastrous social and cultural effects (see, for example, Murray, 1984; Mead, 1992; and the discussions of the right's ideological and discursive strategies in Mink, 1998; Schram, 1995; 2000; Withorn, 1998). But the targeting of AFDC is significant despite its relatively small scope: 'fewer than 5 million adults are on the rolls' with programme costs 'amounting to about 1 per cent of federal budget' in the years before its abolition (Piven, 1998a: 22). This programme, rather than the array of other welfarist things that the US state does, has been systematically constructed as the hegemonic meaning of welfare in the US context. So, social security programmes, covering a much wider range of benefits and a much larger population at much greater cost, are referenced separately – they are not welfare (see, for example, Katz, 1986: 267; Piven, 1997). This does not mean they have been immune from attack and reform, of course (see Clarke, 2001a; Katz, 2001; Skocpol, 1997). Welfare (as AFDC) is discursively constituted as different in terms of the gendered and racialized character of its recipients, referring to lone-mother-headed families, and to black lone mothers in particular (see Neubeck and Casenave, 2001; Gilens, 1999; Mink, 1998; Schram, 2002: chs 5, 6). It was also constituted as different around the moral question of 'desert': welfare was 'unearned', unlike social security programmes based on a contributory model. So, when Clinton announced the 'end of welfare', it meant the ending of AFDC and its replacement by Temporary Aid to Needy Families (TANF) in the PRWORA Act of 1996. The preamble to the Act articulated the purpose of 'welfare' reform in the US context:

1 to provide assistance to needy families so that children may be cared for in their own homes or in the homes of relatives;

2 I have used the slightly archaic sounding phrase the 'New Right' here as a shorthand for pointing to the shifting alliance between different right-wing strands and movements in the USA (and elsewhere). In the US context, it is a way of keeping both neo-liberal and neo-conservative tendencies in view - both of which have been influential in shaping the 'end of welfare' and much more. Picking out either neo-liberalism or neo-conservatism seems to me to miss something of the richness and density of the political and ideological range and repertoire of the Right.

2 to end the dependence of needy parents on government benefits by promoting job preparation, work and marriage;

3 to prevent and reduce the incidence of out-of-wedlock pregnancies and
establish numerical goals for preventing and reducing the incidence of these
pregnancies; and

4 to encourage the formation and maintenance of two-parent families.
(PL 104–93, Title I, Section 401; quoted in Mink, 1998: 66)

I want to emphasize the particular political-cultural conjuncture involved in
the USA. Welfare was given a specific cluster of meanings in which policies,
programmes and a distinctively imagined social demography of dependency
and dangerousness were articulated together in the imagery of 'the underclass'
(di Leonardo, 1998; Katz, 1993; Morris, 1994). It is important to stress the separation between AFDC-as-welfare and social security programmes because the
'end of welfare' in the USA is not the same as the end of *welfarism* (as a political, ideological and institutional formation). It is also not the same as the end
of the *welfare state* (either as an imaginary or as a set of policies, programmes
and institutional practices). I do not mean that they are entirely separate, but
a number of studies of US welfare reform have run welfare, welfarism and welfare state together as though they were interchangeable. For example, Jamie
Peck's (2001) recent study of the rise of workfare is based on the USA as the
'leading/bleeding edge' of reform but elides welfare, welfarism and welfare
states. Blurring these distinctions has analytical and political consequences. It
ignores the specific discursive constitutions of 'welfare' (as AFDC) and misses
the political conditions and effects of defining welfare as a specifically gendered and racialized formation (the demonology of black lone mothers and the
'underclass'). I will return to the 'end of welfare' later in the book, because it
occupies such a central symbolic place in the contemporary politics of welfare.
But, for now, I want to insist that the political accomplishment of the 'end of
welfare' does not make sense without attention to how the *meaning* of welfare
was constructed in a specific political cultural setting.

In a related example, some of these meanings of welfare – and welfare
reform – could also be found in the UK. Here I want to look in detail at a small
piece of 'welfare discourse' in which some strains associated with shifting
meanings of welfare can be detected. In 1998, the Labour government published a Green Paper on 'welfare reform' (and one of its co-signatories was the
Minister for Welfare Reform). Tony Blair's Prime Ministerial preface announced
the principles of reform and struggled with a strange conceptual uncertainty:

> But the principles guiding reform and our vision of the future of the welfare
> state are clear. We want to rebuild the system around work and security. Work
> for those who can; security for those who cannot … *For those of us who*
> *believe the welfare state is not just about cash benefits, but is about services*
> *too* – like health and education – there are hugely ambitious programmes of
> reform under way in our schools and hospitals. (Prime Minister, 1998: iii, my
> emphasis)

This consultation paper announced New Labour's first plans for 'welfare reform' (creating 'a new contract for welfare'). These were mainly addressed to the task of reconstructing the benefits system (unemployment, sickness, and disability benefits and pensions), although other policy areas (education, health etc.) were referred to in passing. But the Prime Minister's introductory remarks strike an oddly uncertain note: are we talking about reforming 'welfare' or the 'welfare state'? Here we encounter the familiar problem of meaning: what is included in the welfare state? Is it about cash benefits – or about services, too? The problem is posed in rather strange terms ('those of us who believe ...'). It is not clear who this 'us/we' might be – or who the others are who do not believe it. This might be thought too obsessive a view of language and the minutiae of its use, but I want to suggest that there may be good reason to treat this sort of linguistic and syntactical discomfort as pointing to problems of articulating difficult discursive repertoires. Here, I would argue that these signs of strain mark the effect of 'discursive borrowing'. New Labour, and the Green Paper in particular, were attempting to appropriate the language of 'welfare reform' from the USA to shape and inflect the reform of benefits in a more 'workfarist' direction (on some of the institutional and policy routes, see King and Wickham-Jones, 1998; Peck, 2001). I would suggest that the uncertain and ungainly formulation of 'those of us who believe' shows the signs of strain in the effort to reconcile the US discourse about 'welfare' (and welfare reform) with an older (and dominant) British/European discourse about 'welfare states' (expressing a larger conception of public welfare provision). The 'welfare state' discourse is also one deeply embedded in the history and self-conception of the Labour Party in Britain – and has proved a difficult terrain for New Labour to address in its endeavours to 'reform' and 'modernize' Britain and 'public services'(see, *inter alia*, Clarke and Newman, forthcoming; Finlayson, 2003; and Chapter 7 in this book).

What welfare means and how its meanings vary ought to be central matters of concern in the study of social policy. Such meanings work across the intersection of the political and institutional realms. Arguments about welfare (and the proper role of the state in relation to it) have been absolutely central to political/ideological shifts in the last thirty years. Those arguments are complexly – and unevenly – connected to changes in the politics, practices, relationships and institutional architecture of welfare provision. So, what are the implications for studying welfare states? 'Welfare' – both what it means and what is done in social policy – is currently unsettled (Hughes and Lewis, 1998). What was 'taken for granted' – produced by the post-war settlements that sustained what Huber and Stephens (2001) call the 'Golden Age' of the welfare state – can no longer be assumed. So our inquiries might explore both the question of how the 'taken for granted' meanings of welfare – and welfare states – came to be settled, if only temporarily, and the contending projects that now attempt to redefine welfare and its relationship to the state. The (once) assumed coherence, unity and stability of the 'welfare state' was a *constructed achievement*, not an essential feature of its institutional arrangement. The current practical political-cultural destabilizations of the meaning of welfare (and welfare state) prefigure and point up the *necessity* of analytic deconstruction. In order to trace the diverse projects and processes of reform, we need to grasp the dynamics of settlement and destabilization.

Shaky ground: unsettled formations of welfare, state and nation

At this point I want to argue for a general orientation to exploring the contested, contradictory and unstable dimensions of welfare states – with an attention to the 'contentious practices' in which welfare is embedded (Holland and Lave, 2001b). By contested, I mean to draw attention to the fact that the welfare states are made – and remade – by complex social and political forces whose alignments vary between societies and over time. Welfare states are not just the institutionalized expression of the balance of class forces or parties. As different social and political projects contend the meaning of welfare (and the forms of its institutionalization), so welfare states are subject to multiple and potentially contradictory forces and pressures. They may be engaged in promoting family life, creating flexible labour, managing collective security, ensuring intergenerational reproduction, regulating the distinction between 'entitled' citizens and 'benefit tourists' and 'false claimants' ... and more. Welfare state 'settlements' represent a temporary alignment of social forces and pressures – a reconciliation of the multiple and contradictory interests and demands within a dominant view of the 'nation' and its needs (Clarke and Newman, 1997; Hughes and Lewis, 1998). But settlements imply the possibility of their becoming 'unsettled' or destabilized. They are vulnerable to coming apart – either because the forces that they attempt to contain may be unmanageable, or because new forces and pressures arise that rock the settlement's foundations. I have long been fascinated by Gramsci's (1971) observation that 'the life of the state can be conceived as a series of unstable equilibria' because it captures this oscillation between settlement and destabilization. The idea of 'unstable equilibria' is a guiding metaphor for my arguments in this book.

Alongside this general concern with the contested, contradictory and unstable, I think there is a need for a more 'conjunctural' analysis. This implies exploring how a specific moment is shaped by multiple and potentially contradictory forces, pressures and tendencies. What is distinctive about the present conjuncture is that all three elements – welfare, state and nation – have been destabilized and their institutionalized meanings called into question. Attempts to change the meaning of 'welfare' take place alongside changes to the meanings of 'nation' and 'state'. How they are – and should be – connected is also contested (for example, in conflicts over the 'proper' role of the state in welfare). There are attempts to create new settlements – to fix meanings, to institutionalize them in new political-cultural formations and to naturalize them as the necessary, inevitable and best way of 'doing welfare'. But these are *attempts* at becoming dominant: they are not yet fully settled. They bump into 'old' or residual meanings, commitments and institutions and are engaged by alternative emergent meanings, which imagine different 'welfare futures' (Hughes, 1998).[3] Conjunctural analysis requires attention to the multiple and conflicted possibilities that are condensed into a particular historical moment – rather than merely reading the dominant trend that links past, present and future as if in a simple linear narrative.

This is a period where various once-settled formations (and combinations) have become unsettled. The shift from 'solidity' to 'flux' is a disconcerting one. The title of this chapter – *standing on shaky ground* – is a metaphor for the analytical problem of dealing with a period in which the 'keywords' have all been put into motion at the same time.[4] It is not possible to simply pick up the shifting and contested meanings of 'welfare' while assuming (hoping?) that the 'nation' and 'state' provide solid and unchanging political and conceptual reference points. It is precisely because the nation and state are both unsettled and subject to conflicting attempts to resettle them that 'welfare' is in such flux. Who gets 'welfare', from whom, subject to what conditions, and for what purposes, are questions evoked by attempts to remake nations and to change the place and role of the state.

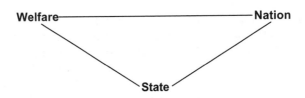

Figure 1.2 *Welfare state/nation-state*

In the post-war period, the configuration of interlocking 'welfare states' and 'nation-states' came to be the taken for granted norm. We understood the institutional density of national welfare states as the developed form of welfare capitalism, even if there were variations (such as Esping-Andersen's 'three worlds of welfare capitalism', 1990), and thought that other places had not yet developed to the advanced point of the European model(s). But welfare, nation and state appeared to be stably and securely articulated, as in Figure 1.2. Welfare was delivered by the state to the people, in pursuit of the national interest, for the purposes of reproducing, maintaining and developing the people. In this form, each of the three terms is implicated in the others. However, this approach makes visible the significance of how the people/nation are con-

---

3 The conception of dominant, residual and emergent meanings is borrowed from Raymond Williams. It is helpful in thinking about how contending meanings coexist in a particular moment. It does risk implying a linear sequence in which residual meanings necessarily decline and disappear. That is not my intention: residual meanings are marked by a history, but may persist or even be revived as re-emergent meanings.

4 The title is taken from a song performed by Etta James ('Shakey Ground' by J. Bowen, E. Hazel and A. Boyd, published by Jobete Music UK Ltd) on the LP Seven Year Itch, Island Records, ILPS 9923, 1988.

strued in the formation of welfare settlements. In the last three decades, each of these terms has been subjected to diverse pressures, forces for change and political-cultural challenges. In what follows, I use the triangle of Figure 1.2 to sketch some of the 'unsettling' forces and processes around the three terms – though they are the subject of rather longer discussion in the rest of the book.

The meaning, desirability, distribution and scope of 'welfare' have been intensively contested through different political projects – ranging from the 'anti-welfarism' of the right to the expansive welfare politics of social movements seeking to make welfare less exclusive, less discriminatory and less punitive. These are crudely summarized in Figure 1.3 (and will be discussed further in Chapter 2).[5]

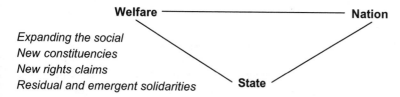

Neo-liberal anti-welfarism
Conservative anti-welfarism
Workfare
Revalorizing the private/familial
Individuation/consumerism

Welfare ——————————— **Nation**

Expanding the social
New constituencies
New rights claims
Residual and emergent solidarities   **State**

Figure 1.3 *Unsettled welfare*

As I argued above, welfare states are also nation-states: they embody conceptions of the 'people' and their 'way of life' – which the state may try to support, reform or improve. States – including welfare states – are part of nation-building (and rebuilding) projects (e.g. Castells and Himenan, 2002; Lewis, 1998a; Ong, 1999). While welfare has been contested, so the nation implied in the welfare-state/nation-state formation has also been subject to new forces and unsettling movements. It has been destabilized by new flows of people, cultures and identities that have disturbed the spatial and cultural boundaries that have been used to mark the 'edges' of the nation (see Figure 1.4). This is not about the 'end' of the nation, but it certainly marks a period of unsettling processes. It is also a period in which nationalism – and nations – are being 'reinvented' and reasserted, even as more relationships and connections (from capital formation to family formation) stretch across national boundaries. Questions of the nation – and the national popular (how the unity of the

5 These political-cultural forces overlap with more conventional accounts of the 'pressures' on welfare states to some extent (e.g. Kvist and Jaeger, forthcoming; Taylor-Gooby, 2001a). They are, however, not identical, not least in avoiding the separate identification of demographic and social change. Such a separation of populations and ways of life from their representation in political-cultural discourse is problematic.

nation – the people – is imagined) – recur across most of the chapters of the book.

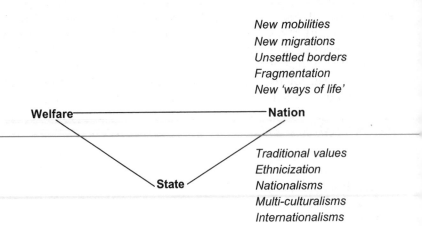

Figure 1.4 *Unsettled nations*

And, of course, the same is true about the 'unsettling' of the state – both in general terms and in its more specific role as the producer and provider of collective forms of welfare. Different processes have affected the state's form and ways of functioning – subjecting it to diverse conceptions of 'reinvention', 'reform' and 'modernization', while relocating it in new systems of governance, beyond and within the nation. Figure 1.5 summarizes some of these (and they are discussed more extensively in Chapters 4, 6 and 7).

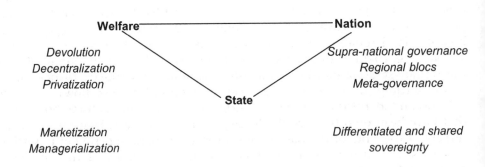

Figure 1.5 *Unsettled states*

In short, each of the keywords – welfare, state and nation – has been subject to a wide range of forces for change, unsettling both their taken for granted meanings, and the institutional forms in which they have been embodied. Each of the terms remains contested: there is no single clear-cut direction in relation to welfare, state or nation, much less in how they are being recombined in new settlements. 'Old' meanings (and the collective identities that they carry) are reluctant to disappear. Surveys reveal continued deep public support for the 'welfare state' – or the collective provision of health care, education, social care and income support (Taylor-Gooby, 2001a). Nations – and their cultural expressions – continue to command loyalty (and intense commitment) in the face of regional and global realignments. Indeed, nations are such a potent source of attachment that new ones are being created. States, as Hansen and Stepputat note, are the focus of sustained, and possibly growing, expectations to 'confer fully fledged rights on an ever growing range of subjects' (2001: 2). This points to the material and symbolic significance of social citizenship. The figure of the citizen is, metaphorically, triangulated by combinations of nation, state and welfare. How they are combined shapes the identity of citizenship: the relationships, the conditions, the rights and the terms of membership. It is this that makes social citizenship so fiercely contested. Citizenship is, as Dean and Melrose (1999: 170–2) argue, a 'strategic terrain' where political projects and popular discourses meet.

These 'old' or 'residual' conceptions coexist – in a more or less conflictual way – with current dominant projects to reform nations, states and welfare. They form blockages or interruptions that the dominant strategies of reform and modernization have to overcome. This is perhaps best exemplified in the potent symbolism of the National Health Service as an embodiment of collective, publicly provided welfare in the UK. There are also emergent meanings, carried in new projects that aim to create new 'solidarities' and new possibilities. These might challenge narrow nationalism, the dissolution of the public realm, the new conditionality of welfare citizenship or the new disciplinary and discriminatory approaches to regulating the social. Raymond Williams (1989) used this distinction between dominant, residual and emergent cultural forms to keep open the analysis of particular conjuncture. It guides us to look beyond the dominant, to recognize what it was trying to displace (the residual or residualized) and what it needed to exclude or coopt (the emergent). This coexistence of residual and emergent formations alongside the current dominant tendencies is a reminder that the formations of welfare, state and nation are unsettled and that their reconstruction is *unfinished*. Settlements – the political-cultural underpinnings of welfare systems – are only ever temporary, however deeply embedded, institutionalized and naturalized they might appear. How they become unsettled – and what projects aim to create new settlements – are critical issues in the analysis of changing welfare and changing states. This is what 'standing on shaky ground' implies – and why it demands our attention.

My aim in this book is to foreground the contested, contradictory and unstable character of the formations being studied in ways that make it possible to think of the processes of change as unfinished. While I believe it is possible to draw out dominant forces and tendencies, I also want to know how they are contested, and what difficulties they have to negotiate when they attempt to construct a new settlement or equilibrium. Equally, while I think it is important to trace such moments of settlement that solidify, institutionalize and naturalize a specific formation, I also want to insist that we understand the conditions that make them temporary. How do they become vulnerable to challenge, destabilization and reconstruction? For me this is the most powerful contribution that the 'cultural turn' can make to the study of welfare states and social policy, and this is the focus of the following chapter.

two

Taking a cultural turn

This chapter takes up some of the arguments from Chapter 1 – in particular the relationships between welfare states and the construction of nations. I am going to approach these issues through a detour around the cultural turn – because cultural analysis makes visible distinctive aspects of the connections between welfare, state and nation. Culture has become a keyword, actively used in both academic and policy circles. Culture is a recurrent way of signifying issues of diversity and difference in complex/modern societies (even though it was first used to talk about simple/traditional ones). Culture works as a rhetorical resource in social and political claims-making (to define distinctive needs and rights). Finally, culture also marks out a significant analytic orientation (as in such phrases as the 'cultural turn' and 'cultural studies'). In all these forms it has enriched and enlivened the study of social life, but it has also been traduced as a deviation and a distraction (too much attention to the ephemeral and 'merely cultural', forgetting the 'real' and 'material'). As is often the case, social policy seems to lag behind some of the other social sciences in arriving at this encounter. The cultural turn has been explored, celebrated and resisted in other fields since the 1970s at least (see, for example, Chaney, 1994; Eagleton, 2000; Jameson, 1997; Ray and Sayer, 1999; Steinmetz, 1999). This chapter:

- considers the conception of culture as property or trait that underpins the dominant uses of culture in social policy (first section);
- examines cultures as cultural formations (second section) and as the results of cultural practice (third section);
- explores the implications of the cultural turn for thinking about how welfare states construct nations – and their 'people' (fourth section);
- takes the racialized formation of welfare in the US as a distinctive example of the connections between nation, state and welfare (fifth section); and
- returns to the issue of the 'cultural turn' and considers some of

the political and analytical arguments that surround it (sixth section).

Encounters between culture and social policy have been going on for some time, at least since nineteenth century social investigators and reformers in Britain worried about the cultures of the labouring and dangerous classes and how they might be improved (see, for example, Lloyd and Thomas, 1998; Pearson, 1974). The term 'culture' has a long and complex history (Eagleton, 2000; Williams, 1988). In the nineteenth century, it circulated widely in public and political discourse. It was used as a term to condemn the instrumentalist utility of industrialization and urbanization that dominated nineteenth century social development in Britain:

> Civilization was abstract, alienated, fragmented, mechanistic, utilitarian, in thrall to a crass faith in material progress; culture was holistic, organic, sensuous, autotelic, recollective. The conflict between culture and civilization thus belonged to a full-blown quarrel between tradition and modernity. (Eagleton, 2000: 11)

In reverse, culture was also used as a term to register the shortfall of 'backward' or 'less civilized' groups from the benchmark of 'civilization' (a.k.a. 'British society'). Investigators and reformers took up culture as a term with which to identify, examine and report on the condition of the 'other' in the British social formation. I have deliberately used 'social formation' here (rather than 'society') to indicate the larger imperial Britain, rather than just the geographical limits of the British Isles or the political limits of the (more or less) United Kingdom. In this sense, Britain's 'others' were to be found in both its domestic and its colonial populations. Techniques, perspectives and concerns were shared between domestic investigators and those examining 'native peoples' in the colonies. Indeed, intrepid investigators examining the slums, sinks and rookeries of London and Manchester were often described as venturing into 'darkest England'. Culture emerged as a concept that linked the practices and perspectives of early sociology, social reform, social administration and anthropology. For example, Henry Mayhew's description of the costermongers of London was as much an anthropological exercise as any of the reports sent back from Africa or India: the representation of another 'way of life'. Such groups were, in di Leonardo's (1998) elegant phrase, 'exotics at home'. Such ways of life were noteworthy because they were different from the (unseen and unspoken) norm. As Eagleton notes: 'One's own way of life is simply human; it is other people who are ethnic, idiosyncratic, culturally peculiar' (2000: 26).

Such 'culturally peculiar' groups enriched the world: exotics set against the dull conformity of bourgeois life. At the same time, their presence (and their 'irrationality') threatened the stability of bourgeois life. As a result they became the objects of governance strategies, knowledges and practices. The culture that marked them as different also positioned them as premodern residues in need of 'tutelage' and 'civilizing' interventions that would assimilate them to the

modern world (Hall, 2002). These views of culture's relationship to social problems typically rely on a relatively impoverished conception of culture, often
eliding it with 'moral condition' or 'lack of morality'. This model of social
investigation, its focus on culture, and its links to the processes and practices
of governing is one that recurs throughout the twentieth century in relation to
different 'social problem groups': aliens; problem families; the delinquent
young; those stuck in cultures of poverty, cycles of deprivation or cultures of
dependency; the underclass; immigrants; ethnic minorities and more.[1] Social
policies have constantly been shaped by the concern to police, reform or
improve the cultures of others.

More recently, 'culture' has been the site of conflict over the significance of
difference. Culture has been used to mark forms of pathological deviation from
the civilized 'norm', but it has also been reworked as one of the means through
which claims may be made on public resources and policy. As Andrew Ross has
argued, culture is one way of identifying and legitimating patterns of need
among social groups:

> Increasingly, respect for people's cultural identities – conventionally associ-
> ated with broad categories of gender, race, sexuality, nationality and ethnicity
> – has come to be seen as a major condition of equal access to income, health,
> education, free association, religious freedom, housing, and employment. For
> some, this need for cultural respect is a necessary supplement to the basic
> human rights pertaining to freedom of speech, assembly, and conscience.
> (1998: 191)

Where culture is the marker of difference, it becomes a strategic resource to be
deployed in struggles around politics and policy. It has been used in attempts
to overthrow exclusions or subordinations, and in campaigns against 'second-
class citizenship'. This has historically been driven by the actions of subordinated or excluded minorities (e.g. in constructing the culturally specific needs
and practices of 'minority ethnic groups'). But it has also been deployed in
defence of majoritarian and/or dominant cultures (for example, in struggles
over schooling where recognition of white, 'traditional', English culture has
been a focus of parental demands). Social policy has been increasingly exercised by questions of 'multiculturalism' (Hesse, 2001a; Lewis, 2000b). As Hesse
has argued, the concern with multiculturalism marks the postcolonial moment
as societies struggle over how to reconcile the unfinished business of decolonization, the movement of peoples and cultures, and the intersections of difference and inequality. Multiculturalism is the site of conflicting representations of what a 'modern society' might look like and how its complexly constituted population is to be governed. Its dominant forms centre around the
problems of accommodating the cultures of 'others' into the 'civilization' of
metropolitan societies (see, for example, the discussions in Baubock, Heller and
Zolberg, 1996; Parekh, 2000). These uses of culture in policy and political discourses typically operate with an understanding of *culture as a property* – something that individuals and collectivities belong to, or that belongs to them.

---

1 Indeed, it continues into the twenty-first century in the UK government's concern with migrant citizens and
the necessity of instructing them in the ways of civic society (Home Office, 2002).

Culture as possession

The idea of culture as the property of a social grouping is probably the most widespread usage of the term. Culture locates people: individuals share the culture of the group to which they belong. The culture links, embeds and shapes them. It also explains people and their actions – and has been used to explain anything from differential propensities to criminality, through more or less successfully performing organizations, to different national welfare systems. Cultures form people: people possess culture, and are possessed by it. This is a very familiar meaning of culture and has some familiar shortcomings (see, for example, Gupta and Ferguson, 1992). It treats cultures as undifferentiated, closed and undynamic systems, and treats relations between cultures as external and non-hierarchical. Each culture is seen as *homogeneous*: it has no internal patterns of differentiation, nor do people within it occupy different positions in relation to the system of beliefs, values and norms. In contrast, many studies of specific cultures (whether national, ethnic or organizational) reveal complex patterns of internal differentiation. Within organizational studies, for example, there are differences between formal and informal cultures; between official organizational culture and occupational cultures; and between the organizational culture and its subcultures. People occupy – or take up – different positions in relation to the formal organizational culture and cannot be unproblematically assumed to share it (no matter how much the organization's management might wish to believe it). Similar processes of differentiation arise in relation to all cultures: gender and age formations cut across the apparent unity of ethnic cultures; differences of class, region, and ethnicity are at work within national cultures.

Secondly, the view of cultures as *closed* is a legacy of the anthropological view of 'traditional' societies which saw them as cut off from cultural contact (in particular, cut off from contact with the 'modern' world). The effect is to treat cultures as stable and bounded systems of meaning. Cultures abut one another rather than interact. Each occupies its own distinctive place in the world. The contemporary flow of meanings across and between cultures suggests that this notion of a closed system cannot be sustained. There is a larger question about whether it was ever a proper view of cultural formation: very few societies lived in such seclusion that cultural interchange (and conflict) was excluded from their 'way of life'. Warfare, border maintenance and trade all contributed to the 'cross-cultural' circulation of symbols, even before the colonial encounter.

This recognition of leaky boundaries also has implications for the conventional view of cultures as *stable* entities. Cultures are viewed as condensed and solidified tradition, impervious to change (except at glacial pace) and reproduced or transmitted from generation to generation. Again, this reflects the old anthropological and sociological distinction between tradition and modernity (static-organic societies versus dynamic-atomized formations). In contemporary settings, however, cultures seem prone to disturbance, flux and innovation. Such innovation includes the constant reinvention and revitalization of 'tradition'. In the present, at least, keeping things the same requires the expenditure of a lot of social effort. This suggests that stabilizing cultural forms, norms and habits is an active process rather than an integral or inertial effect of cultural transmission.

The question about relationships between cultures can be posed in a different way – around processes of *domination* and *subordination*. Cultural exchange and intersection do not necessarily take place as acts of free exchange between equals. As noted above, cultures tend to be observed, ordered and classified from an apparently a-cultural position (the norm of Western, European, British, English civilization). Just as the obsessive focus on 'blackness' obscures the normative status of whiteness, so the fascination with cultures of the other obscures the normative status of the dominant/imperial culture. Cultures become classified around – and below – a dominant point of articulation: 'civilization' functions as the normalized reference point (see Marfleet, 1999, on 'European civilization'). Other cultures are coded as lesser, subordinate, or deviant.

Finally, the conventional view of cultures sees them as *bounded* with only external relationships to one another. This rests on an 'assumed isomorphism of space, place and culture' (Gupta and Ferguson, 1992: 7), in which societies and cultures are assumed to be interchangeable terms and to be co-located in the same space. This has been a convenient fiction in a number of ways – but it will clearly not suffice as an analysis of cultures and their interrelationship. Anthropology (and the imperial lines of connection along which it flowed) was itself a project of cultural intersection and transformation: it took the act of viewing into 'traditional' cultures, observing, interpreting, classifying and reporting on their peculiarities. It brought 'home' images of the exotic, the other and the Oriental (Said, 1979) which became woven into the culture(s) of the West. The cultures of the colonizers and the colonized have been profoundly interlinked – such that neither pole in these relations can be understood as the 'pure' embodiment of its own 'tradition'. For these reasons, questions of fusion, *mélange* and hybridity have come to greater prominence in cultural analysis – and point to the following section on cultural formations.

Culture as cultural formations

One central problem for cultural analysis is how to think of cultures coexisting in time and space. How can national cultures be understood in ways that grasp their internal differentiation (and contestation) and the forms of transnational connection that might shape them? Taking British culture as an example, such relationships clearly shape a culture that cannot be reduced to any essential or traditional 'Britishness' (at least, without entering into the production of national myths). Rather, analysing British culture implies opening out its internal formation. It would mean addressing how a hegemonic 'Englishness' is a structuring principle, cementing the other nation-regions into subordinate places. It would mean exploring how specific class-based conceptions of nation, identity and norms have occupied dominant places in the meaning systems of English-British culture. At the same time, it would involve an examination of how the colonial and postcolonial moments have shaped English-British culture both through the construction of the 'other' and through the appropriation and integration of cultural forms, symbols and practices from the 'elsewheres' of Empire. Tea – as drink and social event – might well provide a microcosm in which social relations (of class, gender and ethnicity) and colonial forms and practices are condensed and ordered as a key element in what Berlant (1991) calls the 'national symbolic'. The 'national symbolic' denotes the field of cultural forms, symbols and practices that make up the idea of the nation – the imagined unity of people, place and ways of life.

This leads us to think of a national culture as a composite, or compound *formation*, not a simple unity. It condenses different elements into a singular formation – with a distinctive internal ordering or structuring. It is what Marx (writing about the circuit of capital in the *Grundrisse*) called a 'unity in difference' or 'distinctions within a unity' (1973: 99). This is different from a simple unity or expressive totality (in which all the elements carry the marks of the whole – like the writing in a stick of rock). In a unity in difference, the whole is made up of interconnected elements, structured in a particular way but not reducible to one another. The analytical challenge here is to grasp both aspects – the unity and its different elements. To focus exclusively on the unity misses the complex structuring elements and principles. To grasp the parts alone means missing the unity. Analytically, this means combining *deconstruction* (taking apart of the unity to reveal its elements and internal relations) and *reconstruction* (understanding how this particular unity is formed, structured and held together).

It is important to understand how the apparently simple unity of a nation or 'British culture' has been constructed and what happens to those who are subjected to its deployment. Cultures define the terms and conditions of membership – who counts as part of an organization, a community or a nation and where they are placed within it. Cultures construct a field of positions – exclusions, subordinations and marginalizations around the normal/universal subject. Cultures circulate norms of social organization – for example, about work, the family and the ways in which they express and embody the 'nation' (see Williams, 1995; Clarke, Langan and Williams, 2001a; 2001b). There is a critical point of coincidence here between cultures and social policies (Saraga, 1998; Lewis, 1998a; Lewis, Gewirtz and Clarke, 2000). As Susser notes in the US context:

> government policies with respect to documentation, immigration quotas, quarantine, legal definitions of indentured servitude, the land rights of indigenous peoples, and slavery were important determinants of differentiation. (2001a: 4)

The cultural turn invites us to think about welfare states as something more than allocative mechanisms for money, commodities and services. Social policies are constructed with cultural resources – knowledges, norms and identities – and they produce cultural effects, not least in the specification of the meanings, conditions and identities of citizenship. Social policies, then, can be examined as cultural phenomena. We can explore the cultural resources they deploy, the cultural effects they aim to produce, and the attempted resolutions of cultural conflicts or contradictions they try to put in place (see, for example, Lewis, 2000b; Clarke and Newman, 1998). Shore and Wright have argued for this view of policy:

> Policies are inherently and unequivocally *anthropological* phenomena. They can be read by anthropologists in a number of ways: as cultural texts, as classificatory devices with various meanings, as narratives that serve to justify or condemn the present, or as rhetorical devices and discursive formations that function to empower some people and silence others. Not only do policies codify social norms and values, and articulate fundamental organizing principles of society, they also contain implicit (and sometimes explicit) models of society. (1997: 7, emphasis in original)

Nevertheless, there remains a difficult question of how to think about the organizing or orchestrating principles of cultural formations. How is a particular unity in difference structured? Within cultural studies, this question was originally answered by an expressive model of class and culture that assumed an identity or a homology between the social group and particular cultural forms, norms and practices. Adapting the anthropological view of culture as the way of life of a social group, this model asked what happened when societies contained more than one group, and where the relations between those groups – classes – were antagonistic. The resulting analyses distinguished between bourgeois and working class cultures, each of which was the distinctive expression of a social class. They were engaged in cultural or ideological struggles to dominate – to become 'the ruling ideas of the age'. This model of class cultures has been challenged by attempts to understand culture as a field of mobile conflict and contestation between social groups (rather than as a battle between different and opposed cultures). This alternative has produced new ways of theorizing the relationship between social positions and the production of meaning. Drawing on a range of theoretical resources (from the Soviet linguist Volosinov to the Lacanian-inflected Marxism of Louis Althusser), a number of writers (notably Stuart Hall, Ernesto Laclau and Chantal Mouffe) have argued for a view of cultural formations as *articulated ensembles* (see Slack, 1996).

Rather than words (or signs) having one fixed meaning, this conception of articulation emphasizes their polysemic character: they have a potential to be given different meanings. In practice, a specific meaning is (temporarily) fixed by the connection of the word/sign into a chain of meaning. It is inflected – given a specific meaning – by where it is located and the associations which are generated by that location. As a banal example, 'freedom' is polysemic: it has the capacity to carry multiple meanings. It is also highly valorized – and is much sought after by a variety of political projects which attempt to appropriate it (and the high value that it carries) and fix a particular meaning (freedom from state interference; freedom from hunger and fear) by locating it within a chain of connections. The formal characteristic of words and signs being polysemic is not the same as saying that each word/sign that we encounter is free-floating, or available to being given any meaning that comes along. Specific words and signs are always attached somewhere, and are sedimented with past meanings. Polysemy is an indication that such accrued meanings are not inevitable, fixed or permanent: they may be undone and remade. But the practices of articulation, disarticulation and rearticulation are active and energetic, and may be resisted and contested. Think, for example, of the discussion of the meaning of 'welfare' in Chapter 1 – which revealed systematic efforts at disarticulating established meanings of welfare and forging new connections. 'Welfare' as collective or mutual provision and involving rights and entitlements (a meaning developed during the twentieth century against class-ridden conceptions of charity and philanthropy) had to be displaced. This disarticulation had to be achieved in order to establish the different meaning of 'welfare-as-a-problem' (a drain of national wealth, the cause of dependency and moral decline, a funding system for an underclass etc.).

From this starting point of polysemy and articulation, it is possible to think of cultural formations as *articulated ensembles*. The concept of articulation draws attention to the constructed and contestable character of cultural formations. Articulations can only be provisional and temporary: they are always vulnerable to projects of disarticulation and rearticulation. However, it is important to say that 'provisional' and 'temporary' are relatively abstract properties associated with the process of articulation. They do not mean – as with the polysemy of signs noted above – that everything is constantly in flux. On the contrary, cultural analysis suggests that some articulated systems of meaning become immensely solidified or sedimented. They become obvious, taken for granted, or naturalized forms of common sense – what Gramsci called 'second nature'. In relation to welfare, meanings around gender and the family, 'race' and nation, and wider biological constructions of difference and deviance have proved persistent and resilient – though eventually challengeable and vulnerable (Saraga, 1998). Other terms have been the site of continuing efforts to articulate them – and rearticulate them – in struggles over welfare. 'Unemployment', for example, had to be constructed and made visible and meaningful as a social problem (rather than an economic fact of life or effect of individual failings) in the late nineteenth century before it could be treated as the object of social policy. In the late twentieth century, it has been the focus of attempted rearticulations towards more individualized conceptions of capacity, orientation and opportunity: from the 'unemployed person' to the 'job seeker' in British parlance (Gazeley and Thane, 1998). Attention to the sedimented, contested and shifting meanings of cultural formations – and their changing articulations – is central to what the cultural turn can bring to the study of welfare states. But the emphasis on contestation and articulation brings questions of process and practice to the fore.

Culture as practice

Most of the views of culture that I have discussed so far emphasize cultures as systems or formations that produce and subject social agents (individuals and collectivities). They are, in Eagleton's phrase, 'quasi-determinist': cultures shape identities, meanings, orientations, knowledges – and, by implication, the possibilities of action. Nevertheless, one critical part of the 'cultural turn' has been an emphasis on culture as actively constructed by social agents. Meanings have to be made – and remade. They require practising agents. Much work in cultural analysis has championed active, practising agency against determinist views of social (or economic) structure. From E.P. Thompson's exploration of the 'making' of the English working class to examinations of cultural innovation, subversion and resistance, cultural analysis has celebrated the active production and contestation of meanings (e.g. Thompson, 1963; Hall and Jefferson, 1976; Hebdige, 1988; Duncombe, 2002; Holland and Lave, 2001b).

This draws attention to culture as the *product of practice*. Practice is understood differently in the varying perspectives that have contributed to the study of culture. In some places it is 'signifying practice' (the construction of meaning through signifying chains, after Saussure). It might be the practice of *bricolage* (after Lévi-Strauss) – assembling new systems of meaning out of existing materials combined in new ways. It might be 'discursive practice' – a concept shared by Foucauldians and linguistic analysts – in which the knowable and sayable are elaborated, reproduced, institutionalized and reinvented (Jaworski and Coupland, 1999). Even where *dominant* meanings are reproduced, the emphasis on 'practice' draws attention to the work that is necessary to such reproduction, rather than treating their reproduction as an inevitable effect of their dominance. Practice – the activities of enunciation and articulation – is a necessary, rather than epiphenomenal, part of the processes of cultural production. Practice is politically and analytically important because it is the site of the possibility of a different outcome – imagining, speaking, signifying, creating an instantiation which is not that which went before. Here, too, cultural analysis points to the fragile and unstable character of social reality that is 'socially constructed' (Berger and Luckmann, 1966). There are, of course, complications here. There are tensions between different perspectives on practice, and between the views of agents as 'cultural guerrillas' or as 'cultural dupes' (Clarke, 1990) or what happens in the 'space between transgression and reproduction' (Holland and Lave, 2001a: 19). Nevertheless, the attention to the productive capacity of agents as practising subjects is a vital contribution of the cultural turn. Agents (of varying kinds) are constantly involved in what Holland and Lave (2001a) call 'contentious practices' – where they refuse to go quietly.

There are links here to the idea of articulation discussed in the previous section, because articulation is itself a cultural or symbolic practice: it designates the work of disconnecting and demobilizing potential meanings, locating and trying to stabilize new ones, and resisting attempted rearticulations from other positions. The concern with practice leans towards what Holland and Lave call 'dialogism' (2001a: 8, following Holquist, 1990). Studies of ideological, discursive or cultural formations tend to focus on the ways in which they constitute, interpellate or hail 'subjects'. Dialogism views agents as 'always in a state of active existence; they are always in a state of being "addressed", and in the process of "answering"' (2001a: 10). People may be summoned, or 'hailed', by dominant positions that tell them who they are, how to conduct themselves and what is impossible. They may become those subjects, but they may also ignore the calls, not recognize themselves as such subjects, or speak back in different voices or accents, producing new articulations. Such a dialogical view seems a better guide to the terrain of cultural politics and ideological politics in which movements, parties and projects try to colonize 'common sense' and selectively connect it to new directions. This dialogical view points towards culture as formed by a 'politics of articulation', rather than being merely the site of the 'politics of subjection'. The issue of practice is central to the cultural turn. It underpins concerns with the constructed and contested quality of cultural formations. It brings to the fore questions of accommodation, negotiation, resistance and contention – rather than merely subordination, subjection and compliance. Finally, 'practice' is a reminder that every articulated ensemble – every formation – is a temporary accomplishment. It took cultural practice to construct it; it takes cultural practice to sustain it; and it is vulnerable to cultural practices that may contest it.

Populating the nation: the dynamics of inclusion and exclusion

In Chapter 1, I argued that welfare states are implicated in the construction of social differentiation across a range of relationships and positions: age, class, disability, gender, ethnicity, race and so on. But they are also about their composition into national formations – how these differences are ordered, organized and managed to produce a 'people'. Welfare states are central to the processes of the construction and practical implementation of definitions of the nation, national membership and citizenship (Lewis, 1998a; Nobles, 2000). Who counts as citizens, what the normal 'way of life' of the nation is, what differences are to be tolerated, erased or redressed, and where the boundaries between states, markets and families are to be drawn: these are all inscribed in the politics, policies and practices of welfare. Through social policies the state tries to prescribe who the people are, what they should be doing and how they should be living. Welfare both reflects normative judgements about the 'nation' and attempts to produce a people who live out those national norms. Welfare, viewed from this standpoint, is part of 'nation-building' projects, even in the context of shifting global and regional conditions of the nation and state.

The conventional view about the relationship between nation and culture derives from the 'organicist' view of nations as a product of the coincidence of place, people and a shared way of life (Gupta and Ferguson, 1992). Nations, then, are *natural* unities – and nationalism is an organic ideology that seeks to build the nation from its natural conditions: the soil, the borders, the culture, the spirit of the people (Smith, 1971). This view draws on the conception of culture as property: it is both a unity, and unifying (it is what the people have in common). This model of nation and culture has had both political and intellectual consequences. In political terms, it legitimates nation-creating claims (establishing the nation that reflects or captures the unity of a people as a cultural or linguistic community); and it legitimates suppression of cultural differences or the forced incorporation of 'cultural minorities'. In academic terms, it has enabled systems of comparison and classification based on different national cultures or cultural types (see, for example, Hofstede, 1980; and the critique by McSweeney, 2002). The 'cultural turn' gives rise to different views of nations – as the product of nation-building or nation-constructing political projects. Nations are not 'naturally occurring phenomena' which only have to be translated into institutional forms; they have to be made. As Eley and Suny put it, nations were

> sometimes a redescription of existing state-organized territorial populations, were sometimes an inspiration, a projection from emerging civil societies, movements seeking to reorder in terms of themselves the political and state-institutional landscapes they encountered. 'National categories' or nationalities became announced and elaborated during the nineteenth century in ever-widening profusion, a process which in global terms during the twentieth century has shown few signs of contracting. (1996: 20)

Politics and culture are interleaved in these nation-building processes – as attempts are made to forge the identity and unity of the nation through defining (and inculcating) its unique culture. Nations create the way of life that they claim to express by combinations of repression, exclusion and education. Nations construct governmental apparatuses to teach themselves about their way of life – circulating a common language, shared symbols, sets of values and norms about conduct. At the same time, they articulate differences – from 'minoritized' internal groups who may not be numerical minorities, but don't speak the language, or don't share the culture, and from external groups who either threaten the nation or pay tribute to its superiority. Nation-building is rarely a one-off process: nations have to be remade in the face of shifting conditions, borders, populations and problems. Gail Lewis has pointed to the unsettled and shifting forms of social relationships in nineteenth century Britain as posing new challenges of reinventing the nation:

> New forms of belonging and ways of imagining the nation became imperative. Who constituted the nation; what the appropriate forms of behaviour were; how new authority codes between the socially 'superior' and 'inferior' (both at

home and in the colonies) were to be produced; and what form the relation between state, economy and the people was to take, were all pressing questions. It was in this crucible of transformation that new forms of social cohesion, stability and dominance were to be produced ... The point is that 'nations' are always made and remade, and that their boundaries, real and imagined, internal and external, have provided the frame within which welfare regimes are constructed and practised. (1998a: 4)

Welfare policies and practices both take place within the framing of the nation, but they are also means by which it is produced and reproduced. They are also one of the settings where conflicts about citizenship, membership and belonging may be fought out – as marginalized, excluded or subordinated groups challenge the dominant terms and conditions of welfare citizenship. Welfare policies and practices embody social assumptions about the composition of the people and about their 'way of life'. The post-war British welfare state was built on a 'social settlement' that connected normative assumptions about work (the expectation of full male employment), family (a strong gender division of labour built on male breadwinner and female domesticity) and nation (a white, Christian, imperial 'race'). The family articulated work and nation through day-to-day reproduction of the male worker and generational reproduction of the 'race' (see, *inter alia*, Clarke and Newman, 1997; Clarke, Langan and Williams, 2001a; 2001b; F. Williams, 1989; 1995). But welfare policies and practices also served to enforce such assumptions: ensuring the proper relations between dominant and subordinate positions (gender and age dependency, for example) and either containing or excluding those who failed the 'normative' conditions (disabled people, improper sexualities, racialized 'minorities'). Welfare states are one of the mechanisms through which the social architecture of the people is managed. Identities are allocated and arranged in their 'proper' places within and beyond the nation.

Nation-building is a recurrent challenge for nation-states. If we accept a 'cultural turn' view of the nation, this is hardly surprising, since the construction of nations is a contingent and contested process. It involves the effort to install and stabilize a particular settlement (a dominant conception of the people and their way of life). Such settlements require 'maintenance work' to keep them in place, but they are also vulnerable to changing conditions – and to the claims of new imaginaries of the people. Nations become unsettled or destabilized – and one of the features of the current period is that destabilization is both more widespread and more visible. Nations are dissolved, reformed or realigned with new borders (and new peoples). Nations are also the setting for revived and anxious nationalisms – as their imagined sovereignty and unity are 'undermined' by regional and global flows (e.g. the EU and new flows of migrating people). The period is one in which new regional and global alignments coincide with the continuing effects of decolonization in the old European empires, creating 'postcolonial states' in the former colonies and the 'postcolonial condition' in the former metropoles (Hansen and Stepputat, 2001; Hesse, 2001a). As Eley and Suny remind us:

> it is especially vital to see how the social relations, patterns of culture, and increasingly racialized discourse of national superiority produced in the colonies and the subordinated extra-European world became powerfully reinserted into the European metropolitan frame. 'Colonial knowledge' in this sense had a crucial bearing on the structure of nationalist politics inside Europe ... The *gendering* of national identity, whether in militarism or warfare *per se*, or in the general ordering of nationalist representations around conceptions of masculinity and femininity, also had key colonialist roots – as, for instance, in discussions around colonial intermarriage, which generate complex bodies of discourse around gender inequalities, sexual privilege, class priorities, and racial superiority, which in their turn became potently rearticulated into nationalist discourses at home. (1996: 28)

National formations are variable in both time and place. They differ between national settlements, and national settlements differ through time.[2] This suggests a rather different view of historical and comparative analysis from the dominant concerns with welfare regimes or typologies of welfare states (e.g. Esping-Andersen, 1990; Huber and Stephens, 2001). It implies first a greater concern with historical dynamics – the transitions, trajectories and tendencies that create, destabilize and modify the 'unstable equilibria' of particular national settlements. But more importantly, it raises the 'cultural' question of the relationship between national formations of the 'people' and national welfare settlements. What Gramsci called the 'national popular' is the setting for political-cultural projects that attempt to (re)construct the nation and (re)define the people in creating new settlements – new bases for economic power, social order and political rule. So, what formations of the people underpin and are articulated by national welfare settlements becomes a vital question for the comparative analysis of welfare states. This is also rather more than attending to the aggregated presence of 'class, race and gender' in welfare policies and politics. It is their mutual and multiple constitution (and their imbrication with other divisions) that shapes the nation/people formation. Karen Brodkin (2001) tries to draw out this distinction in terms of different levels of analysis. She suggests that it might be useful to distinguish between the key social relations or divisions and how they are structured to form a nation: 'if race, gender and class are each key forms of organizing the nation's society and culture, then the organization of these organizations – the ways they constitute each other – is the meta-organization of the nation' (2001: 370).

Racialized formations: the beginning and end of US welfare

I think this is helpful in pointing to the social architecture of 'nations' as for-

---

2 Welfare and social policies are also implicated in the construction of 'regions' as distinctive would-be unities, whether 'Europe' or 'Asia' (Fink, Lewis and Clarke, 2001; Ong, 1999).

mations. The articulation of social differences – the history, significance and effects of particular divisions – will vary between national formations and their welfare settlements. While 'race' – or racialized divisions – may be present everywhere, their place in, and consequences for, specific national formations vary. In earlier writing about welfare and welfare reform in the USA, I argued that:

> Studying the USA reveals the need to think about the way class, 'race' and gender have specific national formations. 'Race' – or what Omi and Winant (1986) call 'racial formations' – is not a natural or universally occurring phenomenon. Rather we need to think about the ways in which forms of social division and inequality are racialized – produced as 'race' – and how the processes and forms of racialization vary from society to society (and historically) ... Racial formation has a specific American form – in terms of how US society is racialized, in terms of the political salience of racial distinctions, and in terms of how 'race' is articulated with other social divisions – of gender and class in particular. The USA's social formation has been distinctive in a number of ways, particularly around dimensions of 'race' and ethnicity. Its history combines a 'settler' society (including the repression of Native American groups) and a 'slave holder' society (including the forced insertion of black Africans into the American economy and social relations). The effects of these structures on economic, social and political development in the USA have been profound, not least in their intersection with the politics, ideologies and policies of social welfare. (2001a: 146)

The distinction between social security and means-tested assistance that proved so central to the later politics of 'welfare reform' was articulated as a structuring principle in the 'New Deal' response to capitalist crisis in the 1930s. The New Deal's work and welfare programmes reproduced patterns of social division – and normative expectations about differentiated social roles, particularly distinctions between men and women in relation to employment, public works and social insurance schemes (Amenta, 1998: 156–7; Gordon, 1994). But they also reinscribed forms of racialized divisions. In particular, African-Americans were effectively excluded from social insurance programmes because neither agricultural nor domestic work were included as qualifying forms of employment, and as Amenta notes, 'in the 1930s, two-thirds of African Americans were working in these occupations' (1998: 159). As Quadagno argues, this results from a political-cultural struggle to shape the limits of welfare:

> Because of Southern opposition, agricultural workers and domestic servants – most black men and women – were left out of the core programs of the Social Security Act. Instead, they were relegated to the social assistance programs, where local welfare authorities could determine benefit levels and set eligibility rules ... Southerners would simply not allow the federal government to dictate standards or set benefit levels. They sought control over any social pro-

gram that might threaten white domination, so precariously balanced on cotton production. (1994: 21–2)

Within the social assistance programmes, class, gender and racial codes shaped the administration of welfare. Gordon notes that 'ADC [Aid to Dependent Children – the forerunner of AFDC] was unique among all welfare programs in its subjection of applicants to a morals test. The most frequent measurement of a "suitable home" was sexual behaviours' (1994: 298). Mink argues that the evaluation of 'moral fitness' was 'encoded with Anglo-Saxon biases' and that ADC delegated wide discretion to:

> administrators and social workers – most of whom were white and middle class. Discretion allowed for the imposition of Anglo-Saxon criteria, as well as for racial exclusion where uplift was seen as either undesirable or impossible. (1990: 110)

Racialized divisions – and racializing norms – thus structured the emergent 'welfare state' in the USA in both policy and practice. Such lines of fracture – and their maintenance – have exercised a powerful shaping influence on the subsequent development of the American welfare system. The enlargement of assistance programmes – and the withdrawal of the 'suitable home' morals test – in the 1960s resulted from the shifting class and racial composition of the USA, especially the shift to an industrial and urban black working class during and after World War II. This shift provided the basis for political, cultural and social struggles organized around 'race' and welfare. Civil rights struggles intersected powerfully with what Piven and Cloward call 'Poor People's movements':

> The welfare explosion [of the 1960s] occurred during several years of the greatest domestic disorder since the 1930s – perhaps the greatest in our history. It was concurrent with the turmoil produced by the civil rights struggle, with widespread and destructive rioting in the cities and with the formation of a militant grass-roots movement of the poor dedicated to the combating of welfare restrictions. (1993: 198)

The New Right's politics of welfare first claimed to be a project to rescue the sensible policies of the New Deal from the excesses and mistakes of the 1960s 'Great Society' expansion of welfare. But, as noted in Chapter 1, it focused explicitly on assistance programmes (AFDC especially), and in the process constructed them in profoundly racialized terms (Mink, 1998; Neubeck and Casenave, 2001). Despite the evidence that most poor people are white, New Right writers and commentators consistently equated poverty (and 'dependency' on public assistance) with African-American (lone) mothers (see, for example, Murray, 1984, whose book was built on an argument that it was appropriate to use 'black' as a proxy for 'poor'). Gilens (1999) has charted the ways in which media representations of poverty shift from relatively sympathetic portrayals of 'white poverty' to sterner – or more alarming – images of black 'ghetto' poverty at different points in political struggles over poverty and welfare.[3] In the rise to dominance of the New Right, the political and public discourse about 'welfare' and its reform became decisively fused with a racialized (and gendered) imaginary about poor people. The 'underclass' – urban, black and dangerous – symbolized the problem of US liberalism and its 'tax and spend' social policies (Clarke, 1991). The 'end of welfare' could only be accomplished through this racialized – and racializing – discourse. In Gilens's terms, 'why Americans hate welfare' is because its dominant representations fuse questions of desert, taxation, race and social fear.

Despite the potency of this fusion of race and welfare, many studies of welfare reform still presume that its politics were about class relations (narrowly conceived); were driven by class interests or class forces (narrowly conceived); and were centred on the intersection of welfare and (waged) work. There is no doubt that the coincidence of neo-liberal politics, the processes of economic globalization, and the 'reform' of welfare towards workfare formed a very favourable terrain for analyses based in and on political economy (see, for example, Gough, 2000; Jessop, 2002; Peck, 2001). In such studies, the dynamics of class and capital accumulation figure as the main forces driving welfare state change. Peck's excellent study of the rise and spread of 'workfare' explores the challenges to 'welfare' and 'welfarism' in the USA (2001: chs 2 and 3). It addresses the role that 'race' and gender play in the constitution of the 'contingent' workforce that 'workfare' strategies seek to produce (e.g. 2001: 22–3), but it treats these as labour market effects rather than being integral elements of the politics of welfare reform.

As a consequence, Peck misses the distinctive political-cultural character of the 'war on welfare' – directed at black, lone-mother-headed families (the 'welfare queens' responsible for producing an urban 'underclass'). Racialized and gendered politics, ideology and discourse were mobilized in the attack on welfare and played a critical role in enabling 'the end of welfare' (see, for example, Clarke and Piven, 2001; Mink, 1998; Quadagno, 1994). The 'end of welfare' constructed new connections between lone mothers and waged work (as in other programmes such as the 'New Deal' in the UK). In the USA, it did so through a particular set of racialized and gendered dynamics – one of whose effects is the 'revival' of black women's role as domestic servants (Boris, 1998; Davis, 2002). But the Personal Responsibility and Work Opportunity Reconciliation Act also established new forms of regulation of the personal, sexual and familial behaviours of lone mothers. The options available to states in respect of the personal conduct of mothers (beyond their labour market 'responsibilities') under PRWORA are summarized by Mink:

> to strip families of cash benefits where mothers do not identify biological
> fathers; to withhold benefits to children born to mothers while enrolled on wel-
> fare; to sanction recipient families that include adults under age fifty-one who

---

3 There is also a line of sociological and anthropological investigation that constructed similarly racializing fusions of poverty, the ghetto and the underclass (for examples, see the critiques in di Leonardo, 1998; Hyatt, 1995; Morgen and Maskovsky, 2003).

do not have and are not seeking a high school diploma; to declare all nonciti-
zens ineligible for assistance; to require drug tests of recipients; to cut benefits to mothers whose children are truant; to treat new state residents under the
welfare rules of their former state; and to provide no cash benefits at all. (1998:
62)

These concerns – aimed at promoting 'family life' – are not reducible to the
work/welfare nexus, or to the post-Fordist regulation of waged labour. It seems
necessary to understand the complex political-cultural construction of 'welfare'
in the USA, especially its development as a distinctively racialized and gendered formation. Without that, it is hard to grasp how 'welfare' could be institutionally and discursively separated from social security to enable its reform,
and how neo-liberal and neo-conservative projects coalesced to bring about
'welfare's end' (Mink, 1998). The saga of the 'end of welfare' cannot be properly grasped without an understanding of the dynamics of the struggles over
the national popular in US welfare politics. From the efforts to 'enlarge' the US
welfare system in and after the 1960s, and the attempt to 'roll back' the partial
(and uneven and contradictory) advances, we must look for the traces that
'poor people's movements' left on the US state (Piven and Cloward, 1993;
Schram, 2002). Nor are 'poor people' the asocial or unmarked (unidentified)
occupants of class positions. As the various social movements have made clear,
becoming poor is one of the effects of social differentiation (see, for example,
Goode and Maskovsky, 2001; Morgen and Maskovsky, 2003). Racializing, gendering and disabling dynamics of difference coalesce with other dynamics in
the production of inequality. The poor have a socially and historically specific
social composition, and are subject to processes of recomposition (Susser,
2001b). What the 'cultural turn' makes visible is the way in which welfare is
about the nation and the people as much as it is about 'work'. Ways of life need
to be supported and enabled – and deviant ways of life need to be disciplined
or controlled by the exercise of power. The 'people' always contain 'problem
populations' who must be managed in the national interest. They may be
included, incorporated or incarcerated – but they are an object of constant fascination for the state.

Making the cultural turn

I have tried to indicate some of the ways in which cultural analysis might
enrich our grasp of politics, policies and practices in welfare states. It enables
an approach that moves beyond treating 'society' as a backdrop or passive context against which welfare states are studied and to which they may 'adapt' in
a more or less appropriate way. From a 'cultural' standpoint, contexts are active
and productive: they frame, shape and constitute what is possible, imaginable,
knowable and desirable because they embody (contested) imaginaries. Such
imaginaries claim to tell us how society is, what it is becoming and how we
should organize to move to the future. As we saw in the US example, they are

national-popular imaginaries: about the people, their virtues and failings, their 'way of life' and how to sustain and advance it. This is a different view from seeing welfare states as more or less rational mechanisms of adaptation to more or less clearly defined 'social trends'. In turn, welfare states 'produce the people' in trying to put the national-popular imaginary into practice. Welfare states embody assumptions about work, about care, about national membership, about who lies outside the nation, about forms of financial arrangement, about families and age/gender dynamics, about forms of difference and how to regulate them, about poor people and how to manage them, make them not poor, or make them less dangerous. This conception of the welfare state as both constituted and constitutive lies at the heart of the 'cultural turn'.

I am using the term 'cultural turn' to refer to the rather diverse sources of interest in the cultural, ideological, discursive or symbolic features of social welfare. There has always been work within social policy around the topic of ideology. However, this has tended to be in the form of ideology conceived as a relatively systematic body of politically oriented ideas which have – to a greater or lesser extent – influenced the development of social welfare (George and Wilding, 1976; Clarke, Cochrane and Smart, 1987). By contrast, the cultural turn in social policy has treated the realm of ideology in a more expansive way – as involving the implicit social assumptions as well as explicit ideological conceptions that have informed the social character of welfare. The cultural turn marks the combined effects of a number of different theoretical and methodological strands. These include structuralist Marxism, particularly in the Althusserian conceptions of ideology and subjects; other varieties of Marxism, for example, the Gramscian concerns with both hegemony and the contested contradictoriness of 'common sense'; varieties of feminist analysis and investigation; poststructuralist approaches to the arbitrary yet conventionalized power of language; the Foucauldian examination of discourses, together with the knowledge–power relations embedded in them; postcolonial approaches to the formation of racialized systems of inequality and identity; and the legacy of phenomenological and symbolic interactionist approaches to social construction, particularly in the sociology of deviance.

Steinmetz notes that many scholars have 'rejected the term culture altogether on account of its vagueness and polysemy. Some favor concepts such as ideology, discourse, hegemony, meaning, interpretation, subjectivity, identity and the unconscious, yet these are no less multi-vocal' (1999: 7). Needless to say, these diverse approaches do not fit tidily, or comfortably, together. But they have all contributed to the possibilities of studying welfare states and social policy in a 'cultural' way, even though they might not use the term 'culture'. Steinmetz makes an interesting argument that:

> [the] cultural turn ... should not be defined by the specific employment of the word *culture*. More important is an understanding of systems of signification and subjectivity as importantly constitutive of social reality ... Social theory is often forced to rely on semiotically overloaded terms such as *culture* whose meaning is overdetermined by changing historical usage, struggles among

discourse communities, and simultaneous existence within lay and academic communities. (1999: 7, fn. 8, emphasis in original)

One reason for stressing the diversity of strands that have contributed to the cultural turn is to resist the temptation to narrow it to one dimension or orthodoxy. The cultural turn is, I think, broader – and less certain – than the 'linguistic turn' or the shift to 'poststructuralism' (see also Steinmetz, 1999: 2). Secondly, this movement towards a constructionist, constitutive or cultural view of social arrangements has retrospectively been identified with a theoretical and political movement away from 'class' (in both its classificatory and its relational senses). However, some of the first steps in this movement were made around a concept of class that tried to link 'social structure' and 'social relations' with the field of culture in the analysis of social reproduction and social conflict. Explorations of the normative formations of social policy and welfare practices challenged the claims about social improvement and social progress that had dominated the study of social policy. Instead, studies revealed the cultural means through which dominant class power and control were enforced and reproduced. A range of work examined the ways in which bourgeois norms or demands were inscribed in the policies and practices of social welfare with the aim of regulating, controlling or disciplining the working class. Such issues were posed in some of the intersections between the new social or cultural history of the 1970s and the radicalization of aspects of sociology, in particular the emergence of a 'radical deviancy' theory associated in the UK with the National Deviancy Conference (e.g. Donajgrodski, 1977; Taylor, Walton and Young, 1973; National Deviancy Conference, 1980). A meeting place for these developments was provided by the idea of 'social control'. This focused work that uncovered the processes through which class relations, positions and power were sustained, defended and reproduced. Social control was also a critical lever for studies that challenged forms of liberal expertise and professional neutrality, prefiguring some of the concerns of Foucauldian studies (the concept was also critically challenged: see particularly Gordon, 1988: ch. 9). In this process, Gareth Stedman-Jones's study of *Outcast London* (1971) forms a sort of exemplary text. It presented a complex analysis of class relations in mid nineteenth century London, and revealed the creation of forms of intervention, particularly the Charity Organization Society, directed at stabilizing – and indeed naturalizing – forms of class control and power (see also Mooney, 1998). This focus on social control gave rise to critical studies of state apparatuses and practices ranging from social work to juvenile justice, education to health, policing to prisons.[4]

These peculiar deviations from the mainstreams of both Marxism and social policy intersected in uneven – and not always comfortable – ways with the

---

4 Because this is, in part, my history, I am sensitive to attempts to rewrite it around different sorts of turning points, whether these are the distinction between modernist and postmodernist approaches or the arrival of Foucault. For example, Hillyard and Watson (1996) suggest that Foucault's *Discipline and Punish* (1979) inspired investigations of the prison by Ignatieff (1978) and Melossi and Pavarini (1980) among others. The duller version is that both acknowledge the appearance of Foucault's work after their own studies had been completed. This is not to deny the real impact of Foucault, but is to suggest that binary distinctions of 'pre-' and 'post-' may risk oversimplifying history (see Clarke, 1991: ch. 2; 1998).

eruption of new politics and new analyses that, in social policy at least, under-took the denaturalization of gender, 'race', sexuality, age and ability. Such work challenged the dominant structurings of social arrangements and identities within social welfare and in the academic field of social policy (e.g. O'Brien and Penna, 1998; Taylor, 1997; F. Williams, 1989; 1996). It emphasized the con-structed – and therefore contingent – character of conceptions of natural and unnatural, normal and abnormal. It demonstrated how social welfare policy and practice have pathologized – defined as deviant – subordinated groups. The result is a series of approaches within social policy that are linked by commit-ments to deconstruct social welfare. They enable us to open up not just how a particular client group is defined; not just how a particular policy is conceived and enacted; but how all the terms of the field are constructed and articulated. From 'consumer' to 'nation', from the 'social bath' to the 'welfare state' itself, we can find examples of how the cultural turn has enhanced and enlarged what studying social policy means (Hughes, 1998; Lewis, 1998a; Hughes and Lewis, 1998; Twigg, 2000).

Nevertheless, this fruitful pursuit of the constructed, cultural or constitutive dimensions of welfare policy and practice has provoked theoretical and ana-lytical splits within the study of welfare – along lines that are familiar elsewhere in the social sciences. These include 'culture versus structure' (Ray and Sayer, 1999); 'modernist versus postmodernist' analytics (Carter, 1998; Leonard, 1997); 'structuralist versus poststructuralist' epistemologies and theories (Hillyard and Watson, 1996; Taylor-Gooby, 1996); 'class versus difference/iden-tity' as the focus of study (Mooney, 2000; Taylor-Gooby, 1996). I have argued elsewhere that engaging in these binarized conflicts is the (non-life-threaten-ing) equivalent of trench warfare (Clarke, 1999b). Trenches are dug; positions are reinforced; tons of highly explosive epistemology are launched against enemy positions; the narrow terrain is traversed back and forth as positions are assailed, captured, overturned. Allegations, accusations and interrogations ('Are you now or have you ever been a structuralist?') replace dialogue and crit-ical engagement as the currency of academic practice.

Instead of reliving World War I, I want to take a cultural turn because it is *within* the cultural turn that these tensions about the relationship between the material and the cultural, or between structure and culture, have been posed most productively. The development of cultural studies (as one institutional-ization of the cultural turn) was structured around the *relation* of the material and the cultural, the economic and the ideological, rather than being based on a one-sided view of the cultural rather than the material, or the symbolic rather than the economic.[5] Cultural analysis did not try to expel the 'material', the 'economic' or the 'structural'. Rather it refused to privilege them as the sole or dominant focus of analysis or as the embodiment of the 'real'. Instead it tried

---

5 This also seems to be true of much of the valuable work being produced within anthropology which finds illuminating and productive ways of examining political, social and economic formations without reducing them to an impoverished 'material' realm or an etherealized 'symbolic' realm (see, for example, Goode and Maskovsky, 2001; Lem and Leach, 2002; Susser and Patterson, 2001; Ong and Nonini, 1997). I would make similar arguments about historical studies that locate themselves in the dynamic intersection of the cultural and material (e.g. Gordon, 1999; Hall, 2002).

to work in and through the tensions, insisting that understanding the economy as cultural, constructed and contingent might be interesting, as well as insisting that the economy did not exhaust real life. Much of the work that has emerged in the 'cultural turn' sought to make this dynamic tension a route to analytical (and political) development. Making the cultural turn involves this sort of balancing act: a resistance to foreclosing difficult and important arguments, an openness to contradictions, and a willingness to live with analytical and political difficulties rather than settling them by theoretical fiat or diktat. I hope that this sensibility – this 'thinking in tension' – characterizes the analysis in this book. If it doesn't, it is because making the 'cultural turn' always involves the risk of falling off on one side or the other. There is always a temptation to be 'merely cultural' or to 'get back to the real'. But the gains of the cultural turn – and the possibilities that it makes available – need to be constantly pursued since they enable us to think differently.

three

Putting people in their place: the contested social in social policy

This chapter builds on the exploration of the cultural turn and what it makes visible in the study of social policy. In particular, it opens up ways of thinking about social divisions and inequalities that go beyond narrow political-economic conceptions of class divisions that have occupied a dominant place in both national and comparative studies of welfare states. As I argued in Chapter 2, conceptions of the nation and people are brought into focus by this approach. Here I want to explore how the national popular is the object of contention in one national setting – the UK. The UK is itself a historical composite – a unity in difference – where many questions of nation, nationality and national identity have been posed around the hegemonic role that England/Englishness has played in constructing Britain/Britishness. In this chapter, however, I take the cultural turn as a route to analysing the politics of welfare, centring on the changing meanings of the 'social' in social policy and social welfare. What sorts of conditions, problems, positions and relationships are 'social'? This chapter:

- explores arguments about the crisis of the welfare state and challenges to its social settlement (first section);
- looks at efforts to desocialize differences and inequalities (second section); and
- considers New Labour's attempts to define and create a 'modern society' in Britain (third section).

The 'crisis of the welfare state' is conventionally equated with the break-up of the political-economic settlements that sustained welfare states in Western capitalist societies, settlements that were often associated with corporatist approaches to economic and social management (e.g. Mishra, 1990; Pierson, 1991). This view foregrounds the political-economic realm as the main dynamic of welfare state change, and identifies political-economic groups (classes, in some sense or another) as the main actors in the process of conflict and compromise over welfare. In the process, a variety of struggles in and around welfare are obscured; a set of problems about how to understand the late twentieth century assault on welfare are forgotten; and some rather crassly economistic views of class are sustained. The reductionism is complex and multiple. Societies are reduced to class relations or differences. Classes are reduced to 'bearers' of class locations, stripped of other identities (as if workers are not also racialized, gendered, sexualized – embodied – subjects). Politics is reduced to encounters between parties identified as belonging to or representing classes (parties of labour or the bourgeoisie). What sort of societies – and welfare states – are these that are only peopled by classes? Here, I want to explore these issues through an examination of what the 'social' in social policy might mean – and how its contested and conflicted trajectory contributes to the politics and analysis of welfare states. I begin by looking at the struggles to challenge the 'social settlement' of the post-war welfare state in the UK, and then explore the implications of those challenges for the ways in which social policy is studied and analysed. I then explore a repertoire of strategies that have been deployed in an effort to 'desocialize' or 'renaturalize' inequalities, before considering the New Labour project of governing in the 'modern world' (Miliband, 1999).

A growing range of studies has demonstrated how welfare states are implicated in the formation, regulation and reproduction of other social distinctions, positions and relations. Welfare states are intimately bound up with processes of family and household formation and maintenance, together with the systems of gender and age relations expected to prevail and be reproduced within these institutions (see, for example, Gordon, 1994; Land, 1997; J. Lewis, 2000; Sainsbury, 1994). In the process, they play a central role in the formulation and policing of boundaries and relations between public and private realms, not least in the regulation of intimacy, identity and sexuality (Carabine, 1996; 2000; Cooper, 1994; F. Williams, 2000). Welfare states are implicated in the construction and recreation of racialized and ethnicized formations of identity, inequality and difference (G. Lewis, 2000c; Mink, 1998; Neubeck and Casenave, 2001; Quadagno, 1994; F. Williams, 1989). Welfare states are significant forces in the construction and management of illness, disability and their differentiation from the norms of health and ablebodiedness (Barton, 1996; Campbell and Oliver, 1996; Pearson, 1974). Welfare states condense, replicate and construct relations of difference – in policies, practices and the forms of power embodied in their apparatuses and agents. Welfare states manage or regulate the social in ways that cannot be reduced to class interests or the balance of class power.

Nevertheless, I want to resist a separation between economic (or material) and cultural (or symbolic) realms as if questions of class, economic distribution and relations are outside culture, while 'difference' is located only in the cultural.[1] If such a split is sustained, we miss questions of how classes are formed, reproduced and peopled – as socially constituted collectivities in specific places and times (see, for example, Gordon, 1999). In such processes, the articulation of racialized and gendered positions shapes the embodiment of class. Processes of household formation, gendered divisions of labour and labour markets also intersect in the production of welfare policies – but not as if labour markets stand outside these other processes. For example, Andersen and Jensen (2002)

---

1 These issues are much debated but I want to emphasize the problems of creating an equivalence between key terms, such that class = inequality = material = economic = fundamental = real.

treat labour markets as economic phenomena. Social divisions only come to life in relation to labour market marginalization and welfare policies:

> Changes in the labour market are seen as one of the most serious threats to the economic sustainability of European welfare states, and to the fulfilment of the ideal of 'full citizenship' among their citizens. Globalisation and technological change ... generate a marked decline in labour market fortunes among lower-skilled and other vulnerable segments of the labour force. This not only leads to social marginalisation, but also becomes a barrier to economic growth. (2002: 1)

In contrast, Susser starts with the cultural – pointing to the socially constructed, contested and variable character of 'labour', and highlighting the interplay between labour markets and social policies:

> we need to consider what in fact constitutes a labor force at different historical periods with different effects on inequality, poverty and social welfare. Nation states, employers, and working class movements define the categories of people available to work differently over time. As social programs and regulations shift, so too do those people who can be viewed as labor ... Alternatively constructions of legitimate dependency and community responsibility, institutionalized in state regulations, entitlements, and cultural expectations of age, gender, and other social identities, protect certain members of the population from accepting the lowest wages. (2001b: 230–1)

Drawing on the discussion in Chapter 2, we might add that the management of national boundaries also contributes to such formations. Migration changes the potential composition of the labour force within particular countries. It changes the potential constructions of the nation: its forms of citizenship, ethnic mix, demography and dynamics of family/household formation (Castles and Davidson, 2000). Different forms of migrant labour (and the different citizenship statuses to which they are allocated or aspire) are also a contested and changeable element for the formations of (waged) labour and (unwaged) care. Increasingly, the nation-states of the West are discovering that demography is not just an 'internal' matter, but is shaped by struggles to traverse and defend borders, and the efforts to regulate the movement of people.

Denaturalizing difference: the crises of the post-war social settlement

One striking feature of the post-war British social settlement is how many of the differences in which the emergent welfare state was implicated were construed and treated as 'natural' – the result of asocial or extra-social factors or conditions. Until the late 1960s, the conception of the social in social policy mainly referred to patterns of socio-economic inequalities (usually constructed as 'class inequalities'). The measurably unequal distributions of wealth, income, life chances, health risks and so on have been the focus of both academic inquiry and policy conflict. This conception of social inequality has also been the centrepiece of popular politics: the development of what T.H. Marshall (1950) referred to as 'social citizenship' was constructed through a set of conflicts, alliances and compromises (see also Saville, 1977). This socio-economic conception forms the core of political and academic arguments about 'redistribution': the possibility and desirability of, and mechanisms for, realigning access to wealth, income and opportunity.[2]

The dominant political formations that were aligned in the construction of the British welfare state – social liberalism, social democracy (and even 'one nation' conservatism) – shared a common view of the 'social'. They understood the 'social' as the site of integrative compromises over the forms of social inequality and forms of social problem that could be grasped within the framing of socio-economic/class inequality (sometimes construed as 'poverty') and its distorting social effects. Below this conception of the social, though, other differences were understood as part of the biological bedrock of human society. Gender differences provided an essential foundation for the desired relationship between work and family. Waged work was the responsibility of the male breadwinner; nurture and home-making the functions of the housewife/mother. The two were linked in marriage, a relationship in which the fortunate alignment of biologically 'normal' sexualities ensured the production of the next generation of breadwinners and housewives. Age differences simply reflected the evolutionary process of the human life cycle (of development and decline). Children were necessarily 'dependent'. Adolescents became troublingly independent, but fortunately grew out of it and emerged as 'normal' adults, only to decline into renewed dependency in old age. Racialized differences were located in the evolutionary biological hierarchy constructed alongside Britain's colonial power. Biology and geography combined in an expectation that biologically and culturally subordinate 'races' should know their place. Finally, disabled people were constructed as the unfortunate victims of biological conditions that rendered them necessarily dependent on (benevolent) medical authority for their maintenance.

This field of differences was structured around biological norms, knowledge and power (Saraga, 1998). Places were ascribed through a naturalization of difference: biology explained that this was 'how women, children, blacks, the handicapped were'. Policy responses might range from the brutal to the sympathetic, but they were framed by biological assumptions. To use the concept sketched in Chapter 2, this was an *articulated ensemble*: a system of positions differentiated from, and subordinated to, the norm of the male – ablebodied, heterosexual, white and preferably middle class (in aspiration if not occupation) providing for his dependants. This complexly defined figure was the 'cit-

---

2 I have been hesitating about calling this focus 'class', because it elides two rather different meanings of that term. On the one hand, there was the Registrar-General's classification of occupations (or other variants) which provided an empirical structure for the measurement of distributional inequalities. On the other there was the Marxist conception of class as a relational formation of capitalist societies which has been influential in the academic study of social policy, though with rather less impact on policy and practice.

izen', the subject of the welfare state's 'universalism' – and others' relationships to welfare were defined by their difference from him. This ensemble was formed through interlocking processes of differentiation, marginalization, pathologization and subordination, as well as exclusion. For example, children were constituted as different from mature, independent adults; as subordinate to familial and public authority (because of their dependence); and as needing both familial and public 'care' (to produce them as independent adults). Within this differentiated biological category, however, there were specific groups of children who were constituted as the objects of special concern: children with special needs; children in need of care, protection or control; delinquent children; and so on. Each of these was differentially positioned in the field of welfare and was practised upon in specific ways. Of course, the 'occupancy' of different categories intersected with a range of other (apparently) non-social markers, particularly those of gender and 'race'. The simple binary distinction between included and excluded is not adequate as a way of capturing the structured field of positions and relationships between them that was embedded in, and enacted through, the policies and practices of the welfare state.

The significance of these constructions lay not only in their ideological or discursive dominance, and their naturalization across a whole society, but also in the way that they were instantiated in the policies and practices of state welfare provision. Welfare institutions produced and reproduced such divisions and the positions resulting from them. Such institutions formed one of the most potent fields of articulation between state power, discursive formations and the fabric of everyday lives. Welfare institutions produced a field of social differentiation with immediate (and often severe) consequences for those positioned by and within it. I want to argue that the 'crisis of welfare' had important roots in the struggles intended to expand and transform, rather than retrench or reduce, state welfare. The welfare states of the mid-1970s were not the same as those of the immediate post-war period. They had been marked by struggles from a range of constituencies around 'welfare': feminist movements aiming to challenge the policy incarnations of the patriarchal family and its gendered division of labour and power; movements of disabled people challenging the policy and practice dominance of the 'medical model'; movements of black people challenging their exclusion and subordination in relation to 'national/racial' conceptions of citizenship; user movements challenging their subordination to bureau-professional power within welfare apparatuses.

Many of these struggles shared a common insistence on the *social* character of patterns of difference, division and inequality. Welfare politics around gender, 'race', sexuality and disability may well have been particularistic in organizational forms and the demands expressed, but they were linked by a commitment to reveal the socially produced or constructed character of difference (Lewis, 2003). These are often referred to as 'new social movements' in keeping with wider sociological theorizing (Pierson, 1991). There are problems with the conceptualization of these movements – particularly the tendency to over-read their novelty; the binary splits between old and new; the distinction between material and symbolic foci of struggle; and that between political and cultural orientations. Nevertheless, problems of conceptualizing such movements should not detract from their significance as challenges to the 'social settlement' of the welfare state (see, for example, the discussions in Lewis, 2000a; 2003; Martin, 2001; Williams, 1996; 2000). As Lewis has argued, the challenge to the 'old' social policy and welfare state was an effect of:

> the insistence by new claims making constituencies ... that the categories, practices and relations of welfare that were previously taken for granted be explored for their emancipatory or subordinating effects. The refusal to treat social differences as pre-social or essential characteristics of particular groups or individuals draws attention to them as the outcomes of processes of subject formation. (2000a: 15)

These movements (and their academic analogues) often asserted the plastic or malleable character of socially constructed differences, identifying them as historically and culturally contingent. This insistence on their 'social' character produces a view of difference, division and inequality as contestable, and capable of being redressed. These struggles arose in part from the contradictions inherent in different features of the social settlement of the post-war years. For example, the '1945' settlement had assumed a homogeneously white British citizenry. This conception of the nation involved an attempt to cast 'race' out into the realms of biology (and colonial geography). From this starting point, it could be assumed that welfare universalism would extend unproblematically to minority ethnic groups through the mechanisms of social assimilation. But the half-hearted attempts at assimilation and accommodation in British social policy highlighted the postcolonial contradictions of trying to sustain a racialized conception of citizenship in the face of a multi-ethnic populace. As Britain moved uneasily out of Empire, so the racialized character of citizenship became increasingly exposed as a contested issue (see, *inter alia*, CCCS, 1982; Castles and Davidson, 2000; Gilroy, 1987). Attempts to maintain the equivalence constructed between 'white' and 'British' encountered struggles against the subordinate status of 'second-class' citizenship. Racialized and minoritized groups were subjected to multiple forms of regulation, from systems of immigration control to focused attention from a range of state agencies (schooling, policing etc.) in a series of practices subsequently defined as 'institutional racism'. Growing evidence of, and struggles for, divergent 'needs' made uneven impacts upon the system of welfare (see, for example, Ahmad, 1993). At some points, such differences were recognized in the form of limited multicultural approaches or in the recruitment of minority ethnic staff identified as more representative of, and better 'attuned' to, the needs of the populations they were expected to serve (Lewis, 2000c). At other points, however, the discovery of 'cultural diversity' exposed minority ethnic groups to the repressive dimensions of state welfare. This was not merely in the form of discriminatory policing, but also in the diagnoses of 'maladjustment' of various kinds in respect of education, social work and health visiting, which in turn necessitated greater intervention or surveillance from the state (Hall et al., 1978; Lewis, 1998b; 2000b).

At the same time, the family became exposed as something other than the happy coincidence of God and Nature. Material shifts in the alignment of family and work and the rise of feminism exposed gendered divisions of labour and power where once only biology had been discerned (Barrett and McIntosh, 1981; Wilson, 1977). These changes included the growing involvement of married women in paid employment (alongside what Beveridge described as their 'vital role' as housewives and mothers); the rise of divorce and remarriage producing serial families; the rise in lone-parent families; the spread of alternatives to the family form – communal living, gay or lesbian households; and so on. In all these ways, conventional patriarchal assumptions about the stability of the family form became increasingly detached from social reality. At the same time, other assumptions about the family were being challenged. These concerned the interior life of families, conventionally understood as the intimate and tranquil 'haven', protecting its members from the rigours of the public world. Led by women's movement campaigns, a less protective interior was made visible. Economic and power inequalities between men and women, and the capacity of the family to produce (and conceal) the abuse of its vulnerable members, were revealed and challenged. These challenges questioned the assumed normality of the family as the focal point of state welfare – making visible the gendered division of labour, the gendered formation of citizenship and its privileged place in the (re)production of racialized identities (Gordon, 1999: esp. ch. 8; Lister, 1997/2003; Yuval-Davis, 1997). In the construction of the welfare state, the family had occupied a double role as an institution that contributed to its members' welfare and as a set of relationships that welfare provision sought to maintain. Both aspects were 'unsettled' by the feminist challenge.

The normalizing assumptions that were built into – and were in turn sustained by – the post-war welfare state had been embedded in a strong distinction between the social and the natural. The ordering of people, positions, relationships and needs grasped most of these as being based in a realm beyond society, a non-social realm of biology; they were simply part of the 'natural order of things'. So the 'normal family' – with its wage-earning, breadwinning, patriarchal head of household and its nurturing, domesticating and domesticated housewife/mother and its other dependants – was not simply 'normal'. Its normality was legitimated and underwritten by reference to these patterns being natural: men's nature being to hunt and gather (even if only the wage packet) and women's biology predisposing them to bring up babies and to mop up what babies bring up. This position was finely articulated by Patrick Jenkin, the Conservative Shadow Secretary of State for Social Services in 1977, at a Conservative Party conference, where he managed to combine biological, legal and religious discourses in a rather desperate reassertion of the old ways:

> Quite frankly, I don't think that mothers have the same right to work as fathers do. If the good Lord had intended us to have equal rights to go out to work, he

wouldn't have created men and women. These are biological facts ... We hear
a lot today about social work – perhaps the most important social work is moth-
erhood. (quoted in Clarke, Cochrane and Smart, 1987: 140)

The same points can be made about the naturalization of other forms of difference. The structuring of age centred on the period of mature independence
constituted by adulthood, preceded and followed by the biologically inscribed
dependency of childhood and old age. The delineation of disability was conceived and codified as biological conditions under the authority of medical
power. The categorization and regulation of sexualities were where the intersection of the distinctions between normal and abnormal on the one hand and
natural and unnatural on the other is at its most dense. All became the focus
of anti-normative – and socializing – challenges. Welfare formed a significant,
though not the only, focus for these movements because it was the institutional nexus in which these divisions were instantiated in substantive and
potent ways. The challenges to state welfare addressed a range of interconnected issues: policies, practices and personnel. Those elements of social relations which had been expelled to the realm of the natural in the structuring
assumptions of welfare provision became the focus for collective social action,
aimed not just at the enlargement of social welfare but at the transformation
of its principles of provision and delivery. In the process, the ideological
assumptions of social policy were exposed and challenged. So too were the
claims that the state and its agents were 'impartial'. The 'organizational settlement' of the post-war welfare state produced institutional arrangements whose
social 'neutrality' was secured by the knowledge, expertise and ethos of bureaucracy and professionalism and their combination in forms of bureau-professionalism (Clarke and Newman, 1997: ch. 1). Williams has pointed to the ways
in which social movements articulated around 'race' and gender developed
complex critiques of state welfare:

> the struggles of many of these groups against relations of dominance have
> themselves focused on welfare provision ... What was also important about
> these social movements was that they were not simply concerned with the dis-
> tributional politics of welfare, but with the very way welfare was organised.
> Racism and sexism operate at state, institutional and personal levels and in so
> far as these specific movements struck a new universal demand it was over
> who controlled welfare and in whose interests. In these terms the campaigns
> of the Women's Movement not only linked conditions within the private sphere
> of domestic and personal relations but also sought to replace the bureaucratic
> and professionally controlled relations of welfare with non-hierarchical, non-
> sexist, non-racist relationships where users of welfare exercised control over
> the nature and delivery of welfare services. (1996: 64)

Similar challenges were developed in relation to disability and sexuality, again
insisting on the *social* character of such identities and refusing the dependent
and pathologized statuses attributed by biological or psychological essentialism

and enshrined in social policy (see, for example, Carabine, 1996; Cooper, 1994; Campbell and Oliver, 1996). The cumulative effect of such challenges might be seen as the 'return of the repressed' in social policy. Each of these dimensions of inequality and division had been ideologically consigned to the realm of the extra-social: they were simply the more or less unfortunate effects of nature. The struggles to make them 'social' opened up new dimensions of partiality and discrimination to critical attention. Such challenges bore particularly on the 'front lines' of state welfare provision, even though they were also directed at the commanding heights of policy-making. Welfare workers, by virtue of the fact that they carried the day-to-day contact between the people and the state, were prone to being captured or coopted by these 'challenges from the margins' and their demands for greater equity or redress (e.g. Newman and Williams, 1995; Taylor, 1993; see also Johnson, 1973, on the instability of state 'mediating professions'). Welfare professionalism became one of the sites in which issues about 'discrimination', 'empowerment' and inequalities of different kinds were played out. The results were often uneven and uneasy compromises: 'matching' black clients with black workers; multiculturalist policies; commitments to 'anti-discriminatory practice'; bureaucratized equal opportunities statements; and so on (Breitenbach et al., 2002; Lewis, 2000c). Nevertheless, this crisis of the *social* settlement penetrated deeply into the organizational and occupational worlds of the 'old' welfare state.

These *socializing* movements had political and policy effects (though rarely the larger transformations that they sought). But they also had profoundly unsettling effects on the naturalizing discourses of difference: they revealed conditions of oppression, subordination and exclusion as socially constructed (rather than natural and universal). Such denaturalization also began to make the 'normal' visible and contestable. The struggles over women's subordination allowed glimpses of how male power was organized and normalized. Disability activism brought the normative assumptions of ablebodiedness into sight. Contesting racialized subordination made it possible to identify whiteness as a racialized position and identity, whose power rested in part on its claimed position as the norm above and beyond its 'racial' or 'ethnic' character. For example, Brah argues that in relation to racialized identities:

> it is important to stress that both black and white people experience their gender, class and sexuality through 'race'. Racialization of white subjectivity is often not manifestly apparent to white groups because 'white' is a signifier of dominance, but this renders the racialization process no less significant. (1996: 105)

Such attempts to transform the conditions of 'second-class citizenship' destabilized the field of welfare positions and the wider framework of constructions of nation, state and welfare. They contributed to the 'crises of the welfare state' through their questioning of what belonging to a (national) welfare state could mean (Clarke and Newman, 1997; Hughes, 1998). Starting from these struggles gives a rather different inflection to contemporary debates about 'welfare reform' (Williams, 2000). It reminds us that the welfare state already had a complex trajectory *before* the arrival of reform, retrenchment, reconstruction and residualization. Bourdieu puts this point nicely when he argues that 'The state, in every country, is to some extent the trace in reality of social conquests' (1999: 33). This is not to argue that the welfare states of the West/North were revolutionized or entirely transformed by these challenges. The changes were uneven, often grudgingly conceded. They resulted in partial accomplishments – accommodations and compromises of different kinds. But certainly those struggles left their traces on welfare policies, apparatuses and practices – and on the political-cultural mobilization of different sorts of groups in contesting the dominant formations of the national popular embedded in social policy in the UK:

> In the attempt to challenge and dislodge the forms of inequality connected to social differences, new social identities and political constituencies have been convened around dimensions of difference. In this sense, we can say that social differences also emerge from the challenges to domination and inequality and the struggle for self-defined identities. Thus social differences are formed in the dynamic interplay between domination and the struggle against it; between the attempt to establish the boundaries of the normal and attempts to dislodge and/or expand those boundaries; between the attempts to limit the criteria of access to resources (including those of welfare) and the struggle to breach or replace those criteria. The result of all this is that previously unrecognized social divisions and identities, such as those formed around subordinations or exclusions attached to race, disability, age and gender difference, have reconfigured the social policy agenda. (Lewis, 2003: 98)

These challenges to the social settlement have profound consequences for the politics of welfare. What the New Right attacked was not only the 'old' welfare state but what it had become – and *what it might have become* as a result of the claims and demands articulated around this field of differences and inequalities. The New Right's anti-welfarism and anti-statism of the 1980s and 1990s were directed never just at the welfare state of '1945', but also at its remade forms of 1965 and 1975. The attacks on 'socialism' and the 'loony left' in the UK (and 'elite liberalism' in the USA) addressed these expanded, and expanding, welfare states. The New Right assault was directed at both the dominant political-economic formation of Atlantic Fordist corporatism that was institutionalized in the construction of the post-war welfare state, and the expansionist and transformative incursions of those struggling to challenge and enlarge its limited welfarism. It is important to register these multiple targets of anti-welfarism. Otherwise we reproduce an ahistorical distinction between the 'old' welfare state and its contemporary 'reform' – which writes out the complex social politics of the 1960s, 1970s and 1980s. This sort of distinction has already been used by New Labour to rewrite the history of the welfare state (e.g. Blair, 1998; Giddens, 1994; 1998). The 'Third Way' constructs a binary opposition between 'Old Left' and 'New Right' which a modernizing 'Third

Way' can transcend. In the process, a whole series of struggles, contestations and political-cultural movements are obliterated (Clarke, Gewirtz and McLaughlin, 2000a: 10–16).

Desocializing difference: the reassertion of inequalities

The expansive – socializing – incursions into the welfare state have been fiercely contested from a range of positions that have attempted to *desocialize* social divisions and to renaturalize inequalities. These 'anti-social' projects seek to locate differences somewhere other than the 'social' – expelling them from the possibility of social and political mobilization and redress. They attempt to locate difference and inequality in discursive realms where they will once again become safe and manageable. They represent difference and inequality as 'really' a matter of economics, biology, geography, culture and history.[3] They overlap, intersect and conflict – but are united in their hostility to the conception of socially contestable divisions. At this point, I only want to sketch these anti-social strategies, since they will return in various political and academic guises during the book. Let us begin with the economic. The revival of economic discourse and its centrality to the political project of neo-liberalism has made, and enforced, two claims about inequality and difference. The first is that economic inequality is a natural, necessary and essential effect of running a free market: there will always be 'winners and losers' because capitalism is an essentially competitive system (Gilder, 1981; see Frank, 2000, on 'market populism'). The second is a rather larger political and philosophical claim, summarized in Margaret Thatcher's view that 'there is no such thing as society', only 'individual people and their families'.

This *individualism* with *familialism* is the elementary form of neo-liberalism – a world of 'possessive individualism' constituted out of individual interests and their interaction in markets (Kingfisher, 2002). This is the fundamental claim about freedom of (buying and selling) choice. It is also the fundamental claim about the most basic or 'natural' state of human affairs. Enterprising individuals seeking to provide for themselves and their families are the elementary form of social life (see also Probyn, 1998, on the 'familialization of the social'). Left to themselves, they will be active, innovative, productive and responsible. Interfered with, they become frustrated, resentful, sluggish and dependent. And, this is a *world*: neo-liberalism claims this state of affairs as a universal condition (see Chapter 5). All people are – or should be allowed to be – enterprising individuals. In the context of welfare provision, this individualism underpinned the challenges to both 'social engineering' and 'monopoly provision' by the state – both of which repressed individual uniqueness and enterprise. At this level, neo-liberalism has no problems about 'difference': it

---

3 It should be clear that these categories overlap with, but are not the same as, academic subjects. 'Economization', for example, refers to the process of making things appear as if they are economic; it is a process of representation. This draws selectively on the work of academic economists for its material, its tactics and its legitimation, but it is not the discipline of economics, and nor do all economists perpetrate it. The same is true for biologizing, geographic and historic strategies and the academic fields to which they are complexly linked.

just does not recognize differences as social. Rather, it understands them as *aso-cial* individual differences of wants: choices to be made by individuals about the particular goods and services that they wish for. Difference is expressed as consumer demand – and only the dynamics of market competition can ensure that those demands are satisfied.

This conception of individual interests and their coordination by the market has underpinned the *economization* of the social – which involves both a reduction (of social life to economic phenomena) and an expansion (of economic relations and processes to rule more of life than the economy). This is a double claim. On the one hand, the economy is the vital condition and dynamic of social life – locally, nationally and internationally. On the other, the rest of social life should be subject to the same processes and dynamics, and not be 'protected' or 'insulated' from market forces, consumer choice and individual freedom of action. More broadly, we have witnessed the saturation of cultures by economic discourse at the same time as economic life has become 'culturalized' (see the contrasting discussions in du Gay and Pryke, 2001; and Ray and Sayer, 1999).

These processes of economization coexist (without much apparent difficulty) with the revival and renewal of *biologizing* discourses. I use the plural here deliberately since there are at least two biologies in circulation that work slightly differently. The first is the renewal – or perhaps mere continuation – of the old biologism. The biology of 'racial difference' (around IQ and other capacities) still legitimates the necessary superiority of the white race over its others; and the socio-biology of gender difference still legitimates masculine dominance in evolutionary necessity (e.g. Barrett, Dunbar and Lycett, 2001; Herrenstein and Murray, 1996; and the critique by Rose and Rose, 2001). The second is the new biologism – practising under the sign of the gene. Here the perfectibility of the organism is promised – offering the capacity to 'design out' flaws of various kinds. The flaws are varied – but seem to be drawn back recurrently to some of the core normative concerns of social order. Genetics holds out the possibility of getting 'gender' right (avoiding too many girls), straightening sexuality (avoiding too many gay genes), normalizing disability/impairment, and eliminating violence and criminality. 'Bad' differences may – it is hoped – prove to be genetically manipulable. There are some striking omissions from such conditions: it should (presumably) be as easy to 'design out' political megalomania, corporate greed, and illusions of superiority and supremacy (and the willingness to act on them). But they appear not to be on the current list of genetic targets. However, these resurgent biologisms aim to take difference back out of the contestable realm of the social and store them somewhere safer – in the laboratory. As Denise Riley (1983: 33–6) argued in the context of views of children's development, biology is understood both as more fundamental than the social (it is an 'underlying' condition) and as occurring prior to the social (expressed in the task of 'socialization'). This double claim – to be before and below the social – makes 'biologizing' discourses potent challenges to the claims of, and on, the 'social'.

The haunting of biology by 'race' persists despite the declining empirical credibility of claims to distinguish 'racial groups' biologically (Gilroy, 2000). There remains, though, the hope – or desperate belief – that 'race' is both 'real' and 'really biological', as if this will hold back the postcolonial moment and its dissolution of national-racial imaginaries. This persistence is also visible in the similar affinity of 'race' and 'place' – a *geographic* anti-social strategy. Mobility, migration and mixing evoke a (colonial) nostalgia for when peoples knew their places: the land, the climate, the culture and the people in their 'traditional' and proper alignment. This imperative is articulated by governments (as they confront asylum-seekers and migrants), by nationalist and racist political forces as they dream of ethnic/racial purity, and by populist media discourses that persist in eliding race, nation and place. The wish that people would stay 'where they belong' is the primitive geography that informs this conception of how race and place are aligned. This spatialization is the recurrent 'elsewhere' of colonial geography that positions 'minority ethnic communities' in a map of origins. In the UK context, of course, these are 'elsewheres': the 'other' places of Asia, Africa and the Caribbean, which serve as the constant hope of racial purifiers and repatriators. This poses the question of the nation – or the imaginaries of the 'national popular' – in complex ways. There is the hope that migrant others might 'return' to their elsewheres ('back to where they *belong*'). But this is shadowed by a fear about the effect of divided loyalties and identifications that may oscillate between here and elsewhere (see Ong, 1999, on fears about diasporic Chinese within 'host' countries and in China).

But, as Gail Lewis (2000b) has argued, the 'minority ethnic communities' identified in multicultural governance are doubly spatialized in governmental discourse and practice. As well as really 'belonging elsewhere' (i.e. not in the UK), they are also understood as occupying *particular* urban spaces : 'inner city neighbourhoods', 'areas of deprivation', zones of 'social exclusion' (the rural remains imagined as white: Neal, 2002). Patterns of settlement, residence and cultural institutionalization are localized – and may be addressed through spatial strategies (community development, neighbourhood renewal, community councils and so on). But localized spaces are separated from the nation: they delimit the presence, visibility and recognition of others.[4]

Conceptions of people and place overlap with *culturalizing* strategies which attempt to register difference as 'merely cultural' (Lewis, 2003). Here the view of culture as possession/property comes to bear most forcefully. Groups are identified with and as a culture, and difference is conceived in terms of a multicultural pluralism.[5] A commitment to recognize 'diversity' means that groups are 'entitled to' their cultures and there is a formalized equivalence between cultures that obscures questions of inequality, power or processes of domination and subordination. Culture (a solidified, stable and homogeneous block) accounts for distinctive social phenomena: the high levels of school exclusion

4 Questions of difference and place are also in play in the other persistent nostalgia – for a time when women, too, 'knew their place' and did not disrupt the public worlds of work and politics.

5 There are connections here with Rose's discussion of 'communities' as a distinctive focus of advanced liberal governmentality (1999: ch. 5). As I have argued elsewhere (Clarke, 2002b), I think this misses critical issues about the colonial and postcolonial formation of community as the locus of governance – and about its contemporary instabilities and contestations (see also Li, 1996).

among African-Caribbean boys; the 'greater tolerance' of South Asian women for domestic violence; the 'entrepreneurialism' of diasporic Chinese; and so on. Culture recapitulates difference to unchanging and unchangeable 'traditions' or 'ways of life' that possess people, even as it may make them the target for interventions by states and their apparatuses. 'Tolerance' of cultural difference as a political virtue runs alongside 'cultural pathology' as a focus of governing those who do not fit the norm. Both mobilizations of 'culture' try to desocialize it, taking it out of the realm of contestation (where inequalities, power, domination and their far-reaching effects might be part of the dialogue).

The final anti-social strategy involves the representation of 'social' difference and inequality as belonging to another (earlier) time. The dominant version of this *historicizing* strategy is a 'been there, done that' view of struggles against inequality. Once upon a time we needed feminism, anti-racism, disability movements and class politics, but – fortunately – they are not needed now. Now is 'new', 'modern', and we need to move onto 'new business' (a central theme in New Labour's conception of history and modernity: Clarke and Newman, forthcoming). The concern with 'equality' is a hangover, a residual militancy that has no place in 'today's world'. A secondary version evokes the 'pendulum' view of history: once there was too much inequality (of whatever variety), but now there's too much attention or resources given to women, black people, disabled people, gays, lesbians and criminals; and 'ordinary people' (a socially unmarked category) are suffering as a consequence. But history's pendulum always swings again ...

I have given a rather shallow account of these discursive desocializing strategies – in part because they are already familiar, and in part because we will be meeting them again at later points in the book. Here I want to emphasize a number of things about them. Although they have all been put to use in 'anti-social' politics and policies in Britain, they are not uniquely 'British' discourses: they flow transatlantically, linking North American and British political cultural conflicts. They may be used differently, but they have been connective in political organizations, in public discourses, and in policy networks. They are strategies that form a repertoire of 'anti-social' possibilities. They are deployed in shifting and sometimes contradictory combinations – but they are put to work in a consistent effort to 'roll back' material and symbolic advances made in the second half of the twentieth century (by different movements in different places at different times). In their assaults on the social they mix divergent conceptions of the present. On the one hand there is a nostalgia for a tidier and more ordered world in which people knew their place; on the other, an enthusiasm for a modernity or modernization that will leave all the untidiness of difference and inequality behind.

Making a modern society: New Labour and the social

These strategies are put to work in political and cultural projects, mobilized alongside other discourses and other imaginaries in the struggles for political power, policy legitimacy and cultural hegemony. However, they are 'strategies' – and strategies are different from outcomes. We should be wary of reading their effects from their intentions. In each I have emphasized that they aim to, attempt to, try to, dispel the 'socializing' claims of social movements. But this is not to say that they succeed. Indeed, one feature of contemporary Western societies (and not only them) is the political and cultural coexistence of contradictory social imaginaries and (potential) political forces, including those committed to 'socializing' difference and inequality. This is not to argue that such discourses are dominant – or that they ever were. But they have certainly refused to go quietly.

I want to think about New Labour's project of 'governing in the modern world' in the light of this view of the social as contested by both socializing and desocializing forces. New Labour has strong continuities with Thatcherite conservatism, not least the commitment to a profoundly neo-liberal view of how the economy, state and society are to be aligned in the context of corporate globalization. Like Thatcherism, it is a project that seeks to create a new alignment of welfare, state and nation – and to establish a new 'welfare settlement' (Lister, 2002a). But New Labour has also had to both address and contain the commitments to expanded senses of both the 'social' and the 'public' that survived – and were even evoked by – the period of Conservative rule in the UK. It has needed to negotiate both the residual attachments to social-democratic welfarism as embodied in public institutions, and the emergent challenges, expressed in social movements, to social democracy's narrow conception of the social (around 'race/ethnicity', sexuality and disability, for example).

Work and family have been dominant principles in New Labour's modernization, expressed in the rhetorical identification of the nation/people as 'hard-working families': 'My passion is to continue the modernization of Britain, in favour of hard-working families' (Blair, in Labour Party, 2001: 3). New Labour celebrated 'work' as the central social, political, economic and personal task (see, *inter alia*, Levitas, 1998; 2001; Lister, 1998; 2002a; 2002b). It is (waged) work that 'inserts' people into social life; connects them to citizenship rights; reduces public spending; provides them with a sense of value and purpose; enables them to act as role models; and, not least, ensures the integration of the national and global economies. The 2001 Manifesto celebrated work's transformative powers: 'Employment's not just the foundation of an affordable welfare state, it is the best anti-poverty, anti-crime and pro-family policy yet invented' (Labour Party, 2001: 24). The centrality of work was registered in the growing role played by the Treasury (and the tax system) in 'incentivizing' desirable behaviour, and its dominance over 'welfare' was symbolized in the renaming of the Department of Social Security as the Department of Work and Pensions.

This 'modern' view of work was a resolutely 'equal opportunity' view, accepting (and reinforcing) patterns of gender change that have undercut the older norm of the male breadwinner (Lister, 2002a: 140–3). New Labour enthusiastically endorsed the challenges to the norm of the white, male, ablebodied worker, claiming that everyone should be entitled to work. Indeed, they insisted that everyone who could work, should work. This conception of the right (and the responsibility) to work was articulated to New Labour's 'modern' view of gender (and disability). But it left unchallenged the distinction between public and private realms – since only paid work in the public realm was valorized. In the process, the apparently infinite flexibility of women's capacity for labour was subjected to new demands, as pressures to be 'economically active' mounted while leaving the distribution and volume of domestic responsibilities untouched. As we have argued elsewhere, the reduction of public provision and public funding for a range of welfare benefits and services during the 1980s and 1990s transferred financial and labour costs to the (uncalculated) private realm (Clarke, 1999a; Clarke and Newman, 1997: ch. 7). From reduced benefit values to substitute labour in relation to health care and education, the private realm (and mainly female work within it) 'bridged the gap' left by public withdrawal. Meanwhile, this pursuit of work as the privileged point of connection between families and the national and global economies prioritized the 'flexibilities' of adaptation to employer demands. Borrowing from the US, 'welfare to work' overshadowed the changing relationships between state and citizen (Deacon, 2002; Peck, 2001). The 'New Deal' for the unemployed was continuously extended to new categories of claimant, and strengthened in terms of its conditionality and disciplines (Finn, 2003). In an echo of New Labour's pragmatic 'what counts is what works', we might suggest that for defining citizenship, 'who counts is who works' (Dwyer, 1998; 2000; Lister, 1998). I will return to some of these issues about work in later chapters in the context of discussing neo-liberalism (Chapter 5) and the state (Chapter 6).

New Labour's modernization also meant trying to rewrite the relationship between state and citizen, while 'reforming' the state. Different sorts of privatizations (as corporatization and familialization) were linked to making the citizen independent, responsible and morally upright. At the same time, the active citizen had to be both hard-working and a 'sceptical citizen-consumer' in relation to welfare services (Clarke, 1997; Needham, 2003). But New Labour also attempted to redraw access to citizenship and the relationships between citizenship, national membership and national identity. These efforts were centrally addressed to processes of migration and asylum-seeking, but they gave renewed salience to postcolonial issues about 'modern societies' being multi-ethnic and multicultural (Hesse, 2001a; Parekh, 2000). Under pressure, New Labour's position shifted from a profound hostility to migrants and asylum-seekers to a more differentiated view which recognized the 'economic case' for useful and productive migrants in a global economy, but sought to intensify the defences against the illegal, the non-genuine, the criminal and the fraudulent. The White Paper *Secure Borders, Safe Haven* acknowledged economic virtue:

> Migrants bring new experiences and talents that can widen and enrich the knowledge base of the economy. Human skills and ambitions have become the building blocks of successful economies and the self-selection of migrants

means that they are likely to bring valuable ideas, entrepreneurship, ambition and energy. (Home Office, 2002: 11)

At the same time, it argued for strengthened borders and for the more actively supported (enforced?) integration of 'new citizens' into the social and political culture:

In an increasingly diverse world, it is vital that we strengthen both our sense of community belonging and the civic and political dimensions of British citizenship ... [Language teaching, education and examination for citizenship] will strengthen the ability of new citizens to participate in society and engage actively in our democracy. This will help people understand both their rights and their obligations as citizens of the UK, and strengthen the bonds of mutual understanding between people of diverse cultural backgrounds. (2002: 11)

New Labour's multiculturalism is articulated around two principles – both familiar from the history of state-managed 'race relations' policies. The first is the commitment to 'tolerance' – the ultimate expression of the superiority of British civilization in relation to the cultures of others. The second is the tight control of immigration – the numeric precondition of both 'tolerance' and 'good race relations' (Hesse, 2001b; Lewis, 2002b). Although this has been justified with reference to the rise of racist/nationalist politics in many European countries including Britain, it also reflects attempts by the centre left to reinvent 'solidarity' around national/ethnic homogeneity.[6] For instance, Wolfe and Klausen (2000) have argued that 'ethnic homogeneity' has underpinned the development of welfare states, because it enables the 'sense of solidarity' that 'creates a readiness to share with strangers'. Similarly Dench's (2003) attack on New Labour's 'meritocratic' orientation juxtaposes 'ordinary white working people' against migration which is construed as a process of 'bringing in people who are not really part of the system'. The rhetorical deployment of the 'ordinary' (against the non-ordinary, strange, others) constructs – or reproduces – a distinctive imaginary, fixing political-cultural identities and solidarities as incapable of being transformed. This figure of the 'white working class' was – equally depressingly – echoed in a piece by one of New Labour's intellectual architects on the day I was drafting this chapter. Peter Mandelson, announcing that 'We need to rethink the welfare state' (what, *again*?), argued:

We need to rethink the role of the welfare state in providing 'cradle to grave' security in a more complex, fractured society where 'entitlements' are not a sufficient moral basis on which to provide a fair system of social protection. We also need to articulate a vision of multiculturalism that speaks to the fears of all communities, including the white working class in industrial heartland areas. (*The Guardian*, 25 April 2003: 24)

6 I am deeply grateful to Ali Rattansi for both drawing my attention to some of these developments and sharing his thoughts on how to respond to them.

Such rethinking has a double politics – legitimating the retreat from collective security in the face of neo-liberal flexibilities, and articulating multiculturalism to the project of constructing Britain as a 'community of communities'. New Labour's response to a rich variety of citizenship claims was a commitment to social inclusion in the conception of a nation as a consensual moral order. To the extent that there are divisions within this social order, they are laid out on a 'horizontal rather than hierarchical model of society' (Lister, 2002a: 137), such that the socially excluded may be enabled to move from the periphery to the centre. Given that New Labour had created the conditions of inclusion, those who remained marginal in some way were there, by definition, either by choice or as a result of their own failings – they were 'irresponsible' in some sense. A gallery of 'self-excluding' groups was constructed: dysfunctional families, 'persistently delinquent' children, school truants, work avoiders and welfare cheats, bad neighbours, aggressive beggars and so on. What these groups had in common was their wilful failure to take up the opportunity to join in as members of a decent and civilized society. Bauman catches this attribution of responsibility: 'It is the fault of the excluded that they did nothing, or not enough, to escape exclusion; perhaps they even invited their fate, making the exclusion into a foregone conclusion' (1998: 85). The excluded failed the 'responsibility' test, preferring to be disorderly and disruptive when they could be like the rest of 'us'. Gail Lewis (2000b) has written of how the unequal patterns of school exclusion affecting young black people were transmuted into the results of moral/cultural deficits and failings in black communities. Equivalent moral codings were put to work around asylum and migration, where the business of government was to test for 'genuineness'. Processes of border control were about sifting the good migrant from the bad (the criminal, the irresponsible, the immoral, the feckless, the 'benefit tourist' and the non-genuine). Those lucky enough to be stamped as authentic may eventually enter the ranks of the included. This distinction (viewed as independent of racial and ethnic characterization) sustained the government's consistent refusal to see any connections between racism and the exclusionary policies, practices and rhetorics directed at asylum-seekers and migrants. These moral codings increasingly found their way into government policies and apparatuses for managing the social order. For example, the 'New Deal' and its requirements for the unemployed; curfews; parental responsibility orders and 'contracts'; school evaluations of parental 'quality'; the calculation of health risks and 'worth'; and the constantly innovative approaches to regulating migration and asylum; were all sites where such moral categorizations were operationalized.

But if these are the dominant trends in New Labour, they are both unstable and cross-cut by different sorts of accommodations to claims made in the name of the social (in both its residual and its emergent meanings). The introduction of a minimum wage and the commitment to eradicate 'child poverty' in a decade speak to the old social-democratic egalitarianism. Legislation on 'hate crimes', the Disability Discrimination Act, and action on gay and lesbian rights show the marks that struggles for rights and recognition have drawn on the state. More generally, the privatized, individualized and familialized nation of worker-citizen-consumers is also the object of activation strategies designed to enlarge the public realm through new forms of representation, consultation and participation (Barnes et al., 2003; Newman et al., 2004). These reflect the persistent problems of a political project attempting to negotiate and contain the contested social. New Labour may be shaped by the wish to create a neo-liberal modernity in honour of globalization – but the national popular is not so easily dragged into line. New Labour consistently encounters residual and emergent mobilizations around conceptions of the social and the public. The two terms are not the same, although they were closely interwoven in social-democratic welfarism. Their contemporary relationship is more troubled because a more contested and conflicted 'social' gives rise to difficult arguments about who the public are, what their collective interests might be, and how they might best be represented (Barnes et al., 2003; see also Fraser, 1997). At the same time, the public realm has been under fierce attack from neo-liberal claims about the moral, economic and political superiority of the private realm (understood as private sector, as market coordination, and as the private/familial: Clarke, 2004). But struggles over the public realm (against different forms of privatization; for the enlargement of public debate, accountability and power; and for the enlargement of who counts as part of the public) are intimately linked to struggles over the social. They are linked because a public realm remains a critical site for mobilizing to contest forms of subordination, exclusion and inequality.

I think this is a rather different view of the 'social' from those visible in Foucauldian studies of governmentality where the 'death of the social' is much discussed (e.g. Rose, 1996a; 1999; 2000). I think that it is important to consider the ways in which 'governmental' action may attempt to manage social formations, may attempt to subject them to regulation, and may attempt to fix the meanings of words and the identities of subjects. But that does not mean that these attempts succeed. Tania Li has argued for the importance of distinguishing the 'project of rule' from the accomplishments, compromises and compliance that are negotiated in practice (1999: 295ff). Foucauldian analyses of governmentality too readily treat these attempts as though they are successful in bringing about the 'subjections' they imagine. In contrast, a more Gramscian concern with hegemony would privilege the partial, contradictory and unstable character of dominant strategies. Similarly an orientation to what Holland and Lave (2001b) call the 'dialogic' would keep open the analytic space in which subjects might be found answering back. There is a question of why any of this matters. After all, the governmentality studies describe many of the key processes of governmental realignments of the 'social' that are in play. I think what matters is the orientation to the processes and the practices of governing. I find the view of advanced liberal governmentality presented by Rose and others too extensive, homogeneous and unified. In this view governmentalities subject populations to their rule. Instead, I want to argue for governing being a more uneven and partial process that has to proceed through alliances, compromises and conflicts in which subjects succumb, sign up or comply – but also resist, or are recalcitrant and troublesome. As a result, its attempted subjections are likely to be less than comprehensive and only temporarily settled. In short, I think we are better informed (analytically and politically) by an approach that stresses a *politics of articulation* rather than a *politics of subjection*. This would give more attention to the construction of social and political blocs; to the political, ideological or discursive means by which social groups are mobilized or demobilized; and to the temporary, unstable and contradictory aspects of 'settlements'.

four

In Chapter 1 I argued that the post-war alignments of welfare, state and nation had become unsettled. For many, globalization has been the dominant force leading to the end of the welfare state and the end of the nation-state. Globalization has provoked enormous controversy both within and beyond social policy about its impact – or not – on welfare states. On the one hand, proponents of 'apocalyptic globalization' announce the 'end of' welfare, state or nation in voices wracked with emotion (whether joy or despair). On the other, sober-toned analysts in comparative social policy (along with other critics and sceptics) insist that relatively little has changed – and that the familiar configurations of welfare, state and nation persist, even if in more straitened circumstances. In this chapter, I am going to take a rather different route through these debates, since they seem profoundly unsatisfactory. Indeed, I fear that they miss precisely the most interesting things about the unsettling and realignment of welfare, states and nations. In this chapter, I will:

- explore the argument between 'apocalyptic' views of globalization and the institutionalist view of national adaptation (first section);
- challenge the dominant view of the state and the market, and look beyond it to the significance of the private realm for thinking about welfare (second section);
- consider the ways in which globalization has unsettled the nation-state (third section).

Apocalypse now?

Strong or 'apocalyptic' theories of globalization claim that it has dissolved the complex of nation-state and welfare state. Political-institutionalist critics restore the centrality of the national by highlighting the specificity of national political and institutional arrangements. But in neither version is the complex of welfare, state and nation explored in terms of their mutual constitution or dislocation. Let us begin with the strong version of globalization. Globalization in the 'apocalyptic' sense is characterized by: the dominance of economics over politics; the power of global capital over nation-states; the installation of markets as dominant institutions of coordination; and the 'end' or dissolution of nation-states and welfare states (see, for example, Mishra, 1999). This view of globalization identifies the power of unleashed free markets (or global capital) to transform the world economically, politically and culturally. The rise of the global economy, in these accounts, dissolves barriers, blockages and borders that might stand in the way of the free movement of capital and goods. Gough describes this as the 'structural power of capital':

> the ability of capital to pursue its goals without necessary recourse to direct action by its agents. We argue that this power rests on its control over investment coupled with its ability to migrate to other jurisdictions with the growing internationalization of economic life. This in turn generates structural power over labour, state revenue dependency and the ideological colonisation of social life. (2000: 101)

Aided and abetted – or even driven – by information technology innovations, capital becomes 'hypermobile', uncoupling itself from its prior local or national moorings. All societies become subject to the same economic imperatives: to open their economies, to attract capital investment, and to create flexible workers. They experience the same political pressures: to create 'low-tax' regimes; to reduce 'unproductive' public spending; to deregulate markets; and to support capital formation and accumulation. Finally, all societies encounter the same cultural pressures towards a global/American culture of consumption. Yeates summarizes this view of globalization and its relationship to welfare states as follows:

> Overall, this account of the relationship between globalization and social policy stresses downward pressures on welfare states and the 'prising open' of social pacts underpinning them. The influence of 'strong' theory's precepts and predictions is clearly evident in the way that the content of social policy is presented as being determined by 'external' – mainly economic – constraints, largely beyond the control of governments; that national political, cultural and social differences will simply be 'flattened' and social standards will plummet by the sheer 'weight' and 'force' of global economic forces. (2001: 26)

Globalization, then, has been predominantly conceived of as an economic process or, more accurately, a process whose primary driving forces are economic ones. With the dissolution of the communist bloc, the world is increasingly envisaged as a single integrated market, in which deregulation works in the service of 'free trade'. Such processes have called into question the role of nation-states, national governments and their public spending programmes (including social welfare spending) in a number of ways. Since the mid-1970s, there has been a rising 'business agenda' (Moody, 1987), in which corporate capital has articulated its demand for 'business friendly environments' (places with low taxes, low regulation and low-cost labour). Such demands have been enforced by 'capital flight': the reality or threat of relocating investment, industrial and commercial processes elsewhere. These views have been installed as 'global economic wisdom' in a variety of supranational organizations and agencies (such as the International Monetary Fund, the World Bank and the World Trade Organization: see Deacon, 1997). Their policies have tended to reinforce a vision of minimalist or *laissez-faire* government, centred on reducing levels of taxation and of public spending and borrowing.

This changing political economy has implications for welfare states. The most pessimistic view is that this new global economy has sounded the death knell for the developed (or 'European') welfare state. Policies of economic and social management can no longer be sustained by national governments in the face of deregulated capitalism. This view of globalization's irresistible force is exemplified in this quotation from Ulrich Beck:

> The premises of the welfare state and pension system, of income support, local government and infrastructural policies, the power of organized labour, industry-wide collective bargaining, state expenditure, the fiscal system and 'fair' taxation – all this melts under the withering sun of globalization. (2000: 1)

But such epochal accounts have their critics. A number of studies have highlighted continuing divergences in national welfare states alongside consistent levels of public spending on welfare, despite arguments that international pressures on national governments are increasing. Keesbergen, for instance, argues that:

> Welfare state research in the early 1990s further documented empirically that welfare states have been remarkably resistant to change notwithstanding the mounting challenges they face. Not surprisingly, a major explanatory problem for these dominant welfare state theories was the persistence rather than 'crisis' or 'breakdown' of the major institutions of the welfare state. Both macro- and meso-institutional theories started to indicate the crucial institutional mechanisms (e.g. path dependency and lock-in) that explain welfare state persistence. (2000: 20)

This more sceptical view of globalization's effects has become an emerging, and increasingly strong, position in comparative and international studies in social policy (see, *inter alia*, Alcock and Craig, 2001; Esping-Andersen, 1996; Huber and Stephens, 2001; Sykes, Palier and Prior, 2001; Taylor-Gooby, 2001a). Esping-Andersen concludes that 'global economic competition does narrow policy choice' but suggests that 'standard accounts are exaggerated and risk being misleading. In part, the diversity of welfare states speaks against too much generalization' (1996: 2). Taylor-Gooby argues that 'Governments recognize limits to their freedom of action, but the practical imperative is that the welfare state should be more efficiently oriented to competitiveness, not that it should be abolished' (2001c: 17). This, then, points to a second approach to globalization and social welfare: one that stresses national political-institutional differentiation. Beyeler argues that the institutionalist approach offers two types of argument against 'deterministic views of the impact of global economic transformation. One points to the role of domestic institutional and political reform capabilities as mediating factors between international developments and domestic change, the other operates with the concept of path dependency and institutional lock-in' (2003: 155).

While accepting the economic trend towards greater global integration, such studies point to the continuing importance of national politics and institutional arrangements for choices over the shape, direction and character of welfare policies. These political-institutionalist analyses have provided a valuable counterweight to apocalyptic views of globalization. They nevertheless have some significant limitations for thinking about the remaking of welfare states. They rely on a view of the state and market as the fundamental (and conflicting) principles of coordination affecting welfare. Secondly, they rest on a view of globalization as an external force to which nation-states adapt. Thirdly, they retain a view of globalization as essentially an economic process, underestimating the complex and contradictory character of contemporary globalization. In these ways, they reproduce the naturalizing assumption that nations represent a unified alignment of place, people and culture (here as political-institutional forms) that I discussed in Chapter 2 (see also Gupta and Ferguson, 1992). Exploring these problems can enable us to think again about welfare states as nation-states in an unsettled world.

Beyond the state or the market?

The political-institutionalist literature has tended to treat the state and the market as opposed principles of social coordination. This view underpins the conception of globalization as an external force acting on welfare states and nation-states. The increased power of capital and/or the international extension of market relations are understood primarily *as a challenge to the state*. The state is seen as having developed as a countervailing power in response to market failure and inequality. This juxtaposition is reflected in Esping-Andersen's (1990) influential conception of the state as securing processes of *decommodification* in welfare, a concept designed 'to capture the degree to which welfare states weaken the cash nexus by granting entitlements independent of market participation' (1999: 43). The market as a means of coordination accentuates 'possessive individualist' ways of being that are mediated by the cash nexus, and which tend towards inequality. In contrast, the (welfare) state tends towards collective and (sometimes) democratic forms of coordination that do not depend on the cash nexus, and offers the possibility for willed redistribution. Nevertheless, the juxtaposition of the state and market in this way embodies a social-democratic view of the state as a corrective to market processes (and to the power of capital). Indeed, Esping-Andersen argued that the social-democratic model 'crowds out the market, and consequently constructs an essentially universal solidarity in favour of the welfare state' (1990: 28). This view is the mirror image of neo-liberalism's representation of the market being distorted by the 'interference' of the state.

Both theoretically and empirically there are problems with this binary opposition. It 'forgets' a long history of Marxist scholarship on how the state's relationship to capital has shaped welfare development (see, *inter alia*, Ferguson, Lavalette and Mooney, 2002; Gough, 1979; Offe, 1984). Marxist theorizations have ranged from seeing the state as 'the executive committee of the bourgeoisie' (in Engels's phrase) to being structurally bound to the 'logic of capital'. Other positions give priority to seeing the state as the (contradictory) site of political class struggle, and as the forum for the temporary reconciliation of conflicting social interests. Such studies have pointed to the ways in which the state is *systemically* implicated in the development and reproduction of capitalism. The state has secured the conditions of capital accumulation. It has institutionalized and legitimated the core interests and orientations of capital (not least in legal forms). It has attempted to create the social (and economic) peace advantageous to continued profitability. These sorts of processes are what the regulationist approach describes as the 'societalization' of forms of capital accumulation (Jessop, 2002: 22–31). Such state action suggests a more complicit, implicated or *articulated* view of the relationship between the state and capital. Surveying this relationship, Yeates has argued that:

> The presentation of the state–capital relationship as one in which capital is essentially in conflict with the state, or hegemonic after defeating the state, is inaccurate. It posits capital always in opposition to the state, whereas it is more useful to see capital and state often allied together, as well as often in conflict … The presentation of capital acting without regulation is also inaccurate: it is bound in various webs of regulations and governance, which it accepts grudgingly, attempts to circumvent and which it very occasionally invites. Indeed transnational capital wishes to secure the support of the state, not to replace the state. (2001: 93)

The state, then, may operate in complex and contradictory articulations with capital. Such articulations may become embedded and institutionalized – as in post-war Atlantic Fordism. But they are always potentially unstable – capable of coming undone as the forces and interests at stake in them change. Indeed, the regulationist approach makes this the centre of the analysis of the crisis of Fordism and the transition to post-Fordism (Jessop, 2002; Peck, 2001).

But there is another important issue about the state versus market distinction that goes beyond questions about the forms of connection between states and capital. The state versus market focus in studies of welfare states has obscured other relationships – and other changes. One of the domains obscured by this focus is the domestic, private or familial realm. The private realm is connected to both the market and the state in the production and consumption of welfare – and in the construction of types of 'welfare subjects' (see G. Lewis, 2000a). A substantial feminist literature has addressed how both political-economic and political-institutionalist studies have omitted the private realm, the family and gender relations from their analyses or have bolted them on as 'residual' categories (see, for example, Daly, 2000; Daly and Rake,

2003; J. Lewis, 2000; O'Connor, Orloff and Shaver, 1999; Williams, 1995). This, of course, takes us back to arguments about the 'social' in social policy discussed in Chapter 3. In terms of thinking about social formations, the way that attention to socio-economic groupings (or 'classes') has obscured gender relations mirrors the way that the state–market focus obscures the private/domestic realm. This is not surprising since the private/public dichotomy is densely interwoven with gender distinctions – both historically and in its contemporary reformulations (Clarke, 2004; Hall, 1998). Nevertheless, the role of the private realm (rather than the private sector) in the production and consumption of welfare disrupts the commodified–decommodified conception of welfare that is located in the state–market distinction. The provision of care or welfare that takes place through personal relations of affection, obligation or duty is neither commodified nor decommodified (Finch and Mason, 1993; Roseneil, 2003).

It should be clear that the relationships between states and markets are profoundly mediated by the private realm. At the most basic and functional level, households have provided the sites of both reproduction and consumption that 'enable' capitalist market economies. They organize care, welfare and social life in ways that are both routine and complex. Both day-to-day and generational reproduction are processes that take place outside the 'public realm' (of state and market). The state, market and private realm exist in shifting and diverse arrangements – not in 'separate spheres', even though they may be represented as such. Neither their variation nor their significance is adequately captured by adding passages about care or women's entry into the labour market to the 'state/market' binary. Such 'bolt-ons' miss the complexity of the relationships constructed through the private realm and how they are articulated with the state and the market.

At the start of this section, I used the rather clumsy formulation of domestic, private or familial realm. I did so because I want to make a distinction between the domestic/private realm and the family; these terms are too often collapsed together. As a result, the hetero-normative *construction of the private as familial* is overlooked (Probyn, 1998). The conception of the private realm as a family composed of a heterosexual couple and their children obscures other forms of personal relationship, household, and support and care (Roseneil, 2003). The private realm has conventionally been imagined as 'the family': the 'norm' that is both supported by welfare states and presumed by welfare states as the site of 'care'. Families have been articulated to welfare states through complex sets of generational and gender relationships that construct varieties of independent and dependent subjects (with different claims and entitlements). In contrast, non-familial, or non-normative, forms of household and relationship have been subject to discrimination, scrutiny, intervention and regulation. At the same time, just as families are not merely settings for gender relationships (they are at least constituted through generations and sexualities as well), so gender relationships transcend the family context. Gender relationships and norms are formed, regulated and contested in the intersections of the private and public realms. They are constructed in gendered divisions of labour; in the organization and control of public and private space; in the representation of (shifting) gender norms in the media; and in the specification of the rights and responsibilities of men and women in social and legal policies. I make these points – banal though they are – because some of the adaptations in social policy analysis to the challenges of feminist scholarship settle for rather less. Instead, gender is equated with the family – and the family is equated with gender (Fink, 2001).

Going beyond such simplifications opens up some of the other dynamics that are at stake in the renegotiation of welfare settlements. I will note three here. First, there is the shifting gendered division of labour – particularly the tendential rise of women's employment. This has implications for the 'breadwinner' models adopted in different welfare states (Daly and Lewis, 2000; J. Lewis, 2000). In particular, it marks a drive towards 'multiple breadwinners' in which increasingly fractured forms of 'flexible' work create the need for multiple incomes to ensure household viability and survival. Such 'breadwinner' changes have consequences for (gendered) familial models of care – either in strongly family-centred welfare systems (such as the 'Mediterranean' states) or in the 'privatizing' initiatives of liberal/neo-liberal states (Kingfisher, 2002; Trifiletti, 1999). The presumed elasticity of women's labour power continues to underpin their simultaneous greater involvement in paid work and the privatization/familialization of 'responsibility' for welfare. To put it gently, viewing 'welfare' as the intersection of state, market and the private/domestic realm makes a substantial difference to comparing how 'welfare states' (or regimes or models) differ, and to what is understood as the contemporary dynamics of change.

Secondly, the 'family' is not a singular and universal form – even though it may be spoken of as such in welfare policies. The normative assumptions about the family have been – and indeed continue to be – part of the contradictory and contested politics of welfare. Household formation (to use a less charged term) is the focus of multiple dynamics – generational, life cycle and life choice changes (the rise in single-person and lone-parent-headed households in the UK, for example). But it is also located in cultural differences – of national and ethnic variation – that are both 'traditional' and changing. Again, in the UK context, African-Caribbean and South Asian patterns of family formation have made a difference – both to forms of family life and to the articulations of work and welfare (see, for example, Brah, 1996; Lutz, Phoenix and Yuval-Davis, 1995). At the same time, they have been vulnerable to differential surveillance and intervention because of their distance from normative conceptions of family life (and the pathologization of difference in policy and practice). In the process, governmental policies towards privatization/familialization reinforce the tensions about different family and household forms. In New Labour's 'modern society', being 'family friendly' oscillates between being (grudgingly) tolerant of diversity and insisting on the 'one best way' (Clarke and Newman, forthcoming; Fink, 2002).

Finally, patterns of family and household formation are being reshaped by processes of mobility and migration in contemporary forms of globalization.

Transnational mobility disrupts the normative sense of family as a spatial form involving co-residence (at least in the nuclear node of parents and children). Migrant workers have always had a significant role in staffing welfare states, even if discriminatory citizenship policies and practices denied them the benefits (F. Williams, 1989). However, current demographic and occupational trends in the Western capitalist societies have produced an increasing reliance on migrant workers in welfare and care work (in both institutional and domiciliary forms). Kofman and Sales (1998) point to the concentration of migrant women in the low-paid, flexible and poorly protected 'service' sector (both public and private). In 2001–2, over 40% of new entrants to the UK's nursing register came from outside the UK, compared with 15% in 1989–90 (Batty, 2002: 21). Some contemporary forms of migration 'stretch' the family across space, creating what Hochschild has called 'global chains of care':

> Such chains often connect three sets of care-takers – one cares for the migrant's children back home, a second cares for the children of the woman who cares for the migrant's children, and a third, the migrating woman herself, cares for the children of professionals in the First World. Poorer women raise children for wealthier women while still poorer – or older or more rural – women raise their children. (2001: 136)

Of course, care work extends beyond childcare: nursing and social care are both part of this transnational process (Yeates, forthcoming). Care in the First World is increasingly commodified (whether it is provided in institutional settings or in the home). It is increasingly performed by (low-paid) migrant workers – who send money back to their families which includes the purchase of care for their own children and other relatives. Such transnational chains are both gendered and racialized, reflecting both the status of care work and its intersection with forms of subordination. Hondagneu-Soleto notes that in the USA, 'domestic jobs ... especially in cities such as Los Angeles, Washington, D.C., and New York – are disproportionately held by immigrant women. These women, many of whom are Caribbean and Latina, are disenfranchised by race, class, gender, and increasingly, by citizenship' (2000: 149). In the process, the family takes on elongated and potentially dislocated spatial shapes – sometimes further dispersed by the fact that men from the same family may be working or seeking work in other places (given gender and regionally differentiated labour markets). This spatial 'stretching' through care chains also points up the problem of thinking of the family as a place – of co-residence, of intimate presence, and with a tight spatial location (the 'home' as a privileged site). Transnational family forms require us to think again about how we conceive of families as social institutions. Such developments return us to questions about globalization – and to the need to move beyond the state–market binary. Aihwa Ong (1999) has argued that transnational mobility requires us to consider mobile people as subjects formed at the intersection of different 'regimes' – of capital accumulation, of states/citizenship, and of the family:

> I view transnationalism not in terms of unstructured flows but in terms of the
> tensions between movements and social orders … I trace the different regimes
> – state, family, economic enterprises – that shape and direct border crossings
> and transnational relations, at once conditioning their dynamism and scope but
> also giving structure to their patterning. (1999: 6)

These regimes do not necessarily fit comfortably together – but each of them
valorizes 'flexibility' in a way that enables people to negotiate forms of
'transnational citizenship'. In this respect, mobility and flexibility are actively
produced (and desired) strategies on the part of subjects – as well as conditions
sought by capital. States form strategies both to promote such flexibilities – and
to deal with the disorderliness that they threaten. Ong traces the dislocations
and disturbances that transnational relations and logics produce for states – but
does not see this as the decline or end of the state as a social force:

> But while such tensions and disjunctures are at work between oppressive
> structures and border-crossing flows, the nation-state – along with its juridical-
> legislative systems, bureaucratic apparatuses, economic entities, modes of
> governmentality, and war-making capacities – continues to define, discipline,
> control and regulate all kinds of populations, whether in movement or in resi-
> dence. There are diverse forms of interdependencies and entanglements
> between transnational phenomena and the nation-states, relations that link
> displaced persons with citizens, integrate the unstructured into the structured,
> and bring some kind of order to the disorderliness of transnationalism. (1999: 15)

In the process, changing family and household formations – and their spatially
stretched varieties – produce new alignments of welfare and work that connect
'state' and 'market' in different ways. These new alignments involve shifting
gender divisions of labour; recurrent migrations and new international divisions of labour; shifting boundaries between public and private realms and
between public and private sectors; and changing patterns of household and
family formation (and state attempts to regulate them). Such changes cannot
be accommodated within the state/market binary – or by 'bolting on' the
family. These processes also remake the relationships between welfare and work
in ways that outrun the external/internal distinction that dominates the discussion of globalization and national welfare states.

Internalizing globalization: the unsettled nation-state

Political-institutionalist approaches see nation-states as the locus of adaptation
to the external pressures of globalization. Beyeler argues that: 'These [institu-
tionalist] arguments do not contend that external processes are unable to affect
domestic policies. Rather they imply that research on the effects of globalization should take into account the role and dynamics of institutions' (2003:
153). This conception of globalization as an external or exogenous force mistakes the *spatial* formation of nation-states in two ways. First, it juxtaposes the

solidly rooted, territorialized, space of nation-states with the mobile, transient and deterritorialized flows of global capital. In contrast, Sassen argues that:

> the global economy is something that has to be actively implemented, repro-
> duced, serviced and financed ... global-economic features like hypermobility
> and time–space compression are not self-generative. They need to be pro-
> duced, and such a feat of production requires capital fixity ... vast concentra-
> tions of very material and not so mobile facilities and infrastructures. (2001:
> 262)

At the same time, the 'external pressure, internal adaptation' conception of welfare state change *misplaces* globalization. Globalization clearly involves flows, relationships and institutions that take place beyond particular nation-states (from transnational corporations to the World Bank, or cross-border flows of people). Nevertheless, these processes, relationships and institutions are also materialized within the borders of nation-states. Corporate headquarters, production and distribution systems, call centres, international and transnational agencies are all territorially embodied within specific nation-states (Yeates, 2001: ch. 3). So, too, are the outputs, products and 'consumables' of global capitalism – from McDonald's burgers to 'world music'. These products may 'change places' – carrying specific material products and cultural formations to be used or appropriated in new locations – but both the producers and the consumers are located within (a variety of) territorial boundaries. The 'external pressure, internal adaptation' model tries to sustain a distinction that limits our capacity to understand the spatial realignments associated with globalization. There are forms and fractions of capital that are already (or wish to be) international or transnational *within* the 'national' space of nation-states. There are political blocs and projects that propound the necessity or desirability of becoming 'global' *within* the 'national' political formation. Similarly, there are 'national' citizens who actively seek aspects of international, transnational and global politics and culture (from international aid, through transnational political alliances, to baseball caps), and there are transnational citizens who seek to locate themselves in more than one national space (Ong, 1999). Globalization is not a disembodied external condition; it is materialized *within and across* nation-states.

Viewing globalization as an internal as well as an external dynamic in relation to nation-states and welfare states underscores the increased salience of borders in the contemporary world (Leontidou and Afouxenidis, 1999). The interpenetration or mingling of the 'national' and the 'global' discussed above indicates the permeability of national borders: their capacity for being crossed by goods, services, capital and people (e.g. Miles, 1999; Wallace, 1999). This permeability is, of course, uneven: borders are more or less open in different places, in relation to different sorts of object and, especially, to different types of people. In some places, and against some sorts of people, they are even reinforced and more intensively policed: Europe's response to refugees and migrants reveals deep political anxiety about such 'permeability'. The current globalization involves new forms and trajectories of mobility of people (as migrations, diasporas and nomadism: see, *inter alia*, Brah, 1996; Castles, 2000; Cohen, 1997; Gilroy, 1993). These call into question the (assumed) unity of nation-states and the 'peoples' that inhabit them. Nations – and their borders – are also on the move, as nations and states fragment, realign or are created anew. All of these tendencies are as visible in the UK as anywhere else. Here, borders – and their 'openness' via the European Union – have been a source of increasing governmental attention and intervention. Much of this has focused on new categories of refugees and migrants – but in ways that build on colonial legacies about the regulation of 'aliens' and 'foreigners'. At the same time, the United Kingdom has been internally recomposed via limited constitutional devolution to create a multinational nation, exposing the tensions around English hegemony within the 'British Isles'. The current migrations, internal divisions and postcolonial concerns about the multicultural and multi-ethnic condition coincide in recurrent anxieties about the 'nation' and the 'people' (Hesse, 2001a; Lewis, 2000b). As I argued in the previous section, such processes also rework other boundaries – between public and private, especially, as families and relationships become spatially stretched. All of these tendencies find their echoes and refractions in social policies: from 'citizenship' tests to the fear of 'benefit tourism' and 'health tourism'; from migrants redressing an ageing demography to the development of 'multicultural' welfare provision; and in the recurrent political-cultural fears about people who are 'not like us' (as if 'us' formed a simple and unified category). Globalization means not the dissolution of the nation-state, but the unsettling presence of the 'world' within the nation-state. The result is that neither the solidity nor the stability of nation-states can be taken for granted (politically or analytically).

Nicola Yeates has argued that globalization is a difficult issue for the study of social policy:

> Its integration into the field of social policy poses questions about many of the assumptions, concepts and theories that have been integral to social policy analysis. Social policy as a field of academic study is ill-suited to thinking beyond the nation state as its theories and concepts were developed in a national context. (2001: 19)

The nation-state is a foundational concept for social policy, and its provenance, applicability and stability are largely taken for granted within the subject. The nation-state provides the unacknowledged conceptual backdrop for most national studies of social policies, politics and ideologies – the metaphorical and literal terrain on which such policy conflicts and developments take place. Welfare states are essentially the result of national histories of political, policy and institutional development (Huber and Stephens, 2001). The nation-state is also the elementary unit of analysis for comparative social policy analysis, built around the (more or less) divergent models, principles, institutions and trajectories of national welfare systems (see, for example, Alcock and Craig, 2001;

Clasen, 1999; Cochrane, Clarke and Gewirtz, 2001; Esping-Andersen, 1996; Kennet, 2001). The growing attention to trends, transitions and trajectories is a distinct shift away from the dominance of static typologies of welfare regimes or models (the classification of difference) within comparative social policy. This more dynamic approach to studying welfare states marks an attempt to capture the processes and directions of welfare state change. As Taylor-Gooby notes, the interest in the adaptation of welfare states to new pressures adds up to:

> the suggestion that welfare systems are successful in adjusting to a changed environment in ways that reflect differences in their current structure and organization and the political and cultural characteristics of the national context in which they developed. Welfare is being 'recalibrated', 'recast', is 'in transition', 'adapting', 'restructuring', 'evolving' or 'being modified', as the titles of recent work suggest. (2001a: 2–3)

But this view leaves the foundational concept of the nation-state in place. The national context remains the privileged site of comparative analysis – and the nation-state remains the focus of attention. While this makes more empirical sense than the 'globalization abolished the nation-state' thesis, it leaves nations and states apparently unchanged. As a result, it underestimates where the contemporary dynamics of welfare make themselves felt. We are encountering permeable borders, the movement of people, and shifting alignments of nations and states – as institutional and constitutional formations, as particular spatial formations, and as unstable and contested national identities. These suggest that, having seen off the challenge of 'apocalyptic' globalization, we might want to think again about the nation-state. That implies thinking differently about globalization – rather than assuming that there is only the 'apocalyptic' version. Appadurai has argued for a more diverse, uneven and unfinished view of globalization:

> It has now become something of a truism that we are functioning in a world fundamentally characterized by objects in motion. These objects include ideas and ideologies, people and goods, images and messages, technologies and techniques. This is a world of flows … It is also, of course, a world of structures, organizations and other stable social forms. But the apparent stabilities that we see are, under close examination, usually our devices for handling objects characterized by motion. The greatest of these apparently stable objects is the nation-state, which is today frequently characterized by floating populations, transnational politics within national borders, and mobile configurations of technology and expertise. (2001: 5)

Akhil Gupta (1998) has argued that attention to instabilities and disjunctures may enable us to escape the forlorn debate for or against the 'disappearance of the nation-state'. This binary choice, he suggests, may be missing the point because 'one can often point to persuasive evidence that leads to *both* conclusions for the *same* cases' (1998: 319). The processes unsettling the nation-state may be *partial and multiple*, and have different effects on particular nation-states. For example, there are distinctive 'destabilizations' that bear on nation-states whose apparent 'territorial integrity' was founded on the interpenetration of the metropolitan core with the colonial periphery. Nation-states like the UK were not a solidified economic, cultural and political unity, where the nation and state had clear and coterminous spatial boundaries. Rather, an ensemble of dispersed economic, cultural and political relations that articulated metropole and colonies enabled the *imaginary* of the sovereign, unified nation-state. These nation-states were political imaginaries but they have been central to the thinking of social sciences. As Sassen puts it: 'Much of social science has operated with the assumption of the nation-state as a container, representing a unified spatiotemporality. Much of history, however, has failed to confirm this assumption' (2001: 261; see also Biersteker and Weber, 1996). Treating the nation-state as a unified block gets in the way of understanding how contemporary movements are reshaping both nations and states:

> State sovereignty, which is today often elided with national sovereignty, actually emerges in a period historically prior to the consolidation of the nation … That this curiously hyphenated entity, the nation-state, does not evoke constant surprise is a testimony to its complete ideological hegemony. Scholarly work has tended to underestimate seriously the importance of that hyphen, which simultaneously erases and naturalizes what is surely an incidental coupling. (Gupta, 1998: 316–17)

In his discussion of the 'postcolonial condition', Gupta makes elegant play with this hyphen between nation and state – and its contemporary destabilization. He argues that this unsettling reveals the contingently constructed coupling of nation and state, such that they become capable of being treated as analytically and politically separable. Within the contemporary processes of globalization, we have seen struggles to abolish nations – and states (in the break-up of the former Soviet Union); to create or recreate nations (from within the former Eastern bloc and in Africa); to detach nations and 'peoples' from states (in the former Yugoslavia and in Kurdish struggles for autonomy); to claim and internalize territory within nations (e.g. the disputed space of Kashmir); and to dismantle former unities of nations and states (as in the move to devolution in the United Kingdom). Much of this comes on top of earlier waves of territorial-political realignments across the relations of 'the West and the rest' in the form of (partial and unfinished) decolonization (Hall, 1992). The consequent insertion of decolonized nations into subordinated and dependent places in the new global political economy further exacerbates the instabilities of nation and state. Such complex and multiple processes can hardly be grasped in the debate about the 'end of the nation-state'. Rather, we may need to pay attention to unfinished, partial and multiple processes of 'unsettling' and to attempts at 'resettling' – the construction of (temporarily) stabilized new formations. Gupta argues that:

> To suggest that the particular historical conjuncture that brought 'nation' and 'state' together into a stable form of spatial organization may be coming to an end is not to argue that forms of 'nation-ness' and 'state-ness' are in danger of disappearing altogether. New, more menacing, racially exclusionary forms of national identity are emerging in Europe and the United States, for example, and statelike functions are being performed by organizations such as the European Union and transnational corporations. (1998: 319)

'Europe', too, can be grasped as a changeable and constructed space (see, for example, Christiansen, Jorgensen and Wiener, 2001; Hudson and Williams, 1999b; Jonsson, Tagil and Tornqvist, 2000). Appadurai suggests that areas or regions, like nation-states, have been treated as unified and stable entities:

> Much traditional thinking about 'areas' has been driven by conceptions of geographical, civilizational, and cultural coherence that rely on some sort of trait list − of values, languages, material practices, ecological adaptations, marriage patterns and the like. However sophisticated these approaches, they all tend to see 'areas' as relatively immobile aggregates of traits, with more or less durable historical boundaries and with a unity composed of more or less enduring properties. (2001: 7)

In the successive waves of remaking during the twentieth and twenty-first centuries, Europe has continued to change in geopolitical shape, in economic formation, in political institutionalization and in the 'European culture' it is supposed to share. There are different constructions of the core elements of that culture − its commitment to liberal democracy, civic republicanism, Enlightenment aesthetics and philosophical values, and Christianity. Each of these has been exposed and contested, either for its hegemonic suppression of alternatives, or for its non-fulfilment in practice (Marfleet, 1999). In 2002–3, controversies surrounded the proposed inclusion of Turkey in the European Union because it is geographically 'elsewhere' and culturally 'non-Christian' and therefore not European in character (see also Will Hutton, 'Onward Christian Citizens', *The Observer*, 9 February 2003: 30). Similar observations might be made about the invention and reinvention of other regions (e.g. 'Asia' and the conception of 'Confucian capitalism': see, for example, Ching, 2001; Ong and Nonini, 1997; Sum, 1999; Sun Ge, 2000). Europe is a complex formation that mediates the global and the national in a variety of ways. These include forming a regional bloc that inserts national economies into the global; providing an economic space that aims to protect the 'social market' of European countries from the bare market of US neo-liberalism; and constructing a social and political space committed to the European 'welfare' model. Schmidt identifies 'Europeanization' as a double process that 'has acted both as a conduit for global forces and as a shield against them, opening member states up to international markets and competition at the same time that they protect them through monetary integration and the single market' (1999: 172).

However, this grasps 'Europeanization' only in terms of economic dynamics; the multifacetedness of the process also requires attention to the political-cultural and institutional dynamics (Fink, Lewis and Clarke, 2001). At the same time the 'Europe' of these processes is simultaneously an entity (which may be recurrently 'enlarged'), a project and a fractious, conflict-ridden coalition – and is not reducible to any of them.

Resettling nation, state and welfare?

I have tried to draw out the links between the unsettling of nation-states and the destabilization of core concepts in the study of welfare states, precisely because the two phrases have been so tightly coupled. But what happens to the study of welfare states as a consequence of this development? I want to suggest several temporary conclusions about globalization as a multiple, uneven and unfinished process. The first concerns trying to draw out what is distinctive about this period of the global: what marks it as different from earlier alignments of the national, regional, transnational? One key element is clearly the rise of forms of transnational capital and the spread of processes of capital accumulation to more places. Here the universalization of capital (and the homogenization of economic space) is combined with the would-be hegemonic place of US corporate capitalism which has attempted to install the neo-liberal model of globalization as the only possible globalization. The rise of supranational institutions connecting and governing the economic and political processes of globalization has created an apparatus through which the US/neo-liberal model can be institutionalized and transmitted. But to focus only there would miss the sense of globalization as a set of connections, flows and disjunctures that combines different tendencies and trajectories. There are other regional formations of capitalism (with other political-cultural imaginaries). And there are other imagined 'modernities' and 'modernizations' that contest the claimed inevitability of neo-liberal globalization. This period or phase of the 'global' is also marked by the continuing dynamics of the 'postcolonial' – the effects of the partial processes of decolonization with their consequences for how the decolonized nations and states are inserted into a global economy. Such contradictory processes affect both the once colonized and the once imperial – unsettling conceptions of 'race', nation and one's 'place in the world' (Hall, 2001). Overlaid on these processes are the effects of the dissolution of the communist bloc – unleashing new, or reinvented, nations and states across Europe and Asia. At the same time, new blocs are being fashioned – creating regional formations that expand, shrink and contest the possibilities of the 'global'. Out of these processes come different imaginings of the world – how it might be liberated (and from what?); how it might be ordered (and subject to whose rules?); and how it might be something other than a market. Such possibilities have to contend with the dominance of the neo-liberal conception of globalization, which is the central concern of the following chapter.

If we equate globalization with neo-liberal globalization – which attempts to subordinate states and national economies to the demands of a world economy – we can see the dominant trends towards what Taylor-Gooby calls the 'competitiveness imperative' driving 'cost containment' and 'activation' policies (2001b: 181). But even there, the 'pressures' are rarely one-directional and homogenizing. I want to argue instead, that as national economic, social and political formations are being realigned in a new network of global relations, they are subject to both homogenizing and differentiating pressures. On the one hand they are under pressure to conform to the (more or less explicit and institutionalized) demands of neo-liberal models of global political economy, or to the conditions of insertion into regional economic-political blocs such as the European Union. On the other hand they are under pressure to have a distinct, and differentiated, trading, cultural and political identity – a distinctive 'place in the world'. Hudson and Williams, for example, have argued that the 'economic' integration of the EU contains dynamics of both homogenization and differentiation:

> these changes in the character of the EU can also be regarded as bringing about a homogenization of its space, seeking to establish the free play of capitalist social relations over its entirety. At the same time, giving wider and freer play to market forces has led to increasing territorial differentiation within the EU. Seemingly paradoxical, these processes of homogenization are enhancing the significance of differences between places in influencing the locations of economic activities and the quality of people's lives within Europe. (1999a: 8)

But, once more, let me insist that welfare reform is not just about the 'societalization' of capital accumulation. It is formed out of multiple tendencies and forces. It has to negotiate national political-cultural formations (from regressive nationalisms to emergent claims on citizenship). It has to deal with national 'bio-politics' (Ong, 1999), organizing the articulation of the private/familial realm with the state and the market. Increasingly, the private/familial is valorized by neo-liberal globalization (as the site of desires, needs and consumption choices). National and regional governments celebrate the familial as the 'foundational' institution that reproduces and secures the 'way of life' of the people even as households overflow national borders. The private/familial is also increasingly the site where the strains and stresses of 'flexibilities' needed to meet the demands of markets and states are condensed. Such forces and processes are not secondary – not after-the-event adaptations to the big 'economy' calculations. They are *simultaneous*: they define the (shifting) character of the nation that has to be 'inserted' into the (shifting) global. In sum, then, the contemporary politics of 'welfare state reform' take place on a ground where established conceptions of people, nation and state are unsettled and contested. In particular, they have been unsettled by neo-liberalism's promise of building a new future founded on liberating people from dependency on the state.

five

Living with/in and against neo-liberalism

I ended the previous chapter by arguing that within the different tendencies and forces of contemporary globalization, neo-liberal globalization is the dominant form. It is important to avoid conflating what might be called 'globalization in general' – the complex of new alignments of places, people and power linked in a series of flows, connections and disjunctures (Appadurai, 1996) – and the neo-liberal *project* of globalization (see Massey, 1999). This distinction is, of course, not an easy one, since the neo-liberal project has been profoundly influential in shaping 'the global' in its image. Neo-liberalism has been the 'business agenda' of the dominant fractions of capital (in both the financial and transnational extraction and manufacturing sectors). It is the 'free trade' agenda adopted by neo-liberal governments, particularly the hegemonic USA. It is the 'Washington consensus' about liberated markets, flexible labour and the diminished role of governments placed at the heart of the major supranational institutions (WTO, World Bank, IMF). Neo-liberalism is a project that struggles to overcome blockages, refusals, resistances and interruptions to the continued expansion of capital accumulation. Some are the results of the stalled and crisis-ridden arrangements of Atlantic Fordism (Jessop, 2002). Some are the socio-technical problems of 'control at a distance' (in a spatially dispersed capitalism). Others can be found in the 'nostalgic/traditional' reluctance of some people to give up valued habits, practices and spaces in the name of modernization, free trade or the new world order (see, *inter alia*, Appadurai, 2001; Gupta, 1998). Still others derive from alternative conceptions of how to organize modernity and local, regional, national and global futures.

This chapter explores the challenge of neo-liberalism in terms of:

- its role as a hegemonic project (first section);
- its spatial and political-cultural unevenness (second section);
- its globalizing or transnational character (third section); and
- its implications for placing the USA and the UK within neo-liberal globalization (fourth section).

Making a neo-liberal world?

Neo-liberalism attempts to define new formations of work and welfare, of state and market, and of public and private around a set of 'freedoms' that are constituted in and through market relations: the freedom to work; freedom from state interference and regulation; freedom of choice. In this sense, neo-liberalism is both widely recognized and understood. It appears as the new 'voice of capital': an ideology that serves to liberate capital from the shackles of governments, unions and regulation. Nevertheless, I think this view of neo-liberalism risks treating it as too coherent and too universal – not least because neo-liberalism appears to offer the chance of overcoming the difficult questions about the connections between economic, political and cultural power. Neo-liberalism promises a return to the 'good old days' when the dominant ideology simply meant the transparent expression of interests of capital. Instead, I want to suggest that there remain analytic problems about how capital 'comes to voice' (and which sections of it speak); about how the liberation of capital is articulated into what Frank (2000) calls 'market populism'; and about how neo-liberalism combines with, displaces or subordinates other political-cultural projects in its attempt to remake the world. I want to argue instead for treating neo-liberalism as a hegemonic project (rather than a singular ideology). This, I think, may provide a basis for addressing both the logics and the limits of neo-liberalism, and the different ways in which people and places live with/in – and against – neo-liberalism.

To view neo-liberalism as a hegemonic project, we need to think about how it goes about trying to make the world conform to its desires. In particular, this means thinking about the different sorts of articulations it attempts to construct: the (re)making of political-cultural formations to the extent that neo-liberalism can command the 'taken for granted' fields of common sense; the construction of political blocs to sustain and carry through the project; the colonization of social and political institutions so that they both embody and emanate its orientations. In the process it is also necessary to pay attention to the processes by which existing, older projects, their political blocs and their forms of institutionalization have been disarticulated, dislocated, and demobilized. Although this has been a project that has been developing over thirty years or more (the realignment of the right and Republicanism in the USA is dated from the mid 1960s by many: see, for example, Saloma, 1984), it may be worth sketching a few key elements.

Perhaps most potently, this project has made crises speak the language of neo-liberalism. Crises, as Gramsci (1971) observed, are not naturally occurring events, whose meanings are clear for all to see. But they do 'create a terrain more favourable to the dissemination of certain modes of thought, and certain ways of posing and resolving questions involving the entire subsequent development of national life' (1971: 184). They are given meaning – they are made to testify – as a result of political-cultural work. Neo-liberalism has been successful at inflecting the meanings of contemporary crises towards its economistic reasoning: whether it be the 'fiscal crisis' of the welfare state ('we can no longer afford ...'); the Asian economic crisis ('too much state subsidy ...'); the 'demographic time bomb' threatening social insurance systems ('too little private insurance ...'); and so on. In a study of the Finnish economic crisis of the early 1990s, Minna Aslama and her colleagues argue that 'politics' becomes displaced by 'economic' knowledge:

> A discourse of economic expertise, then, emerges, stating that the crisis had not been a political one in the sense that there would have been alternatives to the policies. Instead the economic discourse sets economic expertise superior to political discussion ... Monetary policies are considered non-political, and they are seen also as more farsighted and responsible than a 'political' point of view. (2001: 172; see also Prince, 2001, on the 'fiscalization' of policy discourse)

In similar ways, crises across the world have been made to articulate neo-liberal definitions and solutions – setting markets free, putting people to work, deregulating institutions, and enabling choice. We encounter the paradox of the politicized assault on 'politics': the denigration (and even self-denigration) of the capacity of governments, the celebration of aggregated consumer choices over collective decision-making, and the assault on the 'paternalism' of any public policy in the name of (market supplied) freedom. Thomas Frank has called this 'market populism' – the view that:

> in addition to being mediums of exchange, markets were mediums of consent. Markets expressed the popular will more articulately and more meaningfully than did mere elections. Markets conferred democratic legitimacy; markets were a friend of the little guy; markets brought down the pompous and the snooty; markets gave us what we wanted; markets looked out for our interests. (2000: xiv–xv)

Frank recognizes the populist and 'anti-elitist' thrust of neo-liberalism. There has been a sustained effort to naturalize the market as the only, necessary and most efficient coordinator of human activity, from which there results a set of halo effects (business as the embodiment of market dynamism and innovation; management as the embodiment of good business practices). This is associated with the celebration of the figure of the sovereign consumer, freed to make his/her own choices in the face of the dazzling array of possibilities that (only) the market can generate. It is also linked to the insistence on dissolving 'barriers' to free trade and free choice – both for the consumer and for corporate capital. Finally, there is the normalization of 'productivity' and 'efficiency' as the measure of worth and usefulness, though not necessarily of value (Stein, 2001). This applies to both human and natural resources that are understood as 'consumables' (or 'waste' if they are not productive).

This is reflected in neo-liberalism's commitment to 'putting people to work': expanding the range and variety of labour power that can be used in the continuing expansion of capitalist production and accumulation. Neo-liberalism is linked to strategies for:

- the recruitment of new sources of labour (new geographies of production and the 'inclusion' of previously marginalized labour
  forces such as racialized minorities and women);
- the intensified subjection of labour through both machinic and
  managerial control;
- the recomposition of labour (in more fragmented and more
  unequal labour market segmentation);
- the increased flexibility of labour (with new forms of contract; de-
  unionized and non-unionized workforces; legal and illegal migrant
  workers);
- the 'outsourcing' of labour to domestic production or home-working; and
- the devaluation of labour (see, *inter alia*, Beynon et al., 2002;
  Ehrenreich, 2002; Gledhill, 2002; Leach, 2003; Nonini, 2003;
  Standing, 2002; Winson and Leach, 2002).

These realignments of work and workers in neo-liberalism are profoundly connected to the redrawing of boundaries between the public and private (Clarke,
2004). These overlap with, but are not the same as, the distinction between
state and market (as I argued in Chapter 4). The state–market distinction captures the public and private in what might be called 'sectoral' terms: the state
is the public sector, the market signifies the domain of the private sector. Neo-
liberalism has indeed been a critical force in remaking this boundary.
Privatization, contracting out, market testing, public–private partnerships and
the use of public resources to provide 'corporate welfare' are all ways in which
neo-liberal governments have both blurred and redrawn the sectoral boundary
(see, for example, Clifton, Comin and Fuentes, 2003; Crouch, 2003; Whitfield,
2000). But the public/private distinction has other meanings, too. These centre
on the distinction between public and private realms and spheres – and here,
too, the boundaries are constructed and variable.

Neo-liberalism valorizes the 'private realm' in distinctive ways – treating the
family as the natural foundation for the desires, commitments and capacities
that drive both production and consumption. The family underpins the model
of 'possessive individualism' – and the ways in which capacities are understood
as gendered (and distributed by age). Even as the private is celebrated in neo-
liberalism, it is also neo-liberalism's dumping ground. As the public realm –
and the provision of public services – is retrenched, narrowed and constrained
where neo-liberalism shapes policy, so the private realm of families, households and personal relationships is expected to substitute for the state (where
corporate providers see no cream to skim). Kingfisher argues that this is a central dimension of neo-liberalism – and works through a gender dynamic that
relies on the 'infinite elasticity' (Elson, 1994; 1995) of women's labour. This

> entails redrawing the line between public and private such that much of what
> the state supported in terms of reproduction (including not only direct welfare

benefits, but also housing subsidies and educational and health-care programs) is jettisoned or 'reprivatized' (Fraser, 1989: 172) ... In their reconstitution as gender-neutral workers, poor single mothers become increasingly exposed to exploitative working conditions and are increasingly forced to purchase, as consumers, goods and services that were formerly public goods and services – or else provide them on their own. (2002: 48)

The private is also the setting for the renewed exploitation of waged labour – in the rise of both domestic service and home-working (Ehrenreich, 2002; Leach, 2003). Leach has argued that home-working has been the 'model' form of labour for developing the new 'flexibilities' desired in the new processes of capital accumulation. The blurring of home and work in both domestic service and home-working again places women's labour at the centre of neo-liberalism's attempt to remake the world – and intersects with the intensified pressures of daily and generational reproduction (Katz, 2003). The valorized and intensified private realm has one other central role to perform in neo-liberalism's remaking of the world: it becomes the setting where difficult decisions are made and contradictory pressures are, more or less uncomfortably, reconciled.

Neo-liberalism celebrates the expansion of 'freedom of choice' and denigrates the elitism and paternalism of monopoly provider driven public services. One effect is that increasing numbers of increasingly complex decisions must be taken in the private realm – in which people have to learn to act as consumers (e.g. Baldock, 2003; Gewirtz, Ball and Bowe, 1995). Education, health insurance, personal security and various forms of 'risk management' require calculating attention (and calculating capacity) for difficult choices to be made, in circumstances where people may not wish, or have the resources, to be consumers (Barnes and Prior, 1995). Such decision-making is likely to be experienced as time-consuming, energy-draining and potentially dangerous or risky. But this is only part of the intensification of the private, since it is in the private realm that decisions about how to balance multiple pressures and demands have to be made – about waged and domestic work; about its division of labour and rewards; about financial and emotional resources; about different sorts of needs. Of course, at one level, this was always true about the private realm; it is not the invention of neo-liberalism. But what is distinctive is this combined intensification and valorization of the private – as the public realm (in terms of resources, capacities and choices) is drained.

Each of these dimensions of neo-liberalism's project to conform the world bears directly on welfare states. Neo-liberalism does indeed recompose and revalorize 'work' and expects states to 'enable' people to come to work (or enforce the expectation). But both as 'welfare' and as 'states', welfare states embody (or institutionalize) older, counter-hegemonic possibilities. They represent different accommodations with capitalism, so to speak, than those envisaged in neo-liberalism. Rhetorically, welfare states have been made to exemplify the problems of waste, rigidities, lack of choice, and general inefficiency that are the opposite of the neo-liberal imaginary. But they also institutionalize those other possibilities. They employ people: the expansion of women's and some forms of minority ethnic employment from the 1960s in many 'welfare capitalist' societies was heavily dependent on public service growth (see, *inter alia*, Huber and Stephens, 2001; Malveaux, 1987; F. Williams, 1989). Welfare states offer limited forms of decommodified benefits and services and they express non-market-mediated forms of relationship and interaction. They selectively insulate groups of people (more or less grudgingly) from the demands of capital and from market failure. And, as political parties have realized, they provide the potential basis for popular alliances and voting blocs.

In doing so, welfare states provide the symbolic and material expressions (however contradictory and limited) of forms of solidarity, collectivism and citizenship. The project of neo-liberal hegemony required an assault on welfare states not just for what they did, but for *what they represented*. They embodied collective identities and forms of social solidarity in their complexly structured and contested forms of 'universalism'. Meaghan Morris, writing about the attempt to install 'free market economics' in Australia, talks about the sense that:

> We also, just as basically, live in a society where for almost a century the right of all 'citizens' (a concept slowly wrested from the proprietorial control of white men) to a decent living wage, and the duty of the state to ensure it, were *imagined* as fundamental. (1998: 193, emphasis in original)

Morris captures both the collective imaginary of citizenship and the expansive struggles over citizenship discussed in Chapter 3 – the efforts to enlarge it beyond the ablebodied white male norm. This issue of conflicting *social imaginaries* is vital to the question of hegemony. Such alternative imaginaries, and the institutions in which they are embodied, have to be dismantled and demobilized to enable the construction of the neo-liberal hegemony. However, there is a tension between dealing with neo-liberal hegemony in a relatively abstract fashion and the particular national experience to which Morris refers. The national is the terrain of imaginaries of citizenship as a form of social solidarity, while neo-liberalism appears to be (or claims to be) universal/global. However, I want to argue that its practice, and its effects, are profoundly uneven in spatial terms. The construction of neo-liberal hegemony involves political-cultural work on the terrain of (many) national-popular formations. Gramsci's concept of the *national popular* denotes a site of ideological work and struggles to construct the dominant imaginings of the nation, the people, and their (collective) trajectory from past through present to future. Histories are narrated to tell the formation and development of the people; analyses are proffered that describe their current travails; and projections tell how their character, values and potentials will, if properly used, lift them to a brighter and better future. Neo-liberalism can be viewed as a project that seeks to articulate *multiple* national populars: it works *within and across* many nations (Kingfisher, 2002). Each national site poses distinctive problems about its political-cultural formation and each requires distinctive strategies, rhetorics and alliances. Each site requires political-cultural work – including the articulation of discursive fields and the assemblage of political blocs. At the same time, such 'work' also involves the disarticulation of opposing positions, discourses, ideologies – and the undoing and demobilization of the social forces that they engaged. As a result, neo-liberalism is rarely likely to appear alone and in pristine condition. Rather, the processes of articulation within national-popular formations point towards neo-liberalism's imbrication with other discursive resources and its progress through alliances rather than direct rule.

Space, time and difference: uneven neo-liberalism

Catherine Kingfisher argues that 'the story of neoliberalism's globalization' is in practice 'a series of stories characterized by disjointed, disjunctured articulations' (2002: 50). Neo-liberalism enters particular national-popular formations in and through alliances. In these alliances it discovers the discursive repertoire that enables it to 'people' the landscape in more complex ways. Conservative, communitarian, nationalist and authoritarian political-cultural discourses line up alongside liberal, egalitarian and even residually social-democratic discourses to form alliances with neo-liberalism – and sometimes to resist it. Since neo-liberalism claims to define global 'realism' – the true, necessary and inevitable conditions of life in the 'real world' – the range of potential partners is hardly surprising. Both neo-liberalism and its allies need each other. Specific political projects and parties gain a gloss of 'global truth' from neo-liberalism, enabling them to position themselves as representatives of modernity, globalization and the future. For example, in the UK and the USA the subjection of social and political practices to the logic of the 'market' has been enforced through the 'inevitability' of marketization and the 'common sense' of going with its flow as individuals and corporations are 'liberated' from an overbearing state. At the same time, neo-liberalism takes on a particular 'national-popular' aura: it comes to speak the 'local language'. It acquires 'people' rather than mere economic actors for its project. In Kingfisher's terms, the 'preliminary grammar' of neo-liberalism (its general elements) is always embedded in hybrid formations: 'It is, in fact, only in the circulation of neoliberal related meanings and their articulation with other meaning systems that neoliberalism takes on its multiple and contradictory lives' (2002: 12).

Such a view draws attention to the contradictoriness and instability of hegemonic projects. They are alliances – assemblages of political discourses that are articulated *unities in difference*. They are forged in the face of paradoxes, tensions, incompatibilities and contradictions, rather than being coherent implementations of a unified discourse and plan. This implies thinking about neo-liberalism in ways that foreground 'unevenness', rather than a fluid spread across a flat landscape. It may be that the Anglophone countries – the USA, the UK, Canada, Australia and New Zealand – have proved fertile ground for the development of neo-liberal politics and policies. But even there, the outcomes are not exactly the same. As Kingfisher (2002) has argued, studies that examine national variation within the neo-liberal field reveal substantial differences of outcome. This is because neo-liberalism has to negotiate other political formations, other policy legacies and the political forces or blocs in which they have been embedded. For example, the 'New Deal' in the UK aims at re-engaging specific groups of the non-working population in the labour market (young people, lone mothers, disabled people and so on). It attempts to bring 'moral force' to bear, speaking of obligation and responsibility as well as the rewards of waged work. An apparatus of personalized counselling articulates this 'obligation' and seeks to produce a 'return to work'. But it is not (yet) a system of financial or legal compulsion (Lister, 2002b). In contrast, the US approach to workfare has a larger capacity for compulsion and has a more authoritarian approach to the moral-cultural dimensions of aid recipients that need to be 'policed' (Mink, 1998; Abdela and Withorn, 2002). This is not to argue that these reforms are not 'neo-liberal', but to insist that they are *not only* neo-liberal. They are each the effect of specific national articulations. In the UK, neo-liberalism is articulated with the limited 'social democracy' of New Labour's 'Third Way' (and the bloc that it leads – where the residual 'social democracy' might be more extensive than in the party or government). It is also constructed in the face of an emergent 'social liberalism' that appears antithetical to moral authoritarian strains in both Old and New Labour. In the USA, neo-liberalism has coexisted in a dense fusion with neo-conservative tendencies that underpin the moral authoritarianism of welfare (and other) reform.

These are, in a sense, the easy places to find neo-liberalism. In the USA and the UK, it has been articulated into national-popular formations and embedded in the strategies for the remaking of welfare states. Even here, though, it is necessary to insist that neo-liberal reforms have only been partial and uneven – struggling to deal with stubbornly persistent or deeply sedimented policies, institutions and practices that refuse to go quietly. In the UK, the National Health Service has been both an organizational and a political-cultural stumbling block to neo-liberal reform. Too deeply implicated in the popular imaginary of a British 'welfare state' to be the object of a frontal assault, it has been assailed by successive waves of 'organizational' reform. Internal markets, varieties of managerialism, external contracting, public–private partnerships, as well as consistent underfunding and the anorexic quest for 'efficiency' have remade the system (Ferlie et al., 1996; Harrison et al., 1992; Mohan, 2002). Nevertheless, the continued presence of a national, universalist, free health service is both a real and a symbolic affront to the neo-liberalization of Britain.[1] It also is the consistent stumbling block for comparative studies of social policy that seek to allocate the UK to the 'liberal' regime, creating the need for more complex, or hybrid, subcategorizations, such as Ginsburg's (2001) 'liberal collectivism' (see also Esping-Andersen, 1990; Huber and Stephens, 2001; Taylor-Gooby, 2001b).

Beyond the Anglophone countries, neo-liberalism poses different sorts of analytical challenges. It has clearly been a force in the remaking of states and welfare systems in Latin America. It has flowed along the lines of economic and

---

1 I was fortunate enough to be present at a seminar in 1999 addressed by Alain Enthoven, the US adviser who had suggested the internal market as a model for reforming the NHS. His review of 'progress' – or, from his point of view, 'lack of progress' – saw it as a result of the timid and limited introduction of markets. Only a more thoroughgoing transformation of the system by market reforms could rescue it.

political force that have tied Latin American economic and social development into the North American and North Atlantic axes. These are reflected in, and reinforced by, supranational bodies articulating the 'Washington consensus' and enforcing it through fiscal discipline, most obviously in the form of 'structural adjustment' policies. But neo-liberalism has had to negotiate the problems of national-popular politics – and processes of state formation – within the countries of Latin America, as well as the histories of failed 'development' policies of the past. Abel and Lewis (2002: 49) describe 'market liberalism' in a 'tenuous coalition with ethical socialism and social Catholicism' as having been in the ascendant in Latin America. But they raise doubts about its stability – and the capacity of national political projects to survive the dislocations of economic and social 'development' (and the combined prospects of recession and disorder) that are intrinsic to the model. They note that 'earlier versions of liberalism tended to be minimalist in social policy, or, over short periods, treated it as an accessory to stability, only to reject it as a check on macroeconomic efficiency' (2002: 50). Gledhill (2002) explores the instabilities of neo-liberal adaptations in the context of combined national and transnational processes. He points to the contested recomposition of the 'people' within (in shifting distinctions between urban/rural and conflicts over indigenous identities and rights) and beyond the nation (in processes of migration).

In Africa, neo-liberalism looks less like a hegemonization of the national popular than a neo-colonial relationship enforced through supranational bodies like the IMF, the World Bank and the WTO.[2] The policies of 'structural adjustment' required from national governments have consistently forced the reduction of public spending, the erosion of public services and the privatization of the service sector itself. There is a simultaneous stripping out of state capacity, combined with a 'nationalization' of the responsibility to meet rising expectations and worsening social problems.[3] In addition, the conditions of 'insertion' into the global economy create a range of economic, social and political difficulties for the development of welfare policy. As Francie Lund has argued in relation to South Africa:

> In the economic realm, the casualisation of labour, combined with the high formal unemployment rate, means that increasing numbers of people will not get access to formal social protection through their work. There will almost inevitably be a conflict of interests between the organised labour movement in the formal economy, and the new entrants to the informal economy, regarding the social wage. (2001: 236–7)

She goes on to argue that, despite the 'deep and stark' poverty within South Africa, its position as a pole of regional development means that it attracts

2 It should be remembered that the UK was the recipient of an IMF loan in 1976 that carried requirements to reduce public spending, and this might possibly mark the formal 'beginning of the end' of the political-economic settlement of the post-war welfare state.

3 This is reflected in the increasing desire of Northern states to 'contain the problems' of migrants, asylum-seekers and 'health tourists' in the countries of origin, rather than manage them at the frontier posts of the North.

migration from elsewhere in Africa, posing new political and moral questions about citizenship and access to state services (2001: 237). At the same time, Lund's work draws attention to the power of the 'welfare state' idea as a political imaginary – a point of identification and mobilization that figures large in the way people conceive of possible 'solidarities' and expect/hope that states will deliver them. In this encounter, governments get to live out the fierce political tensions between their 'responsibilities to the international community' and the desires of their domestic populations that states should 'confer full-fledged rights and entitlements on ever-more citizens' (Hansen and Stepputat, 2001: 2).

There are similar issues posed in the 'transition' experiences of the former Eastern bloc, where neo-liberalism formed a critical element in the aid/reform/marketization project of the West (Service, 2002; Wedel, 2001). The economic and political-cultural trajectories are different in the 'Second World', since the levels of industrialization and the predisposition to 'liberalize' created a positive orientation towards (at least the first wave of) privatization and market development. Nevertheless, the destruction of state capacity, the undoing of welfare systems, and the intensification of inequalities that resulted suggest some neo-liberal commonalities (Wedel, 2001; Ferge, 2001; Manning and Davidova, 2001; Poole, 2000a). In contrast, it might be suggested that neo-liberalism has encountered different problems of political-cultural formation in East Asia. The development of regionally distinctive or hybridized formations of capitalism have included different (often family-centred) forms of 'welfare capitalism' in which the state has played a critical role in combining economic development and nation-building. Reflections on China's 'marketizing' reforms of both the economy and social policy point to a contradictory mixture of 'state-led developmentalism' (shared with other East Asian societies), and the construction of 'mixed economies' of welfare, with public, private and 'third sector' forms of provision (see, *inter alia*, Deacon, Holliday and Wong, 2001; Smart, 1998; White, 1998). There has been a conscious self-distancing of the 'Asian model' from the neo-liberal (or, more pejoratively, 'Western') model of capitalism and its forms of 'societalization', in favour of 'Asian' and 'Confucian' norms of solidarity and support. While this 'self-Orientalization' may (deliberately) overstate difference, it nevertheless points to different accommodations of capitalist development, political systems and social regime that cannot be easily subsumed within the 'spread of neo-liberalism' view (see Ong, 1999; Nonini, 2003).

Although Northern and Western European welfare states, and their political-cultural formations, may be marked by encounters and accommodations with neo-liberalism, they can hardly be said to have been hegemonized by it. This is true at the level of national welfare states and in the continued defence of a 'European model' of welfare capitalism (Sykes, Palier and Prior, 2001; Leibfried, 2000). Both social democracy and Christian democracy remain potent forms of sedimented solidarity, with relatively deeply rooted national and regional resistances to neo-liberal imperatives (Castells and Himenan, 2002; Huber and Stephens, 2001). These resistances are both popularly based and embedded in (some) political parties and discourses. The resistances are, in some respects, so deeply sedimented in 'common sense' that some social policy analysts have expressed concern that they may inhibit other welfare reforms:

> The key point is that the 'welfare state now represents the status quo' (Pierson, 1994: 181). Any attempt to dismantle it affects entrenched interests and will therefore provoke unpopularity, so governments who wish to contain spending must act indirectly … One influential approach, closely linked with Pierson's and Esping-Andersen's arguments about the entrenched nature of current provision, argues that welfare regimes, once established, tend to advantage particular groups and thus generate policy feedback – an in-built pressure for their maintenance. (Taylor-Gooby, 2001c: 3; see also Esping-Andersen, 1999; Huber and Stephens, 2001, on the 'ratchet effect'; and Kvist and Jaeger, forthcoming)

One reason for sketching these national and regional variations is to avoid the risk of producing a 'symptomatology' of neo-liberalism: the tendency to discover examples of neo-liberal political discourse and policy everywhere in the world.[4] Some of the 'plague spots' or stigmata of neo-liberalism can be detected almost everywhere (a 'privatization' here; a 'workfare' there). But this does not look like a landscape that has been transformed and flattened by a neo-liberal hegemony. It looks more like an uneven and shifting set of accommodations – at the regional, national and local levels – between previously dominant political-cultural formations and that of neo-liberalism (see also Muncie, 2004). It should be clear that a range of political, policy and organizational questions – the 'costs' of welfare, welfare-to-work, managerialism, consumerism and so on – have neo-liberal affiliations. But as Oorschot and Abrahamson (2003) have argued in the context of labour 'activation policies', welfare states have always had a disposition towards encouraging 'willingness to work'. So what is different now is 'not a change in character, but in strength and strictness of the attachment of obligation and duties to social rights' (2003: 301). They argue that this is a more conditional and disciplinary set of relations between states and (some) citizens (Dwyer, 2000; Jones and Novak, 1999; and see also Kosonen, 2001, on 'activation' in Sweden). These mark accommodations and adaptations in European models, rather than a straightforward shift to a neo-liberal 'end of welfare'.

Making the world global: neo-liberalism and the transnational popular

The second reason for this speedy global overview is to provide a basis for thinking about the spatial unevenness of the neo-liberal project as working across different spatial relationships. I think it is useful to see it as simultane-

---

4 I am aware of the superficiality of this sketch, but think that it is important to keep open questions about varieties of capitalism, different national and regional social formations, and alternative modernities. The 'question of difference' matters here, too.

ously a *national* and a *transnational* project. In its national forms, it seeks to hegemonize specific national-popular formations, creating the conditions for governing in a neo-liberal form and direction. At the same time, Kingfisher draws attention to neo-liberalism's 'inherent globality, its tendency to totalize and universalize' (2002: 49). In its transnational form, it seeks to create and enforce a *transnational popular*: an imaginary of a neo-liberal world that represents globalization as it should be. This transnational popular has been embedded (though not without resistances and refusals) in the institutions of supranational governance and in linking networks of administrative-academic policy transmission (see, *inter alia*, Deacon, 1997; 2001; Stiglitz, 2002; Wacquant, 1999). The neo-liberal project of globalization works differentially, in different regions and within different nations. In doing so, it operates through a wide tactical repertoire – ranging from consensus to coercion in relation to its different targets. Put crudely, in the First World, it has worked primarily through the processes of hegemony construction in the field of the national popular – with more or less success. In the Second World, it seized – and attempted to define – the possibilities of 'transition', transforming nations into marketable and marketized entities. In the Third World, it has used fiscal (and sometimes military) coercion to enforce subordinated insertions into the world economy. Wherever it appears, though, it promises 'liberation' and 'empowerment' of individuals, organizations, groups currently blocked by national/governmental inhibitions, allied to a society 'secured' and disciplined by policing and penality. In Wacquant's terms, this is a 'free society' that is

> (neo)liberal and non-interventionist 'above', in matters of taxation and employment; intrusive and intolerant 'below', for everything to do with the public behaviours of a working class caught in a pincer movement between the generalization of under-employment and precarious labour, on the one hand, and the retrenchment of social protection and the indigence of public services, on the other hand. (1999: 338)

Globalizing neo-liberalism imagines a world of free economic subjects, connected by lines of trade, brought into association with one another (rather than being necessarily personally mobile). It should be noted that although the 'individual' is the figure most spoken by neo-liberalism, its dominant 'economic subject' is the corporation – anthropomorphized as a victim needing liberation from the confining shackles of the state's regulation and interference (Grossberg, forthcoming; Frank, 2000).

However, its transnational tactics change the conditions of *national*-popular formations in a number of ways. Transnational neo-liberalism tells 'nations' and 'peoples' about the world – and about their place within it. It also attempts to create the conditions under which such places 'make sense'. It invokes the sense of the necessary, inevitable and irresistible process of 'globalization' and the necessary, inevitable and irresistible pressure to adapt to it. To the extent that it succeeds (through whatever tactics), it aligns a little more of the world, and makes its story look more compelling and more true – both within the specific nation, and for the others who are forced to watch. The weight of *transnational* neo-liberalism makes its incursions into particular national-popular formations more possible. At the same time, because neo-liberal globalization changes the scalar relations of global, regional, national and local, neo-liberalism multiplies its spatial forms. Its transnational form and its national hegemonic projects are accompanied by 'local' neo-liberalisms, as localities try to reinvent themselves as places within the global (as would-be 'global cities', for example) as well as within the national.

Transnational neo-liberalism has been institutionalized in a range of sites and strategies – the institutions of global governance and forms of capital that represent themselves as liberating, enabling and empowering (especially in the global media networks). But having a global project is not necessarily the same as being hegemonic. It is important to note that, despite its claims, neo-liberalism is not always popular. Its arrival has resulted in 'backfires': social explosions, refusals and reactions. These may be directed at various targets – from 'globalization' itself, to national governments 'delivering austerity', to corporate capital in its local/national appearances. Both the 'transnational popular' and the different national-popular formations are contested – by other imaginaries that seek to reinvent 'the people', the 'world' and their futures and to weave new solidarities. These are not always progressive politics. They are sometimes regressive, xenophobic, nationalist and exclusive, but they are also expansive, visionary, internationalist and imagine new collective identities (see, for example, Dryzek, 2000: esp. ch. 5; Gledhill, 2002; Lem and Leach, 2002). In all their various forms, though, they testify to the *instability and incompleteness* of neo-liberal attempts at hegemony.

From laggard to vanguard: rethinking US exceptionalism

The USA occupies a distinctive role in the rise and spread of neo-liberalism, and poses some difficult analytic problems. In comparative studies, welfare in the USA has been treated as an underdeveloped or backward system. Compared with European welfare systems, the USA has been partial, selective, limited and (relatively) underfunded (see, for example, Ginsburg, 1992; Clarke, 2001a). Most of the concepts used to characterize the US welfare system emphasize this: the 'semi-welfare state' (Katz, 1986); the 'work and relief state' (Amenta, 1998); and its status as exemplar of Esping-Andersen's (1990) 'liberal regime'. Much effort has been expended on accounting for this form of US 'exceptionalism': its underdevelopment, its backwardness and its status as 'laggard' among advanced capitalist societies.

The question about US exceptionalism is now a different one. Does the 'end of welfare as we know it' mark the shift from laggard to vanguard? Is the USA now the model of neo-liberal welfare (and social) development? Such a view is offered across a range of policy areas. Peck's (2001) study of workfare is attentive to geopolitical differences but locates the USA at the leading edge of the tendential shift away from welfarism. He argues that 'the U.S. experience – in so many ways paradigmatic – of the crisis of welfare and ascendancy of workfare' (2001: 18) has very particular significance. This is both for its own domestic political formation and because of its status in the internationalization of workfare:

> The U.S. undertones in this reform offensive have been there for all to see – in the adoption of 'welfare dependency' accounts of unemployment and poverty, in the deference shown to reforming states such as Wisconsin, in the macroeconomic alignment between flexible job markets and active/minimalist welfare, in the 'Americanized' language of the reform process itself. This does not mean, of course, that a sudden and total 'Americanization' has taken place, but it does mean that the key coordinates of the reform process, its guiding ideology, its mode of political and media management, and its tactical instincts all derive strongly from the U.S. experience. (2001: 4)

Others have taken a view of the USA as establishing the line of development against which other states can be ranged. For example, Gilbert talks about the movement 'towards work-oriented policies, privatization of social welfare, increased targeting of benefits, and the shift from an emphasis on the social rights of citizenship to the civic duties of community members' being 'evident in almost all of the industrial nations, if not at the same speed or on exactly the same heading' (2002: 5). The examples for this argument are, in practice, disproportionately drawn from the USA, as the leading case. This linear view of trends (and the measurement of more or less progress) replays the old conceptions of 'development' and 'modernization' that were applied to 'Third World' societies in the twentieth century. There, as Massey puts it,

> the standard version of the story of modernity – as a narrative of progress emanating from Europe – represents a discursive victory of time over space. That is to say that differences which are truly spatial are reconvened as temporal sequence. Thus, Western Europe is understood as being 'advanced', other parts of the world as 'some way behind' and yet others as 'backward'. (1999: 31)

Now, the normative line of development is understood to lead to the free market, minimal state, workfarist norm that is the USA. It will be obvious from the arguments above that I think such a developmental model is badly flawed – and its alignment of space and time along an axis of inevitable development is both analytically and politically dangerous. It excludes other lines of development, other potential modernities and other political-cultural possibilities. As Ong argues,

> in the particular ways political-economic and cultural dimensions are combined, it is not possible to talk about a single modernity within the West. The contemporary impassioned conflicts and negotiations over immigrants, multiculturalism, women's rights and the environmental effects of capitalism speak to the composition and goals of development, culture and the nation in different countries. (1999: 31)

The normative conception of development misrecognizes the effort that goes into making the world conform (or, more accurately, *trying* to make the world conform). As I have suggested above, the work of constructing a neo-liberal hegemony is intensive, deploys different strategies, and encounters blockages, resistances and refusals. It has to engage other political-cultural projects – attempting to subordinate, accommodate, incorporate or displace them. To obscure such intense political-cultural work confirms the neo-liberal illusion of inevitability. If, on the contrary, we draw attention to the grinding and uneven struggle to make the world conform – and recognize the limitations and failures of this project – questions of conflict, contestation and the 'unfinished' become rather more significant. Living in a neo-liberal world is not necessarily the same as being neo-liberal. Attention to the different sorts of *living with, in and against* neo-liberal domination is a necessary antidote to 'big picture' projections of its universalization.[5]

We also need to be more careful about how we treat the USA itself. As I have argued earlier, it would be an error to see the USA as the embodiment of 'pure' neo-liberalism. There, too, neo-liberalism is part of a hegemonic alliance or bloc (with conservative/neo-conservative partners) and the character of that alliance explains the 'end of welfare' (and its conditions and consequences) better than taking it solely as a neo-liberal moment. But starting with the USA also provides a differently spatialized view of the new world order that is being sought – and the USA's place within it. One version of this is the uniform, all-embracing and tentacular view of Empire offered by Hardt and Negri (2000). In contrast, Neil Smith (2003) has argued that what we are seeing is the attempt to construct a distinctive form of American Empire, that seeks to create a world safe for US corporate capital (ruling through economic relations rather than by direct military or governmental colonization). I find Smith's view of the geopolitical shape and ambitions of American Empire as an effort to construct a political-economic hegemony (in the articulation of free markets and democracy) more compelling, not least because he is attentive to the blockages, interruptions and failures of these ambitions.

Nevertheless, I think his distinction between geographical colonization and the globalization of US economic power underestimates the links between economic and cultural imperialism – the link that makes globalization always look and sound like Americanism. But his analysis nevertheless grounds 'globalization' in a differentiated and uneven geography – which also provides a reminder about the continuing intractability of some places in the world. The attempt to 'abolish geography' and create a global uniformity (of free trade) keeps bumping into places where formations of people, politics and power are non-compliant. If neo-liberalism is part of this project to liberate corporate capital and maximize its potential, there must be some doubt about whether the military-imperial conception of US world power is entirely consistent with it.

---

5 Anthropology plays a critical role here, since its ethnographic focus on the local and the particular draws attention to different forms of living with/in wider processes, structures and tendencies. Its 'good sense' (in Gramsci's terms) is to refuse to see the particular as merely the exemplification or instantiation of the general.

There are, of course, good material interests that might keep the two projects linked – the collusive interests of the military-industrial complex and the use of force to make the world safe for 'doing business', for example. But there is also a sense in which the two projects might be more loosely coupled – not least in the destabilizing effects of a militarized imperium stomping around the world and demanding its submission. This does not necessarily create a 'good business climate'.[6]

The USA, then, poses some distinctive analytical problems. It requires us to think of it as a complex formation which is simultaneously the 'home base' for the transnational neo-liberal project that seeks to make globalization happen; the command centre for a political-military-industrial unipolar 'world power' insistent on dealing with 'failed states' and 'broken places'; and a political-cultural formation – a 'national popular' – dominated by an alliance of neo-liberalism and conservatism. This alliance rules over a high level of popular cynicism, scepticism, detachment and political demobilization. The USA's spatial reach is enormous – but different in economic, cultural, political and military forms. In addition, it is the centre for a range of political and policy expertise that is 'exported'. The USA is the centre for a field of international policy networks, as well as the forge for the policies that are transmitted through them (see, for example, Peck, 2001; Wacquant, 1999; Wedel, 2001, in relation to workfare, crime control and the post-Soviet transition respectively). It has constructed an apparatus of thinktanks, policy advisers and consultants ready to serve supranational and national governments, NGOs and corporate business in the interests of making the world a better place (which tends to mean, as Wedel shows, making it a little more like the USA).

I suggested earlier that the Anglophone nations have occupied a privileged place in these networks – for political and cultural reasons. They have been early arrivers at the neo-liberal project, so much so that I am tempted to argue that neo-liberalism speaks English. (The English language is also part of the complex neo-liberal transnational popular – and of American economic and cultural globalization.) While there are reasons for attending to these countries as a distinctive neo-liberal bloc, I want to pay specific attention here to the place – spatial and political-cultural – that the UK has occupied in the neo-liberal project. In both social policy and criminological studies, the UK features as a distinctive adjunct to the USA. For example, social policy studies since Esping-Andersen (1990) have located the UK with the USA as examples of the 'liberal' welfare regime, while both Peck (2001) and King (1999; King and Wickham-Jones, 1998) have paid special attention to the US/UK axis in workfare. In criminology, David Garland has identified the USA and the UK as developing a shared 'culture of control' that has been 'shaped by two underlying social forces – the distinctive social organization of late modernity, and the free market, socially conservative politics that came to dominate the USA and the UK in the 1980s' (2001: x; see also Wacquant, 1999).

6 Indeed, in an article written just before the war on Iraq, Hardt (2002) complained that the USA was behaving like an old-fashioned Empire, rather than the new global Empire that its interests required. This perhaps underestimates the contradictions within hegemonic blocs, and the significance of spatial formations.

So, why is this axis so significant, and what enabled it to come about? In the postcolonial period, the UK has been articulated to two geopolitical projects. The first, in (subordinate) alliance with the USA, imagines the UK as part of the 'defence of the free world'. The second, in the European Union, imagines the UK as a formative – and liberalizing – force in the shaping of a regional future (and as part of an 'older' civilization). It would be wrong to pose the relationship between Europe-as-EU and the USA as a wholly antagonistic one: they are, of course, united as the 'First World', as the 'free world', as NATO, as capitalist democracies and so on. Nevertheless, there are signs of strain between the two blocs – over trade, over conceptions of how markets might be regulated and managed, over conceptions of the social and social policy, over culture and cultural hegemony, and over the disposition and deployment of armed force, made particularly visible in the disputes over the war on Iraq in 2003.

The UK has been pulled between these two possibilities while often reviling both: popular anti-Americanism sits easily alongside popular 'Euro-scepticism' in a sort of equal opportunity xenophobia. But the form of articulation that is emerging under New Labour rule marks a distinctive attempt to draw the two blocs into a new alignment. Although the 'special relationship' between the USA and the UK has a long history, it has been politically mobilized in a series of shifting party and personal relationships since the coincident Thatcher–Reagan governments. There were substantial links between Conservative and Republican parties (and thinktanks); subsequently New Labour extensively developed links with the New Democrats (and a whole range of policy thinktanks), while the Blair–Clinton axis proved to be a strong association (see King and Wickham-Jones, 1998). What is striking is the apparent transcendence of the party alignment in the (George W.) Bush–Blair affinity. This very strong US orientation has also been a conduit for neo-liberal discourse, strategy and policy to flow transatlantically (and not solely from the USA to the UK). It has also enabled other discourses (such as communitarianism, for example) to travel. This transatlantic flow has included workfare and other labour market policies; the use of tax credits to 'incentivize' those defined as 'hard-working families'; new crime control strategies; and forms of marketization, privatization and deregulation (see, *inter alia*, Garland, 2001; King, 1999; Peck, 2001; Kingfisher, 2002; Swann, 1988; Wacquant, 1999).

All of this has taken place alongside the shifting and ambivalent relationship of the UK to Europe as a regional bloc. The distinctive feature of the New Labour period has been its insistence on placing Britain 'at the heart of Europe' (rather than on the Conservative 'margins'). The Europeanization of Britain is a more partial and contradictory process than this might imply, since Britain's role at the heart of Europe is to *neo-liberalize Europe*. Britain has sought to install neo-liberal wisdom – and policies – within the EU: to make labour markets more flexible, to reduce the burdens on employers, to liberalize trade and to reduce regulation and 'red tape'. Wacquant describes these lines of flow in a telling imagery:

This wide ranging network of diffusion originates in Washington and New York City, crosses the Atlantic to lash itself down in London, and, from there, stretches its channels and capillaries throughout the Continent and beyond. (1999: 322)

The UK, then, articulates the US-based transnational neo-liberal project in the remaking of Europe. It forms a critical and transformative link in the globalization of neo-liberalism and in the project of neo-liberal globalization.

Neo-liberalism speaks to the renewed sense that 'it's the economy, stupid', as Bill Clinton put it. It allows us to think of how economic shifts and political formations may be connected – as the transparent representation of economic interests; as the rise of neo-liberal (or neo-classical) economics as a public discourse; and as 'economic discourse' permeating or suffusing all other forms of public discourse (markets, consumer choice etc.). But I have also tried to argue that treating neo-liberalism as a hegemonic project might lead to thinking about the instabilities and unevennesses of its achievements. Neo-liberalism intends to subjugate the world – but that is not the same as accomplishing it. The world is also shaped by other forces, projects, ideologies and discourses, and we should be attentive to these alternatives (whether residual and on the defensive; or emergent and assertive). They are both what makes neo-liberalism's life difficult and the source of other imaginaries of the world and its futures. *Living with/in and against neo-liberalism* implies different ways of inhabiting it, cohabiting with it, and attempting to refuse it. While I think that neo-liberalism is, and has been, the dominant global/transnational political force, it is installed more firmly, securely and extensively in some places than others. Its achievements are immense – but still uneven, involving difficult accommodations and remaining contested. Making 'contestation' a feature of the analysis matters: while neo-liberalism may claim that 'there is no alternative', we should not.

six

Governing welfare: systems, subjects and states

Earlier I argued that configurations of welfare, state and nation had been sub-jected to differing forces and directions of change. In the middle of the twen-tieth century, the welfare settlements of most Western capitalist societies sup-ported a construction of the 'welfare state' as a political-cultural imaginary, embodied in a range of institutions, policies and practices. These varied between nations, but the idea of the 'welfare state' expressed a conception of national, collective, social provision. As I argued in Chapter 1, the various assaults on the welfare state have unsettled both 'welfare' and the 'state'. In the process, established formations have been called into question: should the state be the sole or even main provider of welfare? Should state systems, processes and cultures be reformed, modernized or replaced? In these transi-tions, distinctions between public and private have been both blurred and reconstructed, making it difficult to determine the boundaries of the public sector, public services and public provision.

This chapter focuses on the changing 'state' – although it will quickly become clear that many of the analyses of contemporary state change proceed around questions of governance, in which the concept of the state becomes displaced or decentred. Studies of the changing role and form of the state have stressed different processes. For example, some have focused on the changing 'sectoral' balance of welfare provision, pointing to the 'shrinking' role of the state through processes of privatization, marketization and the rise of 'welfare pluralism' (Whitfield, 2000; Rao, 1996). Others have examined the changing relationships and practices of welfare provision, for example by identifying the creation of quasi-markets (Bartlett, Le Grand and Roberts, 1998); contracting (Walsh, 1995); regulation (Picciotto, 2002); or partnerships (Glendinning, Powell and Rummery, 2002) as distinctive features of new welfare arrange-ments. As I suggested in the previous chapter, there has also been the delega-tion of welfare responsibilities, tasks and stresses to the private realm of the individual and of domestic, household and familial relationships.

At the same time, accounts of the changing form of the state have variously described it as 'hollowed out', 'thickened', 'contracting', post-Fordist, 'appointed', and 'managerial' (Rhodes, 1997; Harden, 1992; Burrows and Loader, 1994; Skelcher, 1998; Clarke and Newman, 1997). Others highlighted questions of shifting borders and boundaries – in terms of changing levels of governing (as in concepts of multi-tier governance: Geyer, 2000) or in terms of the boundaries between different social sites (public and private, for example). Not all of these descriptions are specific to welfare: some relate to public services, some to government, some to the state. They suggest processes of transformation in which the state (variously conceived) is changing (in various directions). Many of these issues have been drawn together around the rapidly growing concern with 'governance'. As Daly (2002) and Newman (2001) have both argued, this focus illuminates important change processes in social policy:

> Governance in the first instance invokes an analysis of the state and the 'public' sphere more broadly. A key rationale in the entire field is to ascertain the extent to which a change in governance is associated with or occasions a change in the state itself. The role of the state and in particular its capacities and functions come under scrutiny as do the challenges which increasing social differentiation and the decline of nation state sovereignty throw up for both the state and the centralisation of power. (Daly, 2002: 119)

In exploring these issues, this chapter will:

- examine a conception of governance based on political science (first section);
- contrast this with a poststructuralist focus on governmentalities (second section);
- draw out some concerns about *contradiction, contestation* and the *unfinished* character of governmental projects (third section);
- return to the question of the state – and its dispersed form in the 'modernization' of the governance of welfare in Britain (fourth section);
- examine the implications for how 'statework' of various kinds is governed (fifth section); and
- conclude by returning to the instabilities associated with the rise of the 'new governance' (sixth section).

Throughout the chapter, I will be arguing that while both 'governance' and 'governmentality' decentre the state in analytic terms, there are arguments for thinking again about changing state forms and the changing roles they play. This may require a move towards 'recentring' the state, but in different terms.

From government to governance?

In some ways, the view of governance developed in political science and public administration has the most obvious connections with social policy. It addresses changing mechanisms, relations and processes of governing and, as Mary Daly (2002) suggests, evokes memories of social policy's original incarnation as 'social administration' (Brown, 1983). This political science model narrates a shift from 'government' (understood as direct control) to 'governance' (the indirect pursuit of effects though other agents). The transition is located in a process of the nation-state being 'hollowed out' as power and authority move 'upwards' to supranational institutions and 'downwards' to regional and local bodies (Rhodes, 1997). In the work of Rhodes (1997; 1999) and Stoker (1999; 2000) this approach to changing modes of governing has produced richly detailed studies of governance in practice. It has been associated with a theoretical model that differentiates hierarchies, markets and networks as modes of coordinating social life (Thompson et al., 1991). The approach offers a historical account for the shift away from direct government that centres on government overload, the limits of governmental capacity and the increasing capacity of actors and agencies in (civil) society to resist government direction and to produce desired outcomes. As Peters puts it, this view of governance 'stresses the capacity of social forces to resist the regulations and impositions of the state' and 'extols the virtues of governance systems' that mobilize social or collective resources to 'shape policy at both the input and output stages' (2000: 40–1). In this approach, government has been decentred and must work through, and accommodate to, networks.[1] There is also a more or less implicit historical sequence that sees bureaucratic hierarchy (an integral government) as being superseded by market relations (within and beyond government). In turn, these are being displaced by networks (forms of collaboration, partnership and alliance) that promise to overcome the limitations of both hierarchies and markets. Rhodes summarizes these transitions in UK public services as follows:

> The shift from line bureaucracies to fragmented service delivery systems can be summarised as the shift from government to governance. Governance has become the defining narrative of British government at the turn of the century, challenging the commonplace notion of Britain as a unitary state with a strong executive. The policy of marketising public services has accelerated the process of differentiation and multiplied networks. To the stark choice between hierarchy and markets, we can now add networks. (1999: xix)

At an empirical level, this model has strong elements of plausibility. It catches (some) key shifts in the organization and coordination of public services in Britain. It foregrounds a set of transitions that are visible in the reconstruction of the welfare system, with the shift to markets and internal markets under Conservative rule (Bartlett, Le Grand and Roberts, 1998). It addresses the subsequent attention to processes of collaboration and partnership in New Labour's new principles for developing, organizing and delivering services (Glendinning, Powell and Rummery, 2002; Newman, 2001). It identifies the growing engagement of what Rhodes calls 'non-state actors' in the processes of

---

1 A different model is provided by Kooiman (1993; 2000) who explores the development of co-governing approaches (partnerships, networks and collaboration) as a response to increasing 'complexity, diversity and dynamics' in the social system. These are, however, system properties rather than social formations, and overall the model is limited by its 'systems' conceptions of social life. Not least among these is the assumption of a systemic tendency towards equilibrium, rather than instability.

governing as both corporate and voluntary organizations take on responsibilities for 'delivery', and as a range of stakeholders and partners become involved in processes of consultation, participation and co-production. These studies also draw attention to the complex institutional relations and processes that may be involved in such subsystems. In its British incarnations, this view of governance both anticipates and reinforces 'Third Way' conceptions of moving beyond the state and the market:

> The Third Way stands for a modernised social democracy, passionate in its commitment to social justice and the goals of the centre-left, but flexible, innovative and forward-looking in the means to achieve them ... But it is a *third* way because it moves beyond an Old Left preoccupied by state control, high taxation and producer interests; and a New Right treating public investment, and often the very notions of 'society' and collective endeavour, as evils to be undone. (Blair, 1998: 1)

I have some reservations about this political science view of governance. The first concerns the character of the abstract model that is produced. The model of modes of coordination (and their historical sequencing) tends to be abstracted or detached from the UK context of many of the studies. This both downplays the specific political struggles around state reform in the UK and blurs the differential deployment of other modes of governance in other national settings (and their trajectories through the internationalizing policy networks). At the same time, the modes of governing are treated as occupying the same level of analysis (the 'meso-level' in the terms of Rhodes, 1997: 11). Hierarchies, markets and networks are, so to speak, functionally equivalent ways of conducting the business of governing, though each may be 'fitted' to particular sorts of social context. 'Networks' fit more complicated social contexts, while hierarchies/bureaucracies are better suited to simpler, or more stable, or more traditional social environments. In the process, though, the differences between markets as large-scale institutions, hierarchies as specific forms of organization, and networks as patterns of relationship may be submerged.[2]

The interest in markets as a mode of governance drew intellectual and political legitimacy from the naturalizing conception of markets as coordinating institutions for economic activity, linking demand and supply for commodified goods and services (Carrier, 1997). But in practice, 'marketization' in public services has meant diverse phenomena. It includes the 'externalization' or 'contracting out' of activities; the creation of 'internal markets' with organizational distinctions between purchasers and providers; the creation of 'consumer choice' between competing providers; and the construction of old and new relationships into 'contractual' forms (Clarke, 1999b). Whether these can be adequately grasped as 'markets' in a generic sense is arguable. But the effect of identifying them all as 'markets' is to feed into that simplifying binary dis-

---

2 Thus large hierarchically coordinated organizations may be (corporate) actors in markets, while engaged in inter-organizational networks (price-fixing cartels, for example).

tinction between state and market discussed in Chapter 4. The *political* effect is to promote the (naturalized) supremacy of markets, contrasted with the inefficient and artificial interference of (state) bureaucracies (see, for example, du Gay, 1999; Frank, 2000; Skocpol, 1997).

The governance model's concern with networks similarly risks conflating analysis and normative evaluation. Two examples may suffice to make this point. Networks are regularly described as 'self-governing networks' or 'self-organizing, inter-organizational networks' (Rhodes, 1997: 15), endowing them with an (untested) 'autonomy' and a strong normative value. In these terms, 'self-governing' seems to denote a condition to be prized above being directed by other authorities or processes. Networks appear as both the endpoint of a historical sequence and the most desirable form of governance, despite a very clear recognition that networks can both promote and restrict access to the public domain. They may limit participation, shape (informal) rules of the game and substitute 'private for public' regulation and accountability (1997: 9–10). Networks may also be *collusive*. For example, Wedel (2001) argues that 'reform' in Central and Eastern Europe placed a high value on involving non-state or civil society 'networks', which produced destabilizing patterns of collusion and corruption. In the end, it is unclear whether network governance is an inevitable effect (of social and political change); an adaptive response to government failure (and market failure); or a form of socio-political arrangement that deserves to be pursued or encouraged enthusiastically.

In this view of governance, aspects of the state tend to disappear, or at least fade into the background. This may be an effect of conceptual elisions between 'government' and the 'state' in political theory. The move from government to governance obscures some problems about the forms, roles and capacities of the state. In a discussion of 'governance failure', Jessop (2000b) argues that this flattening of levels obscures relations between 'governance mechanisms' and the 'general state system'. He suggests that, as governance mechanisms are developed and deployed:

> the state typically monitors their effects on its own capacity to secure social cohesion in divided societies. It reserves to itself the right to open, close, juggle and re-articulate governance arrangements not only in terms of particular functions but also from the point of view of partisan and overall political advantage. (2000b: 19)

Reintroducing the state in this way highlights the role of the state in *directing* governance mechanisms and processes, and prevents it dissolving into networks. By distinguishing between the state, (party) politics and governance arrangements, Jessop allows us to see to a more differentiated set of institutions, relationships and practices of governing. This view alerts us to the political choices that shape (and reshape) how welfare is governed. Neither 'governance' nor 'welfare' is the result of depoliticized processes of policy choice and calculation. Governance arrangements may act to constrain or limit the capacity of the state as networks, or actors within them, prove recalcitrant or articulate other objectives. But this view suggests that networks will remain subject to forms of state control (through finance, policy, regulation and evaluation, for example). The state in this sense is engaged in what Jessop calls 'meta-governance': the process of 'managing the complexity, plurality and tangled hierarchies characteristic of prevailing modes of coordination' (2000b: 23; see also Kooiman, 2000). I will return to the question of the state later in the chapter, but before leaving this view of governance, I want to echo the arguments made by Daly and Newman about the 'thin' view of the social that is characteristic of governance studies:

> It is noticeable that theories of governance fail to deal adequately with the issues of diversity and the patterns of inclusion and exclusion through which notions such as 'citizens' and 'communities' are constituted. The conceptualisation of governance and the analysis of the institutions of government tend to take little account of the dissolution of the postwar social settlements around gender, race and class. (Newman, 2001: 171; see also Daly, 2002)

In one sense, this reflects the disciplinary origins of this view of governance: political science and public administration do not bring a richly 'social' view to the study of governance. Nevertheless, as Newman, suggests, it is problematic to lift the changing institutions and practices of governing out of their social locations, especially if changing social dynamics are seen as one of the conditions for changing approaches to governing. In contrast, the view from governmentality brings a distinctive concern with the changing 'social' into view.

Governmentalities: changing subjects

In this section I briefly review the rapidly growing poststructuralist (or more precisely post-Foucauldian) literature on governmentalities (see, for example, Dean, 1999; Petersen et al., 1999; Rose, 1996a; 1996b; 1999). By comparison with approaches based on political science, this perspective returns 'welfare' (as policies, practices and relations) to a more visible place in the analysis. This reflects an interest in governing as the practices of managing populations and their conduct. But in parallel with the governance approach, the study of governmentalities also displaces, or decentres, the state. Instead it insists that governing takes place through multiple agencies, relations and practices. Rose has argued that studies of governmentalities

> focus upon the various incarnations of what we might term 'the will to govern', as it is enacted in a multitude of programmes, strategies, tactics, devices, calculation, negotiations, intrigues, persuasions and seductions aimed at the conduct of individuals, groups, populations – and indeed oneself. From this perspective, the question of the state that was so central to earlier investigations of political power is relocated. The state now appears as simply one element – whose functionality is historically specific and contextually variable – in mul-

tiple circuits of power, connecting a diversity of authorities and forces, within a whole variety of complex assemblages. (1999: 5)

Governmentalities denote relatively structured and coherent relations that link the governing and the governed, which are embedded in 'regimes of practices' with distinctive features. Each form of governmentality (a mentality of/about governing) and its practices feature:

- characteristic *forms of visibility*: those objects/activities on which they focus attention and the ways of seeing those objects;
- distinctive *knowledges*: dominant ways of knowing about objects/activities and populations expressed in specific discourses and implying distinctive relations between 'expertise' and those subjected to, by and through it;
- specific *ways of acting or intervening*: particular 'rationalities' that inform or are enacted in sets of mechanisms, techniques and technologies of intervention; and
- characteristic *ways of forming subjects*: selves, persons, actors or agents. (lightly adapted from Dean, 1999: 23)

I cannot pursue the entire theoretical structure of governmentality here, but I want to underline its anti-reductionist and anti-statist commitments that challenge simplifying assumptions in the social sciences. Governmentality studies have played a significant part in opening up the field of welfare relations and practices in ways that highlight how 'welfare' is implicated in the constitution and reproduction of differentiated subjects (see, for example, Hillyard and Watson, 1996; Petersen et al., 1999). They have also insisted on taking seriously the value of attending to the micro-political processes (the techniques and technologies) of governing populations.

While all forms of liberal governance work at 'arm's length' through the construction of self-regulating or self-governing subjects, rather than through the exercise of direct power, there have been different variants. Harris (1999: 38–40), for example, distinguishes between classical liberal, expansive liberal and advanced liberal governance. Expansive liberal governance involved a (limited) socialization of both economic and social realms under the sign of promoting collective security and is associated with 'welfarism' and the construction of the 'social' as a site of intervention (Rose, 1996b; 1999: ch. 3). In contrast, advanced liberalism is marked by the drive to desocialize both realms. Harris argues that advanced liberalism

> sees 'enterprise' – the enterprising society, the enterprising subject and enterprising economic behaviour – as things which it must actively work to *recreate* … Its task, at least in part, is remedial: it must undo the damage of expansive liberalism and inculcate a political climate in which self-sufficiency is desired and learned. (1999: 44, emphasis in original)

In this remedial work, advanced liberalism economizes other realms, subjecting them to economic (or market) logic, knowledge and practices. What we think of as the social realm has been progressively subsumed by the economic. O'Malley (1996) has described the rise of a 'new prudentialism' that treats citizens as active risk calculators and risk managers, empowered by the retreat of public or collective insurance to 'make their own choices'. The process of economization can be traced in new techniques and technologies (the use of market forms as a means of governing) and in new discursive formations (the reinscription of the citizen as a customer). According to Rose, the fragmentation of the social produces 'communities' alongside 'enterprising selves' as the subjects of governance in advanced liberalism (1999; 2000; see also Probyn, 1998, on processes of familialization). Rose also argues that advanced liberalism constructs new forms of governance in that it:

> sought a new role for the political apparatus as merely one partner in government, facilitating, enabling, stimulating, shaping, inciting the self-governing activities of a multitude of dispersed entities – associations, firms, communities, individuals – who would take onto themselves many of the powers and the responsibilities previously annexed by the state.
>
> The characteristics of contemporary strategies for 'reinventing politics' are familiar: downsizing the state, decentralizing decision-making, devolving power to intermediate bodies such as trusts or associations, privatizing many functions previously part of the state machinery and opening them up to commercial pressures and business styles of management, introducing managerialism and competitive pressures into the residual state apparatus, displacing the substantive knowledge of the welfare professionals by the knowledge of examination, scrutiny and review undertaken by accountants and consultants.
>
> These strategies thus involve the generation of autonomy plus responsibility. They multiply the agencies of government while enveloping them within new forms of control. (2000: 96–7)

Clearly, one does not have to be a governmentalist to have noticed these processes, but governmentality provides a powerful analytic frame through which their intersection and ordering as part of a larger transition can be analysed. It foregrounds the study of multiple and complex apparatuses, knowledges and regimes of practices through which governing takes place. It challenges the view of a changing balance between public and private (or between state and civil society) by treating the 'freeing of the citizen' as a new form of subjection. It promotes a deconstructionist scepticism about the knowledges and forms of expertise that are deployed (and reproduced) in policies and practices. As a result, it provides a valuable antidote to normative assumptions about 'good governance'. Finally, studies of governmentality (or what Dean calls more precisely the 'analytics of governing': 1999: 20–7) locate the shifts in government and governance within a wider programme of remaking modern societies. The government-governance approach tends to abstract processes and practices of governing from specific social/political contexts and conditions. The concern with advanced liberal governance locates changes in welfare policy, relations and systems in a wider dynamic and offers an extended conception of what counts as 'political' that goes beyond the conventional views of party and institutions of government.

Incomplete and insecure: governmentalities and governing

Governmentality has provided a productive basis for a variety of contemporary studies of governing processes and practices (e.g. Cooper, 1998; Ferguson and Gupta, 2002; Li, 1999; Ong, 1999). But I think that the most interesting developments take governmentality beyond its Foucauldian core, overcoming some of its limitations in the process. For me, these limitations centre around governmentality's spatial character; its overunified view of governmentalities; its conflation of strategy and outcome; and, last but not least, the problem of the state. While a powerful deconstructive approach, it reproduces some dominant assumptions within its mode of analysis and main narrative forms. In particular, it takes the form and experience of Western – or perhaps Anglophone – societies as the norm. It might be more accurate to say that many governmentality studies seem spatially indeterminate (see also Allen, 2003, for a critical view about the relation between space and power). But as usual, such indeterminacy tends to result in the generalization of the West as the universal. Viewed from 'elsewhere' (outside the metropolitan centres) the experience of globalized governance is, at least, not very new (Gupta, 2000; Hall, 2002). Both liberal and not very liberal forms of governance have been implicated in the regulation of different forms of 'subject population': coercion coexists with consent and compliance (see, for example, Nonini, 2003, on neo-liberalism and violence). Bringing colonial governance into view also raises questions about the ways in which the management of subject populations involves the exercise of force as well as the invocation of 'autonomous' subjects: the project of 'civilizing' people can be a fearsome process.

The conception of governmentality tends to produce an excessively coherent view of governance – with various projects, strategies and practices treated as instantiations of one form or other of liberal governmentality. The risk is that analysis becomes a matter of revealing example after example of 'advanced liberalism' in practice, each example being treated as no more than another instantiation of the general principles. As a result conflict and contestation are either omitted or contained within the discursive framing of advanced liberalism (becoming merely variations on a theme). I want instead to foreground varieties of disjuncture (temporal and spatial) between different governmentalities and governmental projects. This might draw attention to the variable and contested meanings of welfare and welfarism – rather than simply treat them as a category of expanded liberalism (Clarke, 2000b; and Chapter 3 in this book). It would also mean placing greater weight on contestation (over the logics, forms and practices of governing) as a critical dynamic in the development of governance. Cooper (1998), for example, explores conflicts in which divergent (if overlapping) conceptions of ownership and belonging are mobilized in claims about how critical issues should be governed, and how governing institutions should work (see also Li, 1996, on conceptions of community and property).[3]

Governmentalities tend to be seen as too unified and coherent, bringing about too fast a closure between strategy and outcome. Attempts to make the world conform, to produce self-regulating subjects, systems and relationships, and to install (and stabilize) new ways of being are governmental projects. But they should not be assumed to work. They may produce (conditional and calculating) compliance rather than conformity (Li, 1999). They may summon 'subjects' who refuse to come – or who are too busy doing something else (or being someone else) to bother listening.[4] They may model systems and relationships that turn out to be fractured, fractious and contested. They may create ways of being that fail to displace older (residual) or newer (emergent) alternatives. 'Citizen-consumers', summoned as the subjects of advanced (or neo-) liberalism, may refuse to surrender expansive liberal or welfarist citizen identities, or may resist consumerized positions in the name of global environmentalism and new solidarities. The general principle that I wish to advance is that we should not assume that strategies work as the strategists expect – and we should be attentive to the unevenness of outcomes.

Finally, I think that the decentring of the state in this post-Foucauldian approach inhibits thinking about the reconfigurations of power, authority and governance. Like Jessop (2000b; 2002), I think there are issues about 'meta-governance' – the governance of governance, so to speak – that are located primarily within the state, even as the form, role and practices of states change. The state remains a significant issue – both as the organizing force for meta-governance and as the 'legitimating' agency through which most governmental strategies have to pass to become authorized. This is something other than being 'one partner among many' in the practice of governing. For example, the capacity to require partnerships to take place, to direct them and to evaluate them, marks out the state as a distinctive authority (Glendinning, Powell and Rummery, 2002). The state is also the location of the variety of centralizing tendencies that run alongside, and counter to, decentralization, delegation and devolution, even as it is the organizing force that launches and regulates them (Clarke and Newman, 1997).[5]

I think that governing can be approached in ways that treat instability and conflict as core issues (rather than residual additions after the 'big picture' governmentality has been rolled out and has subjected the world). This implies

---

3 Governmentality studies also tend to focus on the subject positions inscribed in governmental discourses, excluding or subordinating other relations, positions and identities as the source or focus of mobilization. I suspect that this results from treating the 'social' as a field constituted by governmentality, rather than a contested terrain (see Chapter 3).

4 This problem is nicely posed in the title of a paper by David Nugent: 'When States State, Who Listens?' (2003).

5 I am unclear whether governmentalists think that the state has always been one agency among many, or whether the current phase of advanced liberalism is marked by the state becoming one agency among many. The 'anti-statist' orientation of much Foucauldian writing suggests the former, but the quotation above from Rose points to a more 'conjunctural' view of the place of the state. Both, I think, miss something vital about the formation of the state as both a site and a form of organizing power.

thinking about the dynamics of governing as a response to previous blockages, failures and resistances; as producing new contradictions and resistances of its own; and as having to negotiate a landscape that includes 'other' projects, knowledges and practices (Li, forthcoming; see also Smart, 2001, on 'unruly places'). Davina Cooper's (1998) work on disputed governance demonstrates how such analyses might be conducted. She argues that governing bodies 'deal with issues of governmentality that include the reproduction of authority and legitimacy, strategy, resources, obstructions and techniques. At the same time, institutional common concerns are cut across by differences' (1998: 11). She also makes the state contingently visible in the struggles over governing (rather than a monolithic centre of power):

> My conception of the state as a set of articulated identities shares with other approaches a conceptual emphasis on the interrelationship of force, political and regulatory power, dominant social relations and institutional structure … However, how a state functions, in particular, how the western, liberal state actually functions – its relationship to accountability, legitimacy, and authority, for instance – is more contested. (1998: 9)

Such conceptions of the state and its relationships to governing open up important possibilities. In particular, they take us beyond the one-dimensional view of the coherence and completeness of advanced liberalism. In exploring 'governance' and 'governmentality' approaches, I have been trying to construct a critique that accentuates a concern with contradictions and tensions; with the uneven and unfinished character of governmental projects; and with a conjunctural view of how settlement and destabilization might combine to produce 'a series of unstable equilibria'. I have also tried to indicate ways in which, now that the state has been decentred in both governance and governmentality studies, we may need to return it into view as a critical site and agency in the transformations of welfare.

Governing in the dispersed state

In this section, I want to suggest that the shift to new forms of 'governing welfare' in the UK might be seen as a process of changing the formation of the state from integrated to dispersed. This implies thinking about processes of state formation, rather than being hypnotized by a distinction between a monolithic (and unchanging) state and multi-agent governance (Steinmetz, 1999). Instead, I want to look at how emerging governance arrangements and changing forms of state are implicated with one another. At the core of this is a view of *dispersal* as a set of flows from the state to other agents and agencies that have become engaged in the tasks of governing. This process of dispersal involves divergent strategies of reform and generates new sets of tensions, contradictions and potential instabilities. It involves an extensive remaking of both vertical and horizontal relations of power, authority and control to engage diverse agents and agencies in governing. It is an unstable system whose 'organizational glue' is managerialism – understood as an ideology and a set of practices that aim to be both transformative and reintegrative (Clarke and Newman, 1997). Nevertheless, it is a mode of governing where the state is more than residual. Rather the state has acquired expanded capacities of direction, regulation and surveillance over the agents and agencies of governance.

This is a *form of state* that emerges particularly in studies of the UK and other Anglophone countries (Australia and New Zealand, especially). But it is a *model of state reform* that has been internationalized in processes of policy diffusion and transfer. Flynn suggests that there have been strong pressures towards a transnational view of the 'one best way' to manage states, noting that bodies such as the OECD Public Management Group

> have argued that there is a single best way of running state functions, including various lists of features that emulate the operation of companies in a competitive market. These include the use of competition as a way of reducing costs, a more flexible workforce, more charging for services at the point of delivery, performance related pay, short term contracts and so on. Where feasible this sort of approach is made a condition of getting financial help from international institutions, such as the Inter-American Development Bank, the International Monetary Fund and the Asian Development Bank. Even where financial help is not being sought, there are institutions such as the OECD and management consultants that encourage such management methods and assume that there is a single set of problems looking for a unique set of solutions. (2000: 28–9)

This view of state reform has been sustained and supported by armies of consultants and advisers (especially those associated with transnational consultancy and accounting companies). The reforms have been implemented in part by the MBA-badged cadres produced by business schools (again a distinctive UK–US axis). Although implemented very differently in different places, there are some core imperatives about the direction and processes of state reform. Privatization, marketization and deregulation have an intimate, though variable, relationship with the tenets of the new public management (NPM) (see Flynn, 2000; Pollitt and Bouckaert, 2000). The NPM has combined a commitment to reducing the state by externalizing services with a view about how to manage remaining state functions 'in a businesslike way'. Such injunctions have been followed unevenly – in part a function of international relations of power and dependency, and in part an effect of domestic political projects (Flynn, 2000). Even though this agenda has been adopted unevenly – and adapted in practice – state reform has been framed within a very limited range of legitimated possibilities.

The changing governance of welfare has involved a multiplicity of innovations: new policies, new practices, new relationships and new institutional and organizational forms and arrangements. In the UK, we can see changes that include:

- different privatizations: the shift of services to the private sector, and the shift of responsibilities to 'individual men and women and their families';
- the decentralization/devolution of managerial authority;
- different marketizations: the externalization of some activities, the introduction of internal markets;
- the engagement of consumers and proxy consumers in service choices;
- the construction of new forms of inter-organizational and social partnerships; and
- the involvement of service users, communities and socio-demographically specified groups in processes of consultation and participation.

Whether such innovations form a coherent programme of advanced liberalism is, I think, open to argument. They look more contingent and more conflicted – and less coherent – than might be expected. These emerging governance arrangements may be viewed synchronically and diachronically. Synchronically, the current ensemble of governing arrangements is overlaid in complex and contradictory ways, such that it is difficult to draw out one overarching organizing principle. Are the changes about privatization, marketization, familialization, decentralization or centralization?[6] Viewed diachronically, this layering looks like the sedimented institutionalization of successive waves of reform. These waves of reform have been driven by political calculation, by the failures or limited successes of previous reforms (neo-liberal ideologues have always insisted on more), and to some extent they are driven by the problems and tensions generated by previous reforms. The most significant feature for me is that these changing forms of governance are articulated through the state. I mean not that they are unified by the state into some singular and coherent programme, but that the state is both the *object* of reform projects (to 'roll it back' or to 'modernize' it) and the *site* of meta-governance (Jessop, 2000b).

The 'new governance' has multiplied the agencies and sites of governing welfare (Clarke and Newman, 1997; Peters, 2003). It has engaged new providers, fragmented existing institutions into small or medium quasi-businesses, and created decentralized and devolved points of decision-making (from boards of school governors through senior managers to individualized consumers or their proxies). In the process, the vertical and horizontal relationships within which public services are framed have been reorganized. Vertically, such relationships stretch upwards to European and other supranational bodies that are articulated (often in uncomfortable ways) with nation-states and which sometimes speak past nation-states to regional and local bodies, and to individual citizens. At the same time, moves to decentralize management authority (to schools, trusts, community-based organizations,

---

6 Only the depressing trend towards ugly neologisms inhibits me from suggesting that these trends are organized around a principle of *depublicization*: the draining of the public realm's capacities and resources to other places.

partnerships) pushed both resources and decision-making power (or at least responsibility) beyond the intermediate local tiers of government (including local government). In critical areas, too, the shift from client to consumer of welfare services changed the balance of power (and interests and expectations) around the point of service delivery – even if the relationships are something less than full-blown consumerism (Clarke, 1997; Smith et al., 2003). Although these processes have been described as hollowing out the state, the vertical dimension also includes intensified central power. Tighter fiscal control, performance management systems, expanded powers of policy direction, enhanced evaluation systems, and powers of appointment to the expanded array of non-elected agencies through which many public services have been delivered, all contribute to an expanded *central* capacity (Clarke, Gewirtz and McLaughlin, 2000b; Skelcher, 1998).

Horizontal relationships have also been extensively reformed through requirements for contracting, competition and collaboration. Contracting and competition were intended to disintegrate systems of service provision, externalizing some activities to other organizations and creating competition for customers, resources or rankings between providers. To some extent, such fragmenting pressures have been mitigated by subsequent (New Labour) requirements for collaboration and partnership (Glendinning, Powell and Rummery, 2002). Nevertheless, as Newman (2001) argues, this attention to collaboration adds to the complexities that organizations face (since they have to continue to compete) and to the tensions that characterize the system of governance. The effect is to create a 'conditional autonomy' for organizations within this field of relationships – but this autonomy is *highly* conditional and constrained. In particular, it is framed by the increasing array of evaluation, scrutiny and audit agencies deployed by the state as part of the management of performance (discussed further in the next chapter). Above all, this conditional autonomy is governed by the expectation that organizations will manage themselves in a 'businesslike' fashion (Clarke and Newman, 1997; Hoggett, 1996; Pollitt, Birchall and Putnam, 1998). Indeed, in contemporary New Labour approaches, autonomy – construed as the 'freedom to manage' – is explicitly conditional on competitive success. High-performing health trusts, schools and local authorities have been promised enhanced levels of freedom from central direction and scrutiny.

This is a complex and contradictory system of governance (Newman, 2001). It is also *unfinished*. State reform – and the remaking of the agencies, relationships and processes of governing – is a continuing process. The pursuit of strategic aims and objectives produces innovations in governance as governments attempt to refine and enhance their capacity to get the results they want. Innovations also result from the challenge of finding ways to overcome resistances, blockages, opposition and the tendency of individuals and groups to bend or appropriate reforms in unanticipated (and 'inappropriate') ways. The system is also the focus of more tactical adaptations – either to events and problems in the balance of the system, or to matters of political-electoral calculation. What Dunleavy (1995) calls policy 'hyperactivism' – the overproduction of policy initiatives in the interests of being seen to be 'doing something' – is also significant. As Peck argues, the constant turmoil of policy innovation also undercuts potential critics: innovation has already moved policy on by the time that criticisms of previous practice can be formed (2001: 100–3; 358–63). This suggests that the experience of 'permanent revolution' in public services is the effect of several processes in combination. There is an overarching discourse – and practice – of 'change', 'reform' and 'modernization' that attempts to secure both governmental and political legitimacy. As Janet Newman and I argued in *The Managerial State* (Clarke and Newman, 1997: 34–55), a discursive 'cascade of change' links global, national, organizational and personal imperatives about the necessity, inevitability and desirability of change. It remains a compelling discourse, particularly in the way that it has been harnessed to the 'new' and the 'modern' in New Labour. This enables opposition to be readily construed as backward, 'old' or part of the 'forces of conservatism' (Clarke and Newman, forthcoming; Fairclough, 2000; Finlayson, 2003).

Governing work: shifting boundaries

I now want to explore some of the ways in which this new state form and its governance arrangements have involved blurring, dissolving and revising the boundaries between the public and private that had been associated with the 'old' welfare state. But I will do so through examining their intersection with the remaking and revalorization of work in contemporary social policy. From a variety of standpoints, studies have pointed to the new centrality of work: Peck's (2001) analysis of the shift from welfare to workfare; the increasing salience of 'labour market activation' policies across European nations revealed in comparative studies (e.g. Andersen and Jensen, 2002; Taylor-Gooby, 2001a; Zeitlin and Trubeck, 2003); and the New Labour commitment to reform welfare to ensure 'work for those who can, security for those who cannot' (see, for example, Lister, 2002a; 2002b). These focus on work as the *object* of social policy – or workers and would-be workers as the *subjects* of social policy. To these concerns I want to add a consideration of work as the *practice* of social policy: the labours of producing and distributing 'care', 'welfare' and services to the public. Alongside changing forms of governing welfare and changing policies are changing conceptions and conditions of work that involve shifting boundaries about what work means and where it takes place (Mooney, 2004).

Here I want to start with the shifting conditions and location of what might be called 'statework'. State reform projects have sought to get quite a lot of statework out of the state – and I will return to these processes. But what remains as statework *within* the state has been subject to a number of changes. There are processes of occupational recomposition, such as those visible in the National Health Service, aimed at remaking labour processes and forms of occupational and professional power, and seeking to install managerial authority (see, for example, Ferlie et al., 1996; Poole, 2000b). Here processes of changing skill mixes and occupational scope (e.g. extending nursing towards the clinical terrain, while engaging unskilled assistance to perform 'basic' nursing and care tasks) shift occupational hierarchies and the composition and 'flexibility' of the health labour force (Davies, 2004). Most other public services and organizations have experienced variations of these processes. There are common pressures towards managerial coordination; challenges to occupational and professional 'conservatism'; the recomposition of labour forces and the distribution of tasks; and the greater use of unskilled and unqualified labour (e.g. Abbott and Meerabeau, 1998).

Three particular processes stand out for me. One is the continuing universalization of 'management' as the solution to the problem of improving public services (Pollitt, 1993; Cutler and Waine, 1997). 'Making up managers' remains a key process in public services, allied to a new enthusiasm for creating 'leadership' (Newman, 2002). The second is the tendency to shift what were occupational/professional identities to ones that are organization centred. The organization – the trust, the school, the department – seeks to become the point of identification, loyalty and commitment, with externally oriented professionalism being treated as suspect and as a 'special interest' that distracts from the 'organization as common purpose' (Clarke, 1999b). The rise of a competitive-evaluative nexus of regulation (discussed in the following chapter) that requires *organizational* success helps to enforce this identification. Despite this, professionalism (in its public ethos sense) provides a continuing source of recalcitrance, providing one basis for arguments about who 'owns' – or can be trusted with – such services. Echoing Davina Cooper's (1998) examination of contested concepts of belonging, professionals, semi-professionals and workers continue to lay claim to the service, its ethos, or its responsibility to its users. Sometimes these are in the face of new policy initiatives, sometimes in defence of existing labour processes and conditions of service, and sometimes in a challenge to new organizational solutions for public services. For example, health care professionals attempt to speak in the name of patient care; teachers contest curriculum and testing initiatives in the name of children's best interests; while railway workers and firefighters have claimed the public interest in safety in trying to resist various 'modernizations' of their organizations and working conditions. Finally, the processes of state reform have produced new occupations – particularly in the field of networked or partnership governance. These include 'partnership managers', 'community safety officers' and 'neighbourhood managers' (Hughes and Edwards, 2002; Gilling and Hughes, 2002).

At the same time, quite a lot of statework has been expelled from the institutions of the state. Forms of privatization, contracting out and 'trustification' have shifted organizations, labour processes and jobs from the state to the private and voluntary sectors. Through such shifts, working conditions, work processes and the composition of jobs have changed – generally in the direction of cheaper and more flexible labour, exemplified in the 'care work' that grew alongside the private and voluntary sectors' expansion of social and health care provision (both domiciliary and residential). Care work also exemplifies some of the emerging trends of the wider labour market – towards casualization, towards feminization, and towards a growing presence of migrant workers (Mayer, 2000; Yeates, forthcoming). In these processes, sectoral boundaries have been blurred. These may be public services, but they are rarely delivered by public sector organizations, or by public employees, even though they may be purchased with public funds. The drive towards efficiency (most visible in private sector care work) also suggests that such work is subject to flexibility requirements (of contract and managerial discretion). But they are also about new rigidities, for example in the detailed specification of what care work means in practice, often rendering the personal or emotional labour of care work as 'beyond the contract' (Stone, 2000).

These trends intersect with the processes of recruiting new sources of labour to the business of welfare. In particular, the growth of the voluntary sector has meant a continuing need to discover – and manage – new volunteers. The voluntary sector is at the hub of a number of contradictory processes. The shift towards a 'contract culture' has fuelled organizational growth (for favoured organizations) while restricting or inhibiting the 'advocacy' and 'innovation' roles that were previously central to much of the sector. The pressure to become 'businesslike', or to look like a 'well-managed organization', can run counter to the 'voluntary' ethos of the volunteers who may resent attempts to 'modernize' the organization or create forms of managerial supervision and labour discipline (Newman and Mooney, 2004).

At this point, we also begin to see the blurring of the category of 'work' itself. Welfare work and care work are subject to different processes – becoming commodified and decommodified as forms of labour, and regulated by different forms of discipline. The growth of the service sector, for example, includes care work of various kinds – and thus marks a trend towards the commodification of care work (becoming waged labour). But the shift towards voluntary, familial or personal labour marks a trend towards decommodification of welfare or care work as it is taken out of the cash nexus. The growth in voluntary provision and the shift of caring responsibilities to the private setting do not form part of what governments count as 'work', even though they may be vital to the economic calculus of increasing the efficiency of welfare governance. Substituting unwaged labour for waged labour improves the cost structure calculations of services (Clarke, 1999b). Nevertheless, care – in its non-commodified forms – is not valorized as socially useful activity, since it is not waged (Lister, 2002a).

The new governance of welfare, then, throws up some significant – if contradictory – changes in what 'work' means in new occupational, organizational and social settings and relationships. It also blurs and realigns how we understand the distinction between public and private. In one form, it is blurred by 'public services' being funded, organized and delivered by organizations not in the 'public sector' – the results of externalization, contracting and 'public–private partnerships'. But it is also blurred by the double privatizations – from public to private sector, and from public to private realm (Clarke, 2004). It is also blurred by the expectation that public service providers (in whatever sector) will behave more like private enterprises – in being 'businesslike'. The traces of these realignments can be seen in irreconcilable arguments over whether the NHS is being 'privatized' as a result of various 'organizational redesigns': the introduction of internal markets; the use of medical and hospital capacity in the private sector; the creation of 'foundation hospitals' with greater financial flexibility; and so on. The boundaries of the public and private are no longer so clear or settled as they were assumed to be. As I argued in Chapter 5, the private/personal realm becomes increasingly significant as the site for reconciling many of the tensions and multiple pressures generated in the public realm where state and market are being realigned.

Unstable systems and unreliable agents

The 'dispersed state' is at the heart of an unstable system of governance, requiring intense political and organizational effort to keep it from splitting apart. Here I want to distinguish between the instabilities that result from the encounters between the system and its external conditions, and those that are part of its internal dynamics. On the one hand, it is unstable because it is an attempt to find ways of governing conditions, populations and relationships that are themselves unstable and difficult – rather than fixed and acquiescent. As I argued earlier, at least some of the people recurrently fail to 'know their place', even when they are called on to be disciplined, self-governing and responsible subjects. The system is partly unstable because it is shaped by contradictory imperatives, such as accommodating demands for both flexibility and security, or reconciling US and European 'models' of being a modern society. Such political-cultural instabilities contribute to a series of contradictory practices that attempt to translate those multiple imperatives into action. As Newman (2001) has argued, this is a system forged out of incompatible models of governing – oscillating between centralizing and decentralizing tendencies, between competition and collaboration, and regularly unsettled by shifting political objectives. Here, then, the internal dynamics coincide with the projects and problems of governing welfare in the present.

In a dispersed system, the potential sites of contention and instability are simultaneously multiplied and localized. The proliferation of agencies involved in policy, process and practice of services, and the number of 'authorized' decision-making settings (local management, partnership steering bodies, community participation, contracting bodies etc.), mean that the potential sites where conflicts may occur – or be articulated – have increased. For example, Cooper (1998: 96–120) exposes the different notions of 'ownership' deployed in the contested *local* management of a school. But at the same time, such conflicts are *localized* to particular sites and are framed within discursive attempts to distinguish policy and strategy from 'local' implementation and management matters. This distinction has itself proved to be highly unstable. On the one hand, governments find it hard not to interfere in 'operational' matters to achieve political and policy objectives (Harrison et al., 1992). On the other, local or particular interests often demand national/strategic attention to their concerns – and insist on (national) governmental responsibility for policy, resourcing and outcomes.

As both the governance and governmentality approaches suggest, this dispersed system recruits new active agents into the processes of governing (though they view the process and the agents rather differently). It requires people who will 'take responsibility' within welfare organizations and as active citizens. But such recruitment processes are less than perfect. Rather than delivering the ideal subject – self-discipliningly compliant – they create spaces and conditions in which people may think of themselves as agents, and where they may bring other identities, affiliations and attachments into play. As Holland and Lave argue, subjects exist in dialogic relationships, not merely being 'hailed' or 'interpellated', but also 'answering' (2001a: 10). In this process, they may draw on other discourses, vocabularies of motive and political repertoires – which make the outcomes of processes of attempted subject formation or subjugation unpredictable.

Studies of public service management have revealed a range of ways of understanding and acting like managers. Alongside enthusiastic or compliant 'new managers' are also those who 'bend' their conditional autonomy in service of 'local' priorities, fed by emergent demands or residual commitments to 'older' conceptions of public service, need and justice (Newman, 2002; Pollitt and Bouckaert, 2000; Pollitt, Birchall and Putnam, 1998). As Pollitt and Bouckaert argue, the results of managerial autonomy are sometimes 'unforeseen and unforeseeable' (2000: 191). The enhanced spaces of managerial autonomy or freedom – in which managers are supposed to exercise the 'right to manage' – have become the focus of new attempts to discipline, constrain and direct (e.g. through target-setting, evaluation, inspection and audit processes). Relative autonomy always implies the possibility of someone making the 'wrong' choice, no matter how well disciplined they are expected to be.

Similarly, trying to make communities the locus of the new governance encounters instabilities in both the constitution and the practices of communities (Clarke, 2002b). In studies of 'community empowerment', even 'active' communities – and their members – often fail to be the types of agents that the new governance seeks (see, for example, Craig, Parks and Taylor, 2002; Hyatt, 2001). The highly prized 'active citizen' may even turn into an 'activist citizen'. Peters notes that the process of bringing excluded or disadvantaged people into the management and delivery of social programmes 'has also made programmes more difficult to control, and has presented consequent problems of accountability. In some cases, client involvement has left the communities in which programmes are located worse off, as the leadership becomes coopted and leaves the community' (2003: 49). Despite the organicist imagery, 'communities' are contested and changeable constructions (rather than naturally occurring entities). They have shifting and contested memberships which imply problems of activism, leadership and representation (especially when what governance systems seek are 'responsible' representatives). They also have unfixed boundaries – of identity and place – which are the focus of different claims to inclusion and exclusion, and may extend well beyond the imaginary place allocated to them in governance. In the UK, 'minority ethnic communities' are imagined as local, but may be lived as global or transnational formations.

I have tried to emphasize instability and unpredictable agency in this account because both governance and governmentality approaches tend to offer overintegrated accounts of contemporary forms of governing. They foreground the dominant developments, and treat them as if they are effective and productive. Inverting this view, and emphasizing the system of governance as unstable and contradictory, runs other risks – romanticizing resistance, overestimating the spaces for manoeuvre and underplaying the weight of dominant tendencies. Nevertheless, I want to insist that this system of governing is a 'leaky' one that fails to contain and control all that it seeks to manage. It is also one whose integration is ill-fitting and uncomfortable – what Althusser memorably called 'a teeth-gritting harmony'. The system is dominated by a number of tendencies: towards blurring the 'public–private' boundary and enhancing the scope of both the private sector and the private (domestic-familial) sphere. Its tendencies are organized around a mode of dispersal in which funding, policy, strategy and scrutiny are separated from 'delivery'. It tends towards a managerialized view of organizational coordination; and towards the spread of governance among active and 'responsibilized' agents and agencies of various kinds.

Such dominant tendencies construct, control and constrain the forms and spaces of (legitimate or authorized) agency. They also dispel, dislocate and demobilize alternative conceptions of 'governing in the modern world' (Clarke and Newman, forthcoming). They claim inevitability, necessity and natural essentialness as their conditions of ruling in this manner. But it is at this point that I hear the Gramscian 'echo' – the insistence that these are aims and attempts, rather than outcomes. Even where they get results, such outcomes are provisional, temporary and conditional – not the final closure or the successful installation of a whole new system. These are strategies that struggle to dispel 'residual' attachments (to welfarism, social democracy, and conceptions of the public interest being met by public services). They also attempt to contain or incorporate 'emergent' concerns and challenges (around diversity and difference; the impact of intensified inequalities; the failures of privatization; the 'downsides' of deregulated capitalism; and the economic, social and environmental 'responsibilities' of government). The 'new governance' – and its advanced/neo-liberal mentality – has a recurrent struggle with what Thomas Frank rather nicely calls 'the problem of public doubt' (2000: 20). But it is also a system that keeps producing new sources of concern for a doubting public – the failures of corporate accounting and auditing in the USA in 2002 (Enron, WorldCom and the rest) being among the most recent. In the following chapter, I look at some of the ways in which governments in the UK have tried to manage the problems of a dispersed state – and the challenge of 'public doubt'.

seven

Performing for the public

In the previous chapter I noted that the governance of public services is increasingly focused on questions of 'performance'. The management, measurement, evaluation and improvement of performance have become the dominant concern of an interlocking array of organizations, relationships and practices of governing. A number of tendencies are condensed in this rise of performance. Some of these derive from the wider forces discussed in earlier chapters: the effects of corporate globalization and neo-liberalism. Others arise in the more particular encounters between states, governments and publics around the place, role and value of public services. 'Performance' has emerged as a solution to the problems of managing services in a dispersed or disintegrated state form. But this solution has struggled to contain all the pressures that it is intended to manage. I will explore the conjunctural combination of tendencies towards performance through the example of the 'performance–evaluation nexus' in the British state. I will emphasize its place in the New Labour project of governing in the 'modern world': the attempt to modernize British society and its governmental apparatuses. This chapter will:

- look at the combination of forces that have made performance a governmental obsession (first section);
- examine the institutionalization of this focus in the 'performance–evaluation nexus' (second section);
- look at what it means to 'perform performance' in public services (third section);
- explore its implications for relationships between governments and publics around the idea of public doubt (fourth section); and
- conclude by considering the governmental and political instabilities of the performance–evaluation nexus (fifth section).

The performance conjuncture

The governmental concern with the performance of public services is fundamentally associated with the larger dynamics of state reform. As Pollitt and Summa note:

Over almost exactly the same period as performance audit has emerged as a distinct form of audit, the governments of Western Europe, North America and Australasia have embarked upon extensive programmes of public management reform. These have aimed at modernizing, streamlining, and in some cases minimizing the whole of the state apparatus. Although the details of these reform programmes have varied considerably between one country and another, most of them have given a central place to the themes of decentralization and performance management ... This has entailed a widespread rethinking of the balance between the autonomy and the control of public organizations. It has generated a search for mechanisms and incentives that will help realize these new management ideas in practice. (1999: 1–2)

This concern with performance takes specific national forms, shaped by the intersection of global and national dynamics and discourses. A range of tendencies have come together conjuncturally to promote this focus on performance. They include the processes of corporate globalization and neo-liberalism; the 'fiscal crisis' of the state and the discourse of efficiency; the rise of the dispersed state form; and the contested relationships around welfare, the state and citizenship. In different ways, most of these tendencies have featured in earlier chapters of the book. As a result, I will treat them briefly here – but this chapter also represents one way of pulling together some of the arguments so far. It offers a 'conjunctural analysis' of the processes and politics of governing welfare in the UK, tracing the ways in which different forces combine, and are (temporarily) reconciled, as well as looking at the sources of tension, contradiction and instability that may unsettle these arrangements.

As I argued in Chapters 4 and 5, the economic, political and cultural realignments of the world are dominated, though not exhausted, by the structures and flows of a US-centred corporate capitalism. What Frank calls 'market populism' is one of the public voices of this form of globalization: the promise that markets will liberate and satisfy people. For public services, this emerges as the rhetorical (and in some places, practical) 'market test': can publicly provided services compete with the efficiency, flexibility, dynamism and customer-centredness of private sector provision? There are, as many authors have suggested, some problems about whether the market model can, much less should, be applied to public goods and services (e.g. Crouch, 2003; Needham, 2003; Stein, 2001). But, in public discourse, the market 'benchmark' has exercised a dominant influence – as a test and as an aspirational ideal. Neo-liberalism's anti-statist and anti-welfarist tendencies have underpinned a variety of assaults on welfare states, one of which has been conducted via public choice theory, which played a central role in constructing challenges to conceptions of public interest, public goods and public services (Dunleavy, 1991; Niskanen, 1971). Public choice theory contested the idea that public services were governed by altruism, public service goals or professional ethics. Instead, it argued that public institutions were driven by venal, self-interested and self-seeking motivations on the part of clients, bureaucrats and politicians (see, for example,

Friedman and Friedman, 1984, on the 'iron triangle'). Where market populism celebrated the liberatory dynamism of the market, public choice analysis denigrated the ossification of state bureaucracies. Together, they elaborated a moral economy of mistrust about public services, public bureaucracies and public servants (see also du Gay, 1999).

I argued in Chapter 5 that neo-liberalism represented crises as economic phenomena. What O'Connor (1973) described as the 'fiscal crisis' of the state both marked the withdrawal of capital from the 'managed growth' compromises of post-war Fordism and involved the construction of the 'crisis of the state' as an economic/fiscal problem, shaping public discourse around such tropes as 'we can no longer afford ...' and configuring public expenditure as 'wasteful' (mis)use of 'taxpayers' money'. This 'fiscal' discourse has enabled specific forms of political-cultural alliances and a framing of policy debates in terms of fiscal responsibility: what the economy needs, making work pay etc. (see also Prince, 2001). As a result, increased symbolic visibility has been attached to public expenditure, with an emphasis on fiscal control, constraint and consciousness within public organizations.

One particular manifestation of this fiscal consciousness has been the obsession with 'efficiency' in public services. Stein has argued that efficiency has been the key word in the 'attack on the sclerotic, unresponsive, and anachronistic state' that is 'branded as wasteful' (2001: 7). She notes that, in Canada:

> Those who provide our most important public goods are expected to do so efficiently. Physicians and nurses in the hospital where my mother was treated are expected to work efficiently. So are teachers, governments and civil servants. They are constantly enjoined to become efficient, to remain efficient and to improve their efficiency in the safeguarding of the public trust. Efficiency, or cost-effectiveness, becomes an end in itself, a value often more important than others. But elevating efficiency, turning it into an end, misuses language, and this has profound consequences for the way we as citizens conceive of public life. When we define efficiency as an end, divorced from its larger purpose, it becomes nothing less than a cult. (2001: 3–4)

Stein argues that the elevation of efficiency as the dominant goal for public services has displaced and dislocated other vital political debates – about objectives and values, about the means of achieving them and about forms of public debate and accountability. Despite the enlarged debate about public services around quality, standards, improvement and performance in the last decade, efficiency persists as a 'bedrock' value and orientation.

Processes of state reform in this period have emphasized disintegration through various means: privatization, internal markets, outsourcing, delegation, decentralization and devolution, competition between multiple providers, principal–agent contractualization etc. (Chapter 6). All of these have produced a dispersed or disintegrated state involving systems of control at a distance (Clarke and Newman, 1997; Hoggett, 1996). Managerialism has been the dominant organizational strategy (and discourse) for coordinating public services – and 'performance' is a particular development within this framing of organizational control. Performance is one way of naming the problems of control at a distance and the proposed solutions to them. It is identified as a problem emerging in the gap between hierarchical 'command and control systems' and delegated managerial authority. Scrutiny, inspection, evaluation and audit emerge as solutions to the problems of 'arm's length control' (Clarke et al., 2000c).

Although neo-liberalism and its allies have been the dominant forces in challenging the forms and limitations of welfare states, other tendencies have also been significant. As I argued in Chapter 3, struggles have centred on the subordinations, marginalizations and exclusions produced by the normative universalism of welfare citizenship (Lewis, 2000a; 2003; Lister, 1997). Conflicts over welfare citizenship – around axes of age, gender, race and ethnicity, sexuality and dis/ability – have been diverse. But they have raised political-cultural challenges about the relationships between universalism and difference, about the forms and limits of entitlement, and about the discriminatory exercise of power in state bureau-professionalism (Clarke and Newman, 1997: ch. 1; Williams, 1996). These struggles have been made to disappear in political discourses such as the Third Way (Blair, 1998; Giddens, 1998). There, the distinction between Old Left and New Right obliterates a loosely articulated 'New Left/new social movements' formation that voiced challenges to state power, welfare capitalism, and the limitations of citizenship – and gave voice to other conceptions of progress, possibility and modernity.

Such differentiated social identities are increasingly 'spoken for' in the language and imagery of consumerism and consumer choice – a particular variant of how diversity might be construed and contained (Williams, 1996; Needham, 2003; Smith et al., 2003; Stein, 2001). For example, a recent government document on public service reform juxtaposes post-war 'rationing culture' with today's 'consumer culture':

> The challenges and demands on today's public services are very different from those of the post-war years. The rationing culture which survived after the war, in treating everyone the same, often overlooked individuals' different needs and aspirations. Rising standards, a more diverse society and a steadily stronger consumer culture have increased the demand for good quality schools, hospitals and other public services, and at the same time brought expectations of greater choice, responsiveness, accessibility and flexibility. (Office of Public Services Reform, 2002: 8)

The 'consumer' of public services is the neo-liberal appropriation of the struggles around citizenship and difference. It rearticulates difference as the diversity of individual wants, at the same time as constructing the consumer as the antagonistic pole to the producer. I have argued elsewhere (Clarke, 1997) that this image of the 'consumer' of public services involved splitting the figure of the citizen into a number of different identities and interests: the taxpayer, the scrounger and the consumer (see also Commission on Taxation and

Citizenship, 2000). This splitting articulates different pressures on public services:

- the taxpayer, obsessed by cost and the pursuit of 'value for money', necessitates and legitimates 'fiscalization';
- the consumer, seeking ever-higher standards of service, necessitates and legitimates the drive for continuous improvement in performance;
- the scrounger, seeking to exploit public generosity, necessitates and legitimates scrutiny and investigation of claimants.[1]

This refiguring of the citizen produces a complex – and dislocated – conception of the public and the public interest (see also Dean, forthcoming; Humphrey, 2002a). But consumerism may also be associated with a wider field of cultural changes in relationships of power, authority and knowledge. In different conceptions of social and cultural change (from traditional to modern societies, and from modernity to postmodernity), there is a common concern with 'disbelief' as the emergent cultural orientation towards 'authority' (e.g. Giddens, 1990; Lyotard, 1984). Consumerism – as a version of populism (market populism, in Frank's terms) – carries some of this structure of feeling: a disconnection from tradition, convention and authority. Consumerism can be conceived of as both subjugation to corporate capital (via the cash nexus) and the 'empowering' of individual and collective choices (Clarke, 1991: ch. 4; Gabriel and Lang, 1995; Lury, 1996; Smith et al., 2003; Williamson, 1986). But certainly the 'freely choosing' consumer – with expectations of choice formed in the marketplace – is the central rhetorical figure in the remaking of public services around 'performance'.

Together these tendencies have combined to produce a complex crisis of the 'public realm' and it is a crisis that speaks the language of neo-liberalism (Clarke, 2004). These tendencies call into question the value, purpose and organization of public services, and the possibility and character of a 'public interest'. They make problematic a variety of institutional structures and processes through which the public – and their interests – can be represented. The obsession with the performance of public services comes alive in this context – partly because it is shaped by the dominant neo-liberal tendencies (economization, fiscalization, consumerism, marketization and so on). But it also emerges as an attempt to address the failures of neo-liberal strategies – the perceived impoverishment of the public realm, the anti-social meanness of welfare reform, the excesses of corporate and familial privatization associated with Thatcherite Conservatism in the UK. 'Performance' can be understood as an attempt to resolve the problems, contradictions and tensions that emerge in the context where these different tendencies come together, including the

---

1 The policing of 'desert' has increasingly become entwined with managing the boundaries of the nation as 'scrounging' becomes configured around refugees, migrants and aliens, and expressed in images of 'benefit tourists' and (in mid 2003) 'health tourists' taking advantage of 'free' health care in the NHS. (See, for example, Harriet Sergeant, 'The World's Sick Are Flocking to the NHS – and We're Paying', The Daily Telegraph, 23 May 2003: 20–1.)

need to realign neo-liberal governance with a revived (if much attenuated) attention to the public realm.

I will be focusing mainly on the governance of public services in the UK, though it will be clear that many of these processes are international, transnational, and supranational. But they work out differently in specific national political-cultural settings (even as they change the political, cultural and institutional formations of nations and states). What I want to do here is look at how the rise of performance is shaped by those processes and represents a political and governmental project intended to 'modernize' the UK (Finlayson, 2003; Johnson and Steinberg, forthcoming). In the UK, this has meant a programme of reform intended to transform public services into 'high-performance' organizations in the face of *public desire* for public services and *public doubt* about politics, politicians and governments.

The performance–evaluation nexus

These contexts created the conditions in which 'performance' has come to be a central political and governmental concern. In the UK, its roots lie in the state reform projects of the Conservative governments in the last two decades of the twentieth century. The concern with performance sustains the fiscal discourse's attention to the economic and efficient use of resources, albeit tempered by an increased concern with 'quality' and 'standards'. This shift of attention was captured in the second New Labour government's concern with 'delivery', reflecting a political anxiety that the public should see the improvements in services that the government was both resourcing and directing (if at arm's length). Performance sustains the managerial discourse – emphasizing the value, authority and autonomy of managers (and transferring responsibility from the political to the managerial locus). It continues the 'competitive' framing of public services – not just contractually, but in the form of performance comparison (league tables, benchmarking, the distinctions between successful and failing, the melodramatic commitment to 'naming and shaming' underperforming organizations, and so on).

The concern with performance has underpinned the proliferation of scrutiny agencies. These have performed several interlocking functions – evaluating performance, creating comparison, and functioning as both policy enforcers and management consultants (Clarke et al., 2000c; Humphrey, 2002a; Davis, Downe and Martin, 2002). The UK may have the most highly developed system of performance management. It includes audit (both narrow and enlarged: see Pollitt et al., 1999; Power, 1997); inspection (old and new from HMI to OFSTED: Hughes, Mears and Winch, 1996); evaluation (Henkel, 1991); and some of what may be called regulation (Hood et al., 1998; Cope and Goodship, 1999). It is also more loosely connected to the emergence of 'evidence based policy and practice' (Davies, Nutley and Smith, 2000; Trinder and Reynolds, 2000). For convenience, I am going to talk about this cluster of governance institutions, practices and obsessions as the performance–evaluation nexus.

Two slogans – 'value for money' (backed by the holy trinity of Es – economy, efficiency and effectiveness) and 'what counts is what works' – define the period of the rise of the performance–evaluation nexus. They speak to continuities and changes in the governance of public services between Thatcherism and New Labour. The former (value for money) defined the mission of the Audit Commission created in 1983 by the Conservatives (Humphrey, 2002a; McSweeney, 1988). The latter was coined by Tony Blair to define New Labour's 'pragmatic' approach to policy, organization and practice in governing public services (Blair, 1998). Rather than offer a detailed historical account of these developments, I will concentrate on the contemporary configuration of managing public services in a dispersed state in the context of a fractured and fractious set of public orientations.

New Labour has had to operate in a contradictory political-cultural field. New Labour both articulated and tried to contain high expectations about the ending of Conservative rule. It benefited from the release of repressed energy in social movements, trade unions and public service organizations – though it has tried to channel such energy into reasonable and responsible directions. But the 'renewal' of the public realm was a significant focus for New Labour's support, even if this was tempered by a deepening scepticism about (parliamentary) politics and politicians. New Labour emerged as a distinctively contradictory formation: committed to the modern, yet profoundly traditionalist; unevenly liberal and authoritarian; and both expansive and repressively containing. It has sought a carefully managed modernization – constructing a lightly 'socialized' alignment of neo-liberalism, in which flexible working will ensure personal, familial, national and global success. New Labour has seen the performance–evaluation nexus as a way of negotiating some of the social and political contradictions of managing public services in the 'modern world' (see, for example, Mandelson, 2003; Miliband, 1999; Office of Public Services Reform, 2002; and the discussions of modernization in Clarke and Newman, forthcoming; Finlayson, 2003; and Newman, 2001).

New Labour's response to the dilemma of desire for public services and doubt about politics and governments has been to combine tight fiscal control with an emphasis on improving standards (Boyne, 2003). Performance management, evaluative scrutiny and a (rhetorical) commitment to pragmatic, evidence-based, policy-making form the core elements of this modernizing strategy. These elements are both marked by continuities (especially with the Major governments) and intensification: New Labour does it more and more often. In terms of governmental discourse, New Labour (like others) proclaims a virtuous circle of evidence-based policy-making, systematic evaluation and performance management. The performance–evaluation nexus is thus both a governmental project – aimed at realigning public services in a neo-liberal dominated 'modernity' – and a political project that has to modernize British Labourism and attach it to neo-liberal globalization. As a governmental project, it addresses the problem of managing public services in the aftermath of neo-liberal reforms that have not always proved either effective or popular. As a political project, it has to engage a contradictory and fractured public that nevertheless wished to go beyond the stalled political-cultural project of Thatcherism. This drive towards modernization has been directed from within a profoundly centralist state structure and by a profoundly centralizing party formation. The characteristics of the British state enable a 'central command system', and centralism has been the unifying thread of New Labour's approach to party discipline, political management and governmental power (on the significance of state constitution, see Taylor-Gooby, 2001b; 2001c).

In this context, the performance–evaluation nexus has been developed to resolve some political and governmental tensions and contradictions of modernization. First, it attempts to address public anxiety and alarm about the availability and quality of public services, itself partially the effect of 'fiscal constraint' and the pursuit of 'efficiency' since the mid 1970s (Stein, 2001: 97). The reform of the state has been dominated by a commitment to aligning public services with a consumerist view of state–citizen relationships. This combines a stress on increasing quality and enlarging choice with providing the 'information' on performance that would enable the citizen-consumer to make effective choices (Needham, 2003; Office of Public Services Reform, 2003).

Secondly, as I have suggested already, the performance–evaluation nexus represents a solution to the problems of managing a dispersed and fragmented system 'at arm's length'. Withdrawing from the direct provision of services, and from the direct control of the organizations involved in provision, created new problems about how control might be exercised through other means. A rich diversity of mechanisms has emerged – contracts, commissioning, internal trading, market dynamics, partnerships, targets, outcome measurement and, of course, 'more and better management'. But the growth in scale and scope of evaluative systems suggests that governments find them a useful means of managing 'at a distance' (Power, 1997). Certainly, their number and scope have increased substantially under New Labour.

Thirdly, the performance–evaluation nexus offers the latest version of how to take 'politics' out of policy and practice choices. New Labour has claimed pragmatic decision-making ('what counts is what works') as a distinctive virtue, transcending the 'dogmatic' or 'ideological' politics of Old Left and New Right (see, for example, Blair, 1998). Rational, pragmatic, evidence-based decisions can supplant 'ideologically driven' policy-making. Since even politicians seem to think that 'politics' is a dirty word, corrupting rational decision-making, there is a recurrent search for the technical fix that will insulate policy choices from the passions, dangers and seductions of politics. From Royal Commissions, through scientific-professional expertise, to businesslike managers – policy-making has passed through a variety of such technical fixes. In turn each fix has proved vulnerable to destabilizing processes. On the one hand, politics tends to rear its ugly head recurrently (since governments are also political, as are the 'hard choices' of policy). On the other hand, the 'above the fray' technical fix is vulnerable to social, political and cultural challenges to its mode of authority. This may be social scepticism about how great (or good) the 'great and the good' are, or doubts about the trustworthiness of experts and the competence of managers. Claims to authority are always only claims and are always susceptible to challenge.

Finally, the performance–evaluation nexus offers one way of solving the (party) political problem of 'public doubt'. Governments have a political need to demonstrate that they are taking public services seriously (since publics continue to want services) and that they can 'deliver' services, standards, quality or improvement (promises may vary), while trying not to be directly responsible. As Miller argues in the context of New Labour's 'Best Value' inspections of local government: 'Underneath all this is a clear political agenda. This concerns the need to find ways to get the public in their capacity as voters to acknowledge that the money being spent on local government is well spent' (2003: 6). The performance–evaluation nexus provides a means of delivering the evidence that testifies to governmental effectiveness. Information for the tax-payer-voter takes its place alongside information for the citizen-consumer.

So, the performance–evaluation nexus provides a governmental practice that aims to resolve multiple tensions in the new governance of public services. However, the performance–evaluation nexus generates its own distinctive instabilities: some internal to the project itself; some that emerge in the practice of doing performance; and some that occur at the point at which the nexus encounters the contested field of public and political discourse about public services. What Harrison (2002: 476) nicely calls the 'aspirations of control' encounter expanding frontiers of uncertainty and instability.

Performing performance

Evaluation is accompanied by an array of more or less extensively discussed problems about the nature of the 'technical fix' (see, for example, Boyne, 2003; Davis, Downe and Martin, 2001; Humphrey et al., 1999; Humphrey, 2002a; Paton, 2003; Pollitt, 1995; Power, 1997; Stein, 2001). *Epistemological* arguments surround the validity and viability of a positivist view of the social world (which includes organizations) and the capacity of (social) scientific methods to represent social reality. However, evaluation remains firmly located in an 'objectivist' orientation (Paton, 2003). There are *methodological* arguments about the best and most appropriate ways of conducting measurement and evaluation of organizational performance that achieve multiple objectives, or are least intrusive or distorting in relation to the organization being evaluated. Associated with these methodological issues are what might be called the *technical* problems of implementation – the processes in which inspections, audits, evaluations are carried out which may be prone to social, political, organizational and personal instabilities that call into question the particular outcome. Idiosyncrasies of personnel, setting and practice may disturb the reliability or validity of the result of evaluation (and/or measurement).[2] Finally, there are sets of *organizational* issues about measurement and evaluation that have to be addressed in the performance–evaluation nexus. These include the dysfunc-

---

2 Of course, some critics would argue that all events are particular, all evaluations are idiosyncratic and thus these are more than merely technical issues. The technical definition rests on an assumption that there exists a 'normal' state of affairs from which deviations may occur. For some of us, the normal is a more problematic construction.

tional and distorting effects of the act of evaluation on organizations, social actors and the wider society (Power, 1997).

This is all conventional wisdom in the world of evaluation, where most of these problems are seen as resolvable in theory and, eventually, in practice (see, for example, Pawson and Tilley, 1997). 'Measurement churn' (Paton, 2003: 48) results from various factors: technical improvements in measurement/evaluation; the shifting knowledge base of evaluation; the shifting political/policy objectives to be measured; and the tendency of measurement systems to degenerate (not least as organizations learn how to manage the processes through which they are being evaluated). This process of 'continuous improvement' makes evaluation a moving target – such that criticisms are accepted but deferred. Evaluation is always/already about to be improved. The next model will resolve the difficulties, so the current outcomes stand (but only provisionally).[3]

However, these instabilities of evaluation can be viewed as more than technical or organizational problems. If we view performance as a process of collective construction of representations of what is counted as 'performance', then a different set of meanings about performance is opened up (Paton, 2003). Not least, we might take seriously the theatrical sense of performance – the idea of 'putting on a show' – as a way of thinking about the performance–evaluation nexus. This builds on the social constructionist or constructivist perspective on organizations, evaluation and audit that provides an alternative epistemological and analytical starting point to the objectivist view of evaluation and performance (e.g. Paton, 2003; Power, 1997). It self-consciously foregrounds questions about performances, performers and audiences that are obscured – or too readily closed off – within the evaluative framework. For me, it is particularly significant because it intersects with at least some aspects of organizational and popular common sense about performance evaluation – those elements that are sceptical about the politics, processes and claimed outcomes of evaluation. That is to say, I think a constructionist perspective is not simply an 'academic' matter, but also exists in practical forms in knowledges and beliefs about the ways in which organizational and social knowledges are collectively constructed (and are contested). I am tempted to suggest that 'we are all social constructionists now', even if only partially and tactically. This uneven perception of the 'constructed' character of social and organizational knowledge falls within Gramsci's view of common sense as a complex and contradictory field of ideological deposits and traces which involves elements of 'good sense' as well as reactionary, regressive or conformist conceptions of the world. In this context, I will suggest that scepticism about authoritative truth claims may well contain a degree of good sense.

What difference does it make to think about performance being performed? Let us begin at the beginning: states need to demonstrate that they can perform like states. Hansen and Stepputat (2001) have pointed to the general tensions between the erosion of the state's capacities and the increasing range of

---

3 Though their provisional quality will only be visible to those who follow the arcane discussions of measures, methods and technical implementation, and to those who bother to read the footnotes.

demands being made on states. Such demands emerge from diverse 'stake-holders' (from supranational agencies to subordinated and excluded groups within, or on the borders of, nations). They point to the different trajectories of Western and 'postcolonial' states in Africa and Asia, and suggest that

> The modern states of, say, Western Europe are today more diverse, more imprecise in their boundaries *vis-à-vis* other forms of organization, more privatized or semi-privatized than ever before, more integrated in supra-national structures and yet apparently stronger than ever before ... The neo-liberal attempts to restructure and trim the apparatuses of postcolonial states, originally designed for 'low intensity governance', along similar lines, however, have rarely produced a similar flexibility and enhanced capacity. The predominant organization of postcolonial governance as 'command policies' has meant that IMF-prescribed delegation of powers to the local level of the state more often than not has produced deep fragmentation, lack of coordination, and an undermining of the notion of the state as a guarantee of social order.
> (2001: 16)

In both forms, though, states are vulnerable to challenges to their ability to perform – to act like a state. The contexts in which states have to demonstrate their 'stateness' have become more problematic, just as the forms of states have become more attenuated. Here I want to take up this question of how states perform like states. What follows is a relatively skeletal consideration of how performance has been constituted as something to be performed in the context of a dispersed state.

At the most general level, states have to perform like states for a range of audiences, located in different settings and formed in different relationships to the specific state. States have to demonstrate their competence and capacity to ensure that they are taken seriously as states. They must perform for domestic/electoral audiences – the 'people' in their more or less complex and inclusive forms. They must perform for audiences drawn from other states – the field of international and intergovernmental relations (of conflict, collaboration and competition). States also have to perform for an increasing array of regional and supranational organizations and agencies (from the European Union to the Organization for Economic Cooperation and Development); and for national and transnational formations of capital (who do not necessarily share a point of view on the performance). Finally, they have to perform for diverse forms of mobile and 'transnational' people (Ong, 1999). These range from the transnational corporate 'business class', through tourists, to flows of migrants (who may evaluate the performances of several states on their travels).

So, states need to act like states – but this does not necessarily mean performing 'performance'. 'Performance' – as something to be measured, managed and evaluated – is one current version of what a state should look like and it is addressed to both national and transnational audiences. To mix metaphors: performance is an international currency (allowing competitive comparison between states), but it also can be spent in the local markets (particularly the electoral ones). Nevertheless, the question of performance as electoral currency is a reminder that states are not monolithic blocks, particularly in the context of dispersed state formations. They are ensembles of structures and relationships, processes and practices. The pressures to 'perform' bear differently on different elements of the state system: service providers need to achieve high standards of 'delivery'; partnerships need to demonstrate the results of 'joined-up working'; and governments need to perform like governments. One contemporary genre of governmental performance is the 'management of the performance of public services'. The typical features of this genre include:

- government as the people's champion;
- the (neo-liberal) antagonism between producers and consumers;
- scrutiny by independent 'watchdogs';
- management as heroes and villains (responsible for transformational success or implementation failure);
- success stories contrasted with 'failing' organizations (which may always be redeemed or 'turned round').[4]

Performance thus becomes a vehicle for putting on a *governmental* show – setting standards, showing evidence of quality and improvement, celebrating success, and 'naming and shaming' the backsliders. But, I will argue later, the audiences for such governmental performance are always in the position of simultaneously evaluating two things: performance evidence, and the performance – the display – of governmental authority/capacity. To continue exploring the dispersed state, service providing organizations have to 'put on a show', too. They have to represent themselves as 'high-performing organizations' for multiple audiences: the users, consumers and beneficiaries of their services; other competitor or collaborating organizations; and central government and its scrutineers.

The performance–evaluation nexus has become central to the governance of public services in the UK. Although we have seen forms of marketization and privatization, the dominant tendency has been towards the creation of a dispersed and organizationally fragmented system of providers managed through quasi-competitive processes, subjected to state funding, state targets and state evaluation. Evaluative agencies audit performance, provide comparative evaluations, define success and failure, and provide information for 'consumers' of services (in the absence of market information). This system combines vertical and horizontal relationships in a distinctive field of tensions. Evaluation is centrally driven – a 'top-down' set of scrutiny processes. These are legitimated by a claim to be in the interests of the public: taxpayers, users and consumers of services (implying a 'bottom-up' set of pressures – though they are rarely directly embodied, except as 'cases' or 'vignettes'). The horizontal relations are

---

4 Neo-liberalism has naturalized these narratives, with its distinctive agents (producers and consumers); its motivational system (self-interest); its rhetorical juxtaposition of markets and monopolies; and its liberation theology of choice and competition. This discourse provides the dominant conception of the interrelationship of the public, public services and government.

primarily competitive or quasi-competitive between organizations – reflected in rankings, league tables and so on. This competitive conception of performance persists despite an increasing emphasis on partnership, collaboration and joined-up working (Newman, 2001; Glendinning, Powell and Rummery, 2002).

In this context, performing performance becomes a central organizational objective. It is impossible to stand aloof from the evaluative-competitive nexus, since it has resource and reputational consequences. As Paton argues, the concern with performance places extra demands on organizations and their managers:

> [Managers] cannot rely on performance in terms of self-evident operating results to secure the confidence of government agencies or other key stakeholders. Performance in the other sense – that of acting to convey a particular impression and evoke particular responses – becomes important. In other words, managers have to give increasing time and attention to securing the confidence of key audiences by building relationships with them and projecting favourable accounts of necessarily ambiguous activities and figures. (2003: 29)

Performance management thus comes to preoccupy organizations in two senses. First, how to manage the organization to achieve the targets, goals, standards or elements of performance that are expected, demanded or contracted. Secondly, how to manage the presentation of the organization's performance in ways that testify to its achievements and effectiveness. Of course, 'failure' may be the result of either or both forms of management. The failure to achieve and the failure to represent achievement effectively may both result in poor evaluation results. I do not mean to suggest that this is new: Corvellec (1995), for example, discusses how organizations have produced 'narratives of achievement' for a variety of audiences. What is distinctive is the way in which the performance–evaluation nexus makes this a constant and significant focus of attention – and is generally associated with higher stakes being attached to evaluation outcomes. Nor, let me be clear, do I mean to suggest that 'performing performance' is a superficial, arbitrary or unreal process. Performance – as Rob Paton argues – is socially constructed in specific social circumstances and involves the construction of agreed conventions about what counts as performance (and evidence). Such agreed conventions may be arrived at through different routes: by negotiation or by authoritative imposition.

This implies organizational attention being directed to issues of compliance and calculation. Organizations must comply – and willingly – with evaluation regimes. Visible foot-dragging, reluctance or even recalcitrance are themselves evidence of 'producer capture' and the defence of privilege on the part of special interests. Compliance necessitates calculation – how to present the organization, how to make the fit between the organization and the evaluative categories, and how to manage the 'face-to-face' encounters of inspections, audits and site visits where they are part of the evaluative regime.

As a result the process involves a distinctive dynamic between collaborative and adversarial orientations. It is adversarial because of contested views of evaluative judgement and its consequences and because of the different interests that have to be mobilized in and through evaluation regimes (concealed in the benign claim that 'we all have an interest in improved public services'). These differences of interest and perspective make for adversarial encounters as evaluators demonstrate their forensic skills of investigation, while the evaluated struggle to establish the 'truth' of their organization. Humphrey argues that her study revealed that 'Joint Reviewers and local authorities approached the entire (self-) review and (self-) reform process from diametrically opposed assumptions, irrespective of the end result of the review' (2002b: 470). She goes on:

> The Joint Review team conceptualizes itself primarily as an improvement agency, as it aspires to work hand-in-hand with senior managers to the benefit of all stakeholders, and reviewers make frequent reference to their 'free consultancy services', pointing out that it is central government which shells out £55,000 per review. Local authority staff treat Joint Reviews as an inspection agency sent to deliver a public judgement which could make or break individual careers and organizational reputations, so that the position statement becomes a written examination, the interview session becomes a staff appraisal, and the entire process can be pervaded by the stage-management of performance. (2002b: 470)

As such, evaluation is both a grand drama (putting public providers to the test) and a micro-drama, playing out in the interactions of particular organizational actors. But the process is also collusive. It requires that all the parties accept the legitimacy of each other's roles. It requires that all collude in the representation of the process as non-conflictual.[5] All actors have an interest in a well-conducted process with good outcomes. Evaluators may advise and prompt the evaluated on how to achieve 'quick wins' or present success in the pursuit of legitimation (Humphrey, 2002a; 2002b). Wedel discusses the dynamics of 'collision and collusion' in the post-Soviet aid processes – and provides a telling example of 'transferable skills' in the management of performance. Donor agencies set targets for recipients:

> Central and Eastern Europeans were prepared to handle this. An entire language was developed under communism to describe the practice of creating fictions to please authorities. Russians speak of *ochkovtiratel'stvo* (literally, to kick dust into someone's eyes), meaning to pull the wool over someone's eyes or to fool the observer, boss or do-gooder ... This practice had a long history under communism, and continued unabated in postcommunist times ... The responses of officials and managers under both regimes were similar: just as they had engaged in certain 'fictions', ranging from subtle readjusting of figures to outright falsification, to meet prescribed targets under central planning, so they employed the same kinds of fiction in the aid process to please the Western consultants and the donor community. (2001: 74–5)

5 However, the naming of 'conflict' may be possible as a negotiating manoeuvre or tactic: representing the other as aggressive, conflictual or engaged in 'axe-grinding'.

More generally, evaluation requires that all participants collude in the representations of objectivity, independence and transparency that deny the negotiated character of the process, the evidence and the judgement. In practice, of course, the edifice of objectivity proves more unstable than this model of co-construction might suggest. Both parties are likely to discover outrages, infractions and infringements of objective and disinterested evaluation. Such interruptions may well be negotiated as part of the process – comments and concerns being 'taken account of'. Occasionally they spill over, causing public ripples beyond the particular site of the evaluation. OFSTED investigations were the most frequent sources of such spill-over into the wider realm of public and political discourse, although recently they have been displaced by debates about the effects of targets on NHS performance. Newspaper headlines such as 'Hospitals Faking Cuts in Casualty Wait Times' (*The Observer*, 11 May 2003: 1) and 'BMA Chief Attacks "Obscene" Pressure To Hit NHS Targets' (*The Observer*, 26 June 2003: 2) point to the unstable micro-politics of the performance–evaluation nexus. Occupational groups and organizations try to negotiate their own (counter-)claims to authority and legitimacy. The media provide one vital context for contesting the constructions of performance – with organizational, occupational and governmental claims all vulnerable to being viewed sceptically (reflecting the persistent instability of claims to represent the 'public interest').

There have also been running controversies about targets and testing in primary and secondary education; and about the value and usefulness of performance comparison, rather than league tables, for police forces (see, for example, *Guardian Education*, 11 March 2003: 6; *Guardian Society*, 26 February 2003: 7). These controversies are articulated through raising questions about the methodologies of evaluation, the presentation of results and the dysfunctional or distorting effects of evaluation. They point to the problem of maintaining the micro-social order of evaluation, but they also point to the problems of how such micro-orders are articulated into the wider political discourse of evaluation as a key feature of 'modern governance'. This leads me back to my concern with the relationship between performance management and the political conjuncture.

Success and scepticism: the problem of public doubt

'Success' is central to the performance–evaluation nexus. Success is both an effect of, and a dynamic in, the process of evaluation. Evaluation seeks to produce success in general (systemically), while also distinguishing between successes and failures at the organizational level. The dominant regime of evaluation in the UK is comparative and competitive. It is a process that evaluates performances against 'success criteria' (targets, standards, benchmarks etc.). The setting of targets, the scrutiny of organizations and the measurement of performance are both constructed and constitutive processes. Targets, criteria and the modes of their implementation in the practice of evaluation are contestable, even though the process and its results are represented as 'categorical' (Paton, 2003: 29; see also Humphrey, 2002a). Schram and Soss (2002) have explored how the evaluative criteria for welfare reform in the USA were framed and applied in practice. The selection of caseload levels and programme leavers as 'outcomes' reflected particular views about welfare, poverty and dependency (obscuring other possibilities such as poverty reduction: 2002: 193). Schram and Soss highlight the political significance of 'success':

> The discursive processes that we have highlighted ... merit close attention because judgements of policy success and failure are more than just political outcomes; they are also political forces. Beliefs about which policies are known failures and which have been shown to succeed set the parameters for a 'reasonable' debate over the shape of future legislation. Reputations for developing successful ideas confer authority, giving some advocates greater access and influence in the legislative process. Public officials who are able to claim credit for policy success hold a political resource that bestows advantage in both electoral and legislative contests. (2002: 200)

The construction of evaluation as a process of coordinating a dispersed state creates 'success' in a number of different ways. It is, first, a process that is about the production of success (and failure): the comparative-competitive model of performance evaluation is intended to rank 'winners and losers'. Secondly, the process predisposes people to attempt to be successful. Organizational analysts have long known that 'what gets measured is what gets done', by focusing organizational performance on the criteria of evaluation. Thirdly, the process produces many actors with an interest in 'success': the government and specific ministers (demonstrating their capacity to 'deliver'); service heads (demonstrating their capacity to 'improve' the service); organizations (demonstrating their relative effectiveness); and managers/leaders in organizations (demonstrating their ability to innovate, improve or 'turn round failing organizations').

In such a success-oriented field, the discourse of success is likely to be widely deployed. Perversely, scrutiny agencies also have an interest in success in two ways. They need to demonstrate that scrutiny 'works' – improving the performance of the service. They also need to show that earlier recommendations (of policy, practice or organizational design) have had the desired effect. Paradoxically, scrutiny agencies need to both promote success and look 'tough' by identifying 'failure', so as to resist charges of 'producer capture' (see, for example, arguments over how to compare and represent police performance: 'Figures of Fun or Real Ratings?', *Guardian Society*, 26 February 2003: 7). Scrutiny agencies need to demonstrate their 'independence' in order to acquire credibility. This involves complicated triangulations of the relationships between such agencies and 'interests', and may involve narratives of 'standing up to' such interests, especially central government (Clarke, 2002a; Humphrey 2002a).

Finally, as Schram and Soss argue, 'success' is a political resource. It is a resource that matters to organizations, managers and political representatives, especially in competitive or marketized systems of service provision. 'Success' provides a competitive edge – in relation to resources, political access and 'consumers' (directly and indirectly). The reputation of educational providers (schools or universities) has significant 'business' effects – and organizations expend effort on being 'successful' and on managing their *reputation* for success. Organizations must tell 'success stories' (and suppress or invalidate non-success stories) as a condition of organizational reproduction and development.

The effect, I suggest, is a 'success spiral' in which all participants to the process have an inflationary interest in producing 'success'. But in such an inflationary context, there are potential problems about how audiences perceive and respond to success claims. There are a number of potential disjunctures between performers and audiences that give rise to problems:

- *Reluctant readers.* Although scrutiny agencies publish their reports, commentaries and evaluations, these seem not to have reached the 'general reader'. There remains a gap between the imagined 'active citizen-consumer' scrutinizing performance evaluations, and the everyday practices of service users, consumers and citizens. A survey for the Office of Public Services Reform 'revealed that the public has a generally low recognition of inspectorates' with OFSTED the most recognized, by 17% of those surveyed (2003: 23). Evaluation reports primarily circulate in political and policy networks so that taxpayers/consumers mainly get to know about them in mediated form.

- *Mediating media.* The evaluation of public services is reported through mass media in a context of journalistic ambivalence (if not cynicism) about government. Media treatment of the reports of scrutiny agencies ranges from celebration of their 'watchdoggery' to cynicism about both government and producer interests (the 'burying of bad news'; the celebration of 'massaged' good news; or the effects of producer capture in producing obfuscatory comparison).[6] Mass media that combine political-economic antagonism towards public services and journalistic cynicism about politics constitute a difficult and destabilizing setting for governmental 'success stories'.

- *Particularized publics.* Evaluative reports have to coexist with particularized experience of public services (I use 'experience' to refer to what people 'know' about services, and not just their first-hand encounters). This disjuncture is unpredictable: people may be concerned about the state of schools, but think theirs is fine; they may

6 Hackett (2001) discusses contemporary media reporting of social and political issues in terms of the images of 'watch dogs, mad dogs and lap dogs'. The images are compelling and indicate the media's problem of claiming 'independence' in the name of the 'public interest' – a dilemma that they share with the scrutiny agencies.

read about rising health care standards, but have dire experiences; they may read about policing improvements, but be a multiple victim of crime. People are unlikely to read 'evaluations' from the standpoint of the abstracted taxpayer/consumer. Positions in relations of social difference and inequality may also affect the readings they make: this is a differentiated public.

• *Corrosive cynicism or systematic scepticism.* Mistrust has become an increasingly significant condition of public discourse and one that has been accentuated in the acrimonious encounters between 'spinning' politicians and 'cynical' journalists (neither of whom score very highly in surveys of which occupational groups are trusted by the public). Politicians (sometimes) bewail cynicism and depoliticization; journalists bewail cynical attempts to manipulate the public (and themselves). As a result, 'evaluations' of public services appear in an unstable field of political representation. They are vulnerable to media or public cynicism ('they would say that, wouldn't they?'). But they are also vulnerable to scepticism – a more active questioning about how the evaluation was produced, what interests shaped it, how and when it is being deployed, and what its consequences might be. In the current period, I think it can be argued that both cynicism and scepticism condition relations between the public, public services and government. They form what Thomas Frank refers to as the 'problem of public doubt' (2000: 21).

I think that doubt defines one of the basic relationships between people and power. It marks a sense of distance and disbelief. It identifies a reluctance to accept what the powerful claim as the truth. Doubt manifests itself as both cynicism and scepticism (the former a demobilizing orientation that simply suspects all claims; the latter a more active orientation to different claims and their causes and consequences). I do not mean that doubt is the only relationship between people and power. It coexists with many other orientations (belief, acceptance, identification, attachment) and with other dispositions – adaptation, accommodation, compliance and recalcitrance. Doubt is politically 'indeterminate': it is attached to no particular political position and may indeed be a self-distancing from all positions. If 'public doubt' is indeed a widespread condition, it both poses the problem that the performance–evaluation nexus attempts to solve, and creates some of the conditions under which the strategy might fail. As I argued earlier, the performance–evaluation nexus is constructed as an attempt to demonstrate the capacity of states/governments to deliver in the face of sceptical audiences. The principle of 'performativity' (Lyotard, 1984; see also Ball, 1998; Harrison, 2002) involves the attempt to substitute pragmatic and objective 'evidence' for the failed or failing 'meta-narratives' of progress. But it is difficult to stabilize the conditions of production and reception of such 'success stories' – because they are evidently constructions and thus contestable in general and in particular. The 'success spiral' of the evaluation regime further accentuates the potential for doubt since it tends to expand the 'credibility gap' in which claims become understood as 'rhetoric' detached from 'reality'. As governments (and organizations) seek to solidify their 'truth claims' through objective data and independent evaluation, they encounter 'doubters' who refuse to believe in objectivity, independence and the claims that they underpin (Clarke, 2001b; 2002c).

But it would be a mistake to take 'public doubt' as the only – or even the dominant – orientation of publics to public services. Public doubt coexists with public desire (for services and for their improvement) and public commitment (to public ideals of service). This, too, is a political pressure on governments and service providers and takes a specific conjunctural form in the UK in the hope (aspiration? expectation?) that New Labour would restore or revive public services after eighteen years of Conservative degradation. But this coexistence of commitment and cynicism is, it seems, unstable and unpredictable – posing difficult challenges of political calculation and address. How do governments persuade people that they have invested in, modernized and reformed public services (and improved their standards) when people don't believe what governments tell them?

Performance anxiety: governing in doubt

There are both governmental and political problems associated with this performance–evaluation strategy – and they combine to create a distinctive field of instabilities and tensions. Some of these are intrinsic to how the nexus has taken shape in the governance of UK public services. The current performance–evaluation nexus is structured around a centralist, consumerist and objectivist model of control at a distance – and this locks it into several paradoxes. Its centralism runs into dilemmas about local responsiveness or innovation. Its consumerism produces difficulties from the antagonism towards producers, and towards professional autonomy and judgement in particular. Its objectivism runs into organizational and public scepticism about the construction of evidence. Finally, its organization-centredness creates tensions around the promotion and evaluation of partnership, collaboration and cross-organizational (and cross-departmental) working. These are the internal problems of performance evaluation as a governmental project, but it also has to operate in a social and political context where there are both fractured and conflicted conceptions of the public – not all of which can be dissolved into the taxpayer/consumer figure. There are competing conceptions of the public and multiple claims to authority that base themselves on different claims to represent the public interest. Here the 'governmental' project becomes inextricably intertwined with the 'political' project of New Labour.

New Labour's political style has some features that undermine its claim to be promoting the virtuous circle of evidence, evaluation and performance management that drives continuous improvement. This is more than an observation that all political projects are contradictory or incoherent; these inconsistencies bear directly on the conditions of the governmental strategy. New

Labour has had a distinctively 'hyperactive' approach to policy-making, with a stream of initiatives and innovations that have promoted a sense of 'permanent revolution' in public services. This creates a problematic relationship between evaluation and constant innovation (or 'policy churn': Peck, 2001: 15). By the time that the results are obtained on pilot or experimental policy developments, the policy has moved on (e.g. Education Action Zones: Dickson et al., forthcoming).

New Labour governments have also adopted distinctively 'evangelical' tones when proselytizing for modernization and reform. This both reflects the contribution of Christian or 'ethical' socialism to New Labour discourse, and expresses the 'reforming zeal' that characterizes Tony Blair's personal/political mode of address. For example, he has talked of the 'forces of conservatism' resisting reform, and has described the 'scars on his back' incurred in his efforts to 'modernize'.[7] Each particular reform – and the overall conception of modernization – has been presented in tones that are rarely 'pragmatic', but speak instead to a certainty about the 'one best way' that must be driven through (Newman, 2001). At the same time as sounding evangelical, New Labour is also perceived as excessively calculating. The most obvious problem about New Labour's attempt to govern a doubting public is the imagery of 'spin' (see Finlayson, 2003: ch. 2; Gewirtz, Dickson and Power, forthcoming). It is constructed as a defining feature of New Labour's political style. The term has been used to mark the achievements of 'media management' and to denote a cynically calculating view of how to address the public (via the media). The image of spin both reflects and intensifies the mediated field of public doubt, scepticism and cynicism. Any particular government announcement is preceded by this reputation – such that its 'truth claims' are always/already rendered provisional, contingent and contestable.[8]

In trying to dispel the image of sophisticated news and information management associated with 'spin', New Labour sometimes proclaims an enthusiasm for 'common sense', which it tries to contrast with elite wisdom (liberals, the chattering classes, media cynics and so on). Appeals to 'common sense' run counter to evidence-based anything, rather than being the opposite of populism. In contrast, Home Secretary David Blunkett defended his attack on judges for being 'out of touch' as 'It's not populism, it's just good common sense' (The Guardian, 14 May 2003: 1). New Labour's populism mobilizes a selective use of anti-elitism as a discursive strategy for reform. The 'elites' being challenged – in the name of egalitarian modernization – are particular, rather than general. They have included the judiciary, universities and doctors. I do not want to deny they are elites, but they reflect a very partial view of con-

7 'But collectively, all those who see themselves as progressives need to remember who the real enemy is – Tory reactionaries – the defeatists, the pessimists, the cynics' (Tony Blair, 'Progress and Justice in the 21st Century', Inaugural Fabian Society Annual Lecture, London, 17 June 2003: 6).

8 This analysis was developed before the war on Iraq and its political aftermath in the UK, where issues of doubt, mistrust, scepticism and cynicism have become part of the everyday content of public discourse about politics. I wish this made me prescient, but I think that it would be more accurate to point to the dislocating effect of the war – and the efforts to manage public opinion associated with it – on the balance of political forces.

temporary elites – leaving out of account economic, political and (some elements of) cultural elites. This selectivity constitutes the space for other sceptical and cynical views of New Labour that address its fascination with power and money, the problem of 'croneyism' in political appointments and favours, and its obsessive and authoritarian centralism. The same point about selectivity might also be made about who is included in the imagined 'people' spoken for in New Labour's populism – typically figured as 'hard-working families'. In this imagining of the people, New Labour has had to simultaneously address and contain the pressures for a more social (if not socialist) conception of the world – and a more expansive view of public services within it (Clarke and Newman, forthcoming).

What are we to make of this situation? If the above description is roughly correct, the performance–evaluation nexus is operating in a political-cultural context characterized by contradictory impulses. Commitment and cynicism, or support for public services and scepticism about political discourse, coexist in unpredictable combinations. This conjuncture combines long historical cultural trends and the contradictions of a particular political-cultural formation. On the one hand, the mediated rise of scepticism and the decline of deference coincide with struggles to move beyond the false universalism of welfare states to engage a more differentiated and more mobile set of publics. On the other, we have the particular features of the post-Thatcherite political-cultural formation of a 'modern Britain': the cracked and straining joints of a Third Way conception of neo-liberal modernization, in which dogmatic pragmatism coexists (contradictorily) with reforming evangelism and a profoundly regressive populism. Attention to the national and conjunctural features of governing makes visible how wider forces become condensed in particular contexts to produce particular strategies for governing. Conjunctural analysis enables us to see the particular alliances, and hybrid formations, in which neo-liberalism is materialized and put into practice. It also reveals their limitations: the instabilities, disjunctures, contradictions and refusals that continue to make stabilizing neo-liberal modernity a difficult, and unfinished, project.

eight

I embarked on writing this book as a way of bringing together three obsessions. The first was a view that the subject of social policy is the academic setting where big processes and powers, grand concepts and theories come together with the constitution and lived experience of personal lives. It is this distinctive mixture that makes social policy matter as a subject. The second was a commitment to 'thinking again' about welfare states – because social policy deserves richer intellectual resources than the dominant or conventional wisdom provides. The third obsession was the desire to find ways of taking what I think has been productive, exciting and enabling from the 'cultural turn' and to put it to work in the process of 'thinking again' about welfare states and what has been happening to them. In this final chapter, I want to reflect on what happens when those three obsessions come together. Perhaps it would be more accurate to say what *I hope* happens when they come together, since outcomes cannot be read off from objectives.

The cultural turn has provided me with an orientation to thinking of welfare states as *constructed* (rather than natural, necessary or inevitable); *contested* (by different social forces, and from different social positions); and *contradictory* (as a result of trying to manage contradictory environments and contain contradictory pressures). In some respects, many analysts of welfare states would agree with some, if not all, of these points – although they may not want to make them the centre of their analysis. But for me they are the focus: they organize how I look at welfare states, and what I look for. They draw my attention to the complex relationship between the political-cultural conditions – the settlements – that underpin welfare states and their elaborate institutionalization in apparatuses, policies, personnel and practices. This orientation also makes me think about welfare states as *unstable equilibria* – requiring attention to what temporary balance has been constructed (and how), and to the forces, pressures and tensions that might unsettle the balance. But there is a fourth conceptual 'c' to go alongside constructed, contested and contradictory which moves this analysis rather further from the conventional views: the understanding that welfare states are *constitutive*. They create (not just reflect) arrangements of social divisions and differences, identities and inequalities, relationships and resources. Welfare states normalize a conception of a 'way of life' and the people who live it. They promote it, they naturalize it, and they enforce it. In the process, we can see not just 'welfare states', but the alignment of welfare, state and *nation*.

Making the nation visible changes how we think about welfare states. This is more than the acknowledgement that welfare states happen in particular national places, or have different national political-institutional paths or trajectories. The national in this mundane sense is the stock in trade of comparative social policy. But thinking about welfare states as connected to nation-building means treating nations as also constructed, contested and contradictory (rather than a natural unity of people, place, culture and state). Welfare states are one of the means through which the people of the nation are defined, classified, managed and 'improved'. They are also one of the places where the distinction between the people and its others is produced in policy and practice: the distinction between citizens and non-citizens. This is the strong sense of thinking about welfare states as nation-states, because it takes us towards a view of nation-states as the results of processes of formation – and reformation. In Chapter 1, I argued that deconstructing welfare states (and their shadow, nation-states) was a way of seeing welfare states as an articulated ensemble of welfare, state and nation. Such ensembles were put together differently in different places – and were coming apart because of the destabilizing forces that unsettled each of the elements (welfare, state and nation) and the ways in which they were articulated. The settlements underpinning post-war welfare states in the West produced both complex institutional arrangements and political-cultural imaginaries. Distinctive conceptions of nations, people and forms of collective identity and solidarity were institutionalized – and became the site of identifications and cultural investment. They became the dominant and 'taken for granted' meanings of welfare states – even as they came under challenges that sought to extend, enlarge and transform them.

But these settlements – and their institutionalized forms – were temporary and unstable equilibria, no matter how solid and naturalized they appeared. I have traced the variety of forces contributing to the destabilization of those alignments of welfare, state and nation. It is important to insist on this as destabilization – not dissolution or abolition, not 'the end of ...'. We see the welfare, state and nation triangle being traversed by projects that seek to realign them in new configurations: here a more 'conditional' welfare, a more 'enabling' state, or even a more 'multicultural' nation. These projects aim at creating new settlements – but in the present conjuncture this is distinctively difficult given how extensive and complex the unsettling/destabilization of all three elements has been. Although the dominant tendency may be towards an alignment centred on neo-liberal globalization, it is hard to pull, or force, all the elements around nation, state and welfare into this alignment. It is hard because each of them is simultaneously the focus of residual and emergent political-cultural attachments and mobilizations (regressive nationalisms, commitments to public services, expansive new solidarities, new insecurities alongside old insecurities and so on). So, one recurrent argument of the book has been the importance of distinguishing between the ambitions, aims and objectives of political-cultural projects and the outcomes – which tend not to live up to the objectives. As a rule, the world usually turns out to be more intractable and recalcitrant than is envisaged in the 'grand plan'. If the starting orientation for this way of analysing welfare states is about the constructed, contested and contingent character of social formations, the end point is a view of reforming/remaking projects as *uneven* (spatially and institutionally); *unfinished* (both in being incomplete and ongoing); and *unstable* (new settlements proving hard to achieve – and even then they will only be temporary).

So what difference does it make to think like this? I believe it has a variety of academic and political implications – for how the subject of social policy is practised, for how public and academic debates about welfare states intersect, and for how we think about the political-cultural field in which different futures for welfare, state and nation are contested. To engage with these implications means considering the problematic politics of intellectual work – especially those forms of intellectual work that are lodged in academic institutions.

Shaky ground, wobbly ivory towers?

The relationship between intellectual or academic work and politics is persistently difficult – not least because of the tendency towards an oscillation between self-abnegation and self-aggrandizement on the part of academic writers.[1] The most developed form of self-abnegation is the denial of any connection between academic work and politics – the pursuit of a detached, objectivist social science. Such a view persists, especially in the field of policy research and evaluation studies where (social) scientists are merely, in Loren Baritz's (1998) phrase, the 'servants of power' (Morgen and Maskovsky, 2003; Schram, 2002). All academic work has political implications. There is no hiding place where the peaceful pursuit of objectivist science or social science does not connect with the world. Since the world is a complicated, fractured, fractious and politically conflicted place, someone will always find the political implications of academic studies. As a result, some degree of political-cultural reflexivity on our part is probably a good idea. There are no guarantees about the consequences or uses made of any piece of work. Even in the purest, most refined act of academic writing, meaning cannot be fixed or secured against 'alternative' readings. But some thought about the contexts (and never just academic contexts) into which ideas may emerge ought to be part of our professional culture. That implies, at least, some thought about where 'evaluation research' might be located, what it means to 'study downwards' as well as 'study upwards', and whether we should tell (and in the process, reinforce) the stories of the powerful.

1 On the other hand, I don't want to lavish too much time and attention on this subject, since it can be a deeply self-regarding issue. We should be attentive to our responsibilities – not least those of occupying relatively privileged positions (in terms of both material security and the relatively limited, and shrinking, socially sanctioned space to think). But we should also consider our relative marginality in terms of politics, political culture and mediated public culture.

On the other hand, many writers seem to think that politics will automatically flow from their observations or that the political value of their writing can be certified by 'being on the right side'. Asserting politics in academic work 'short-circuits' the difficult relationship between theory and politics – as if the relationship is not difficult and tenuous. Wendy Brown has argued that this premature closure of the gap between theory and practice risks devaluing the proper role of 'theory' – to engage critically and reflexively with the present:

> What happens when we, out of good and earnest intentions, seek to collapse the distinction between politics and theory, between political bids for hegemonic truth and intellectual inquiry? We do no favor, I think, to politics or intellectual life by eliminating a productive tension – the way in which politics and theory effectively interrupt each other – in order to consolidate certain political claims as the premise of a program of intellectual inquiry. (2001: 41)

I am sympathetic to this view of an engaged separation of politics and intellectual work – though I think Brown is clearer about the separation than how the engagement is made and renewed as a 'productive tension'. Since we do not have a direct injection mechanism to politics, perhaps investing a political sensibility (reflexive, critical, sceptical) into our work is as close as we can get. Searching out the forms, strategies and seductions of power – and the forms of negotiation, accommodation, resistance and recalcitrance that people deploy in relation to domination – are important features of academic work. They 'denaturalize' the present and make it available as the product and possibility of human agency: people making history but not under circumstances of their own choosing still seems a reasonable starting point. Certainly, this view of a critical social science (and cultural studies) is one that has informed my own writing and teaching: a commitment to questioning the forms and practices of domination, and making the intellectual resources for such scepticism more widely available. This may be the best we can hope for (and it is certainly preferable to depoliticized academic work).

But I think we also need to recognize the ways in which academic work – and academic workers – are part of the contexts that we study, especially when we are dealing with the welfare state, public services and public institutions. Academic institutions are themselves bound up in the unsettling of formations of welfare, state and nation. Colleges and universities exist in a contradictory relationship to the state and the public realm: they are materially, symbolically and organizationally part of it and they are (sometimes) privileged points of reflection on it. While I do not think that all we might need to know about welfare states can be derived from a study of universities, it does seem odd not to reflect on the conditions and relations of intellectual production as part of the transformation of welfare states and public services. If the spaces for critical work are being squeezed and made more uncomfortable or untenable, that reflects their place in the struggles over the public realm. Changes in its funding, its organization, its management and its subjection to new political-cultural projects have all reshaped the conditions and possibilities of academic work. But so, too, have the challenges to, and dislocations of, hierarchy, authority, power and the processes of cultural reproduction that the universities embodied. 'Progressive' struggles in and against the university were never just about thinking better thoughts. They were also about transforming the conditions and relations of this power/knowledge complex (and changing how it was peopled). There might be a degree of ambivalence here, as we try to both protect and transform sites of knowledge and power. Can we discern new relationships, new alliances, new forms of communication, engagement and debate that neither reproduce the old elitist and paternalist conception of academic privilege, nor succumb to the neo-liberal, market populist, new managerialist remaking of the university? I am not proposing to settle those questions here, but will point to some more modest possibilities of thinking about welfare, state and nation differently.

Imagining the consequences

The attempt to 'rethink' welfare states in this book is intended as an intervention into three overlapping contexts: the subject of social policy; the wider academic study of welfare and welfare states (which extends well beyond social policy); and the uneasy borderland between academic, political and public discourses about welfare states. Each of these matters, but matters differently, so I propose to discuss them in turn – beginning with my 'home ground' of social policy.

Social policy is a difficult subject, dominated by its history as the product of Fabianism – but also profoundly shaped by the difficult struggles to escape that legacy. I am tempted to argue that it forms an academic microcosm of the unsettling of the welfare, state and nation complex of post-war Britain. Its dominant forms centred on the normative assumptions about the alignment of welfare, state and nation in the careful management of social progress – and steady eradication of social problems. It valorized quasi-scientific neutral expertise: knowledge about the social, how to administer it, and how to intervene in it. So the Foucauldian critique of social policy – as an exemplary site of governmental knowledge – is powerful (see, for example, Hillyard and Watson, 1996). But it misses the fractured character of the subject that arises from the multiple challenges to both the formation of welfare, state and nation – and its Fabian knowledge/power complex. As a subject, social policy has been traversed and reworked by Marxist critiques, feminist challenges, anti-racist and latterly postcolonialist interventions, and attacks on the normative assumptions about ablebodiedness, heterosexuality and adulthood. Analyses based in and on different social movements and tendencies have disrupted the dominant organization of knowledge in social policy (Lewis, 2000a). In different ways, they have opened up social policy as a field in which different combinations of policies, practices and power can be studied: how do welfare states produce, reproduce or redress structured differences and inequalities?

In that sense, this book builds on a whole array of critical scholarship within social policy. Such work often opens the boundaries of social policy as a subject, forging connections to other subjects (sociology, most obviously) and to other developing bodies of knowledge (feminism, poststructuralism, and just possibly postcolonial studies). I have drawn on this work to consider what has happened to the foundational categories of social policy – welfare, state and nation – in the struggles to destabilize and realign them across the turn of the century. In doing so, I have tried to take what I think is valuable from the cultural turn to unsettle these terms as conceptual categories within social policy. We (students and scholars in social policy) need to recognize that we stand on intellectually 'shaky ground' as well as political-cultural shaky ground. We cannot, and should not, build on such foundations. We should instead inspect them and consider their temporary, constructed and shifting character (and their contemporary realignments). In particular, I think that making 'nation' visible as a core category – and making its shifting and contested quality central to how we think about welfare and state – is an essential step for social policy. It enables us to think about the articulation of the inside and outside of the nation – and about the shifting boundaries and borders through which that distinction is organized, managed and policed. It allows us to think about processes of racialization, through which the identities of the nation – and its others – are forged and challenged. It might help us to think about how a complex of positions, relationships and identities is nested together in constructions of the people/nation and its ways of life. They are what make 'citizenship' such an important – and such a fiercely contested – concept in social policy (and welfare politics). All these questions enhance the scope and range of studying social policy. They raise important questions about the relationships between equality, difference and social justice (and enlarge the field of who might have a stake in such arguments). They may also help to prevent the risk of social policy reverting to a Fabian norm.

I think this matters in a number of ways. Social policy has been a contested subject because of its hybrid character: the 'applied social science' that combines social analysis and governmental preoccupations with policy and administration. It is contested because welfare states and what they do have profound consequences: they shape, constrain, enable, regulate, reward and punish. As a result social policy is shaped by a tension between 'improvement/progress' and 'challenge/critique': trying to provide useful knowledge that will enable the state/welfare to work better, and trying to reveal what the state/welfare does – or fails to do – to people. That tension still seems to me to be an important one, even if most of what I do falls into the challenge/critique end. But it is important because it draws us back to thinking that the complex apparatuses, policies and practices of welfare (within and beyond the state) exercise powerful influences on how people live their lives. The conditions attaching to benefits and services, the resources that flow through them, the relationships of power and authority in which they are embedded – and the social identities and norms that they produce or modify – command our attention because they make a difference to how people live. They are the focus of critical challenge and engagement because they could make a difference to how people might live differently. Because social policy inhabits this point of conjunction between big institutions and processes, big theoretical/analytical issues and the ways in which people experience the state, welfare and nation in the making of personal lives, it remains a subject that needs to be engaged and contested.

But, of course, social policy does not 'own' the study of welfare states. It has always been 'junior' to the grand social sciences: politics, economics and sociology, in particular. To some extent then, the arguments of this book have been directed to the ways in which welfare states are conceived and studied in these other places – or in the borderlands between social policy and other subjects. The lines of intellectual flow linking politics, sociology, economics and social policy are well established and extensively travelled. But, as I have been arguing, the forms of analysis – political economy, political institutionalism and their kin – provide rather thin conceptions of welfare, state and nation. Escaping the view of welfare states as distribution systems (even contested distribution systems: Huber and Stephens, 2001: 17) means attending to the range of what states do by way of 'welfare' – and how the relationships between welfare and state come to be forged and unsettled. It means taking seriously the constitutive capacity of welfare states, not just their role in reproducing or redressing inequalities. Finally, it means taking 'nation' seriously as a formative element in the welfare, state and nation combinations. Nations are both more and less than the comparative model's view of them as unity of place, people and culture aligned in a trajectory of historical development. They are, as I have suggested, constructions: *imagined* unities of people, place and culture. Welfare states play a significant role in installing, reinforcing and naturalizing such imaginary unities. As a result, welfare is also one of the places where the unsettling of state and nation is felt – where conflicts and challenges about membership, borders and boundaries, and future directions come to be played out.

To make these ways of thinking again matter for the study of welfare states, I have found myself increasingly borrowing from other academic subjects – anthropology, cultural studies, social and cultural history in particular. Studies of welfare, states and nations in these subjects embody more directly the 'cultural turn' and the orientations that it offers. I do not, of course, wish to suggest that such subjects are wholly and unproblematically associated with my orientations here; they, too, are contested and contradictory fields. But they do offer analytical orientations, theoretical resources and substantive studies that have enriched my approach to welfare states – and have enabled me to think again. As I argued in the Introduction, 'border crossing' is an intellectual strategy as well as a spatial one. There are blockages, inhibitions and even forms of policing that interrupt academic border crossing, too: I am sure that some people will not recognize this work as 'real' social policy. Academic disciplines are increasingly subject to forms of disciplinary regulation, but I think the advantages to be gained from being marginal and mobile far outweigh the difficulties. I hope that this book demonstrates why taking the 'cultural turn' is worth the trip.

The cultural turn does something else to the study of welfare states in the grand social sciences. It disrupts their tendency to frame welfare states – and their transformation – within closed systems, finished histories and reduction-ist explanations. A universalizing globalization, an all-powerful capital, an inescapable advanced liberalism – all of these stitch together the present and future, leaving us nowhere to go. Our only choices are to find ways of living with/in them. For me, the emphasis on the uneven, unfinished and unstable character of change – the effect of constructed, contested and contradictory processes – is an important challenge to such tendencies. It insists on the potential for systems to fail or for projects not to achieve closure. This atten-tion to the incomplete and contradictory in analysing projects, systems and formations allows us to sketch the 'fault lines' in the present. It can show the internal and external conditions that prevent 'totalization' – the contradic-tions, the limitations, the refusals, the counter-tendencies, and the instabilities that constitute the conditions for *other* possibilities and other political-cultural projects. It is this orientation to the unfinished and unstable – as a precondi-tion and a result of analysis – that I have tried to stress in writing this book. Pragmatically, this orientation links Foucault's interest in identifying the 'lines of fragility in the present' (1984: 36), or what Brown calls a 'field of openings – faults, fractures and fissures' (2001: 103), with Gramsci's concern to disen-tangle the overlaid, compound and contradictory traces that are condensed in a conjunctural moment.

Finally, the cultural turn makes visible the intersections between academic and popular discourses about welfare states (and their nations). Welfare states are both institutionalized formations (apparatuses, policies, practices) and political-cultural imaginaries (symbolizing unities, solidarities and exclusions). In both aspects they are subject to diverse forms of challenge. They face differ-ent political projects that seek to realign their institutionalized forms and to reinvent their imaginaries (new unities, solidarities and exclusions). Many of these projects speak in the name of modernization in one form or another: the need to bring about the end of welfare in a neo-liberal/neo-conservative USA; the 'welfare reform' of socialized neo-liberalism in the UK; or the modern nation-building welfare state of Finland. But welfare states are also the locus of 'residual' attachments and political-cultural investment, precisely because they express forms of collective commitment (and address individual need). The desire for welfare states persists: in countries where they are being dismantled, in countries where they still command political support, and in countries where they are part of the imagined future.

I have put 'residual' in qualifying quotation marks here because I think there is a difficult argument about the status of such commitments and attach-ments. For some, these attachments are merely residual – the diminishing traces of social democracy, expansive liberalism, welfarism or collectivism (see, for example, Rodger, 2003; and the discussion in Dean, forthcoming). They have certainly been the focus of active campaigns to residualize them (aca-demic as well as political-cultural). In one sense, what is remarkable is the per-sistence of these desires for public, collective welfare, given the battering they have taken in the dominant political discourses over the last thirty years. I think 'residual' rather underestimates their persistence – their refusal to surrender to insistent privatizing, individualizing, familializing strategies. Against this 'residualizing' view of popular support, I want to suggest two alternative possibilities. One is that persistence in the face of sustained efforts to dismiss and demobilize pro-welfare-state sentiment demonstrates its political-cultural resilience: *marginalized* is not the same as residual. People continue to view welfare states as part of the social and public fabric of life – a legitimate political aspiration still given political voice outside the centres of neo-liberalism. Even in those centres, it persists as an orientation outside 'official' discourse – the political-cultural dominants that circulate in political and media apparatuses.[2] A second possibility is that popular support for welfare states combines both residual and emergent orientations: not just a nostalgia for the 'old' welfare state, but a recognition that the need for forms of collective security and social solidarity may have increased alongside (and even because of) the individualizing, privatizing and dislocating tendencies of neo-liberal economic disorder. They may also include new solidarities – within and across nations – that form desires and demands for collective welfare. The larger political problem is how such orientations, attachments and expectations are to be articulated (or brought to voice) within a field of public political discourse that actively seeks to silence, marginalize and demobilize them – to turn them into residues.

But the politics of welfare are not just about welfare and the state; they are also formed around contested conceptions of the nation and its future. The unsettling of the nation (and its relationships to welfare and state) means that political conflicts over welfare very quickly take on the character of conflicts over the nation. These include the relationship between traditional values and modernity; the tensions between conceptions of the nation-as-race and multiple ethnicities that centre on the 'problem of multiculturalism'; the policing of borders and boundaries; and the way in which mobile people are represented as 'social policy' problems (benefit seekers, welfare cheats, health tourists). The nation is not only a racialized question; it involves arguments over family and household formation, internal differentiation (e.g. social exclusion; naming and classifying different socio-demographic groups), and the construction of the 'normal' way of life that policies and practices will promote. But the nation is almost always a racialized – and racializing – focus, particularly so where the postcolonial metropolis is also a focus of contemporary migrations.

As I argued in Chapter 3, the articulation of welfare and nation in Europe is being reworked by the politics of the centre left and the right around 'ethnic homogeneity' as the precondition of social solidarity. The cultural turn might enable us to think about these categories and the relationships between them as constructed and contested. Ethnicity – and its purity – is a form of political-cultural nostalgia: reinventing the nation–race equation as a cultural (as well as biological) unity. Homogeneity is the wish of various cultural fundamentalisms, involving authoritarian fusions of religious, cultural, ethnic and national identities with state power. These seek to hold back the unsettling

---

2 Though I do not underestimate those dominants, or the increasing closure of the circuits in which political, corporate and media power intermingle, producing a sense of disconnection between mediated public discourse and micro-public discourses. This fusion of power and process underlies Carl Boggs's (2000) analysis of the 'end of politics' in the USA.

effects of mobility, mixing, *mélange* and the new solidarities that they make possible. For social democracy to try to reinvent itself on these grounds is both a denial of modernity in its diasporic form, and a refusal to recognize a clear lesson from its own political past. Solidarities are not naturally occurring phenomena: they are the result of political-cultural work that builds connections and identifications. Social democracy in its many European forms has had to build solidarities across social divisions – notably those of class and gender – to sustain the construction and enlargement of welfare states. But in contemporary struggles, the speed with which conflicts around welfare can be recuperated to the question of the nation is profoundly alarming. It is one more reason why social policy (and its relatives) needs to attend to the nation as a constitutive element in the making and remaking of welfare states.

Welfare, state and nation remain powerful focal points of political-cultural projects. They are central to attempts to 'modernize', while being the core of attempts to defend 'older' values and identifications. No-one can leave them alone – because they both symbolize and embody particular versions of the relationships between people, places and power, and because they articulate powerful stories about the relationships between past, present and future. They link large-scale conceptions of the nation and the world with the intimate arrangements and possibilities of personal lives. Their contemporary unsettling emerges from the conjunction of their internal contradictions and the shifting conditions to which they have been exposed. Almost everyone might agree that welfare states cannot go on as they were – but the desired future combination of welfare, state and nation remains contested. The 'future of welfare' remains unsettled because it is a point of condensation for many relationships, projects and imagined possible futures that outrun neo-liberal privatizations, regressive familialism or revivalist nationalism.

Crossing shaky ground: how to live with the unfinished

Truth claims – as poststructuralists know – are more difficult to sustain in a world of competing claims and especially in political formations where deference to authority has declined. Part of the 'good sense' of common sense is a readiness to doubt the statements of power in all its authoritative guises – including, of course, the claims of academics. Chapter 7 was the last substantive chapter in this book not because it had the most particular focus, but because it posed these issues of doubt, scepticism and cynicism most explicitly.

People inhabit their social conditions in complicated ways that include cynical, critical, sceptical and mistrustful relationships to all sorts of truth claims. Such 'semi-detached' positions are not necessarily a basis for political mobilization. I would argue that there are significant differences between cynicism and scepticism in terms of their potential political effects. Cynicism is a depoliticizing – and demobilizing – orientation that denies the possibility of making a difference ('They would say that, wouldn't they?'), while scepticism is a more actively interrogatory orientation ('Who says so, and why?'). Scepticism expects attempts to confuse, obfuscate, mislead because such tactics are the predictable masks of power. But it also admits the possibilities of political choices, political action and political effects – even if conditionally and cautiously (on cynicism, see Chaloupka, 2001; Giroux, 2001).

This is a way of returning to some of the starting points of the book. I do not think that a sceptical stance, an attention to shifting and contested meanings, or a 'deconstructionist' orientation are solely academic positions. On the contrary, they form part of the repertoire of 'common sense' that people use for negotiating the claims to truth that power makes. In keeping with the 'dialogic' view that I sketched in Chapter 2, I think processes of subordination and subjection are usually tempered by the distance of the subordinated and subjected. This view was profoundly shaped by that strain of English Marxist social history that summoned up the Levellers and Diggers from the seventeenth century revolutions and introduced us to the 'making of the English working class' (Hill, 1991; Thompson, 1963). The 'good sense' of many anthropological and historical studies lies in their attention to the incompleteness of attempted subjections. They identify the recurring refusal of people to 'know their place'. Critical distance is not the sole prerogative of academics.

Keeping it to ourselves leads to a 'revelatory' mode of academic writing. We are tempted to reveal that a 'taken for granted', naturalized and powerful element of a particular social order is, in fact, a social construction, a discourse or a stratagem of power. This mode implies that participants may not have noticed – that they may be so subjected to the ideological, discursive or power effect that they are wholly incorporated. As a friend of mine, recently retired from working in local government, put it, it's a certain tone of academic superiority. It implies that you academics are smarter than we are, and you can see through the disguises of power where we cannot. If that is our effect on our readers, we should take note. This is not, I think, to argue that all people are all-knowing, all of the time. 'Common sense' is always particular, uneven, fractured, contradictory and in flux; it is neither simply regressive, nor wholly composed of 'good sense'. But it does matter – both analytically and politically – whether one treats social actors as wholly subjected and incorporated into the dominant trends, or whether instead we see them as at least partially characterized by forms of distance, scepticism and a capacity for recalcitrance. A different view of the politics of academic work follows. A wholly subordinated/incorporated mass needs 'deprogramming' and 'bringing to truth'. Subjects who suspect their subordination – and glimpse the workings of power – need a politics of articulation that works with what they know to enlarge the possibilities of thought and action. It is here, of course, that the right (in its neo-liberal, neo-conservative and radically regressive combinations) has enjoyed such success – with its populist diagnoses of decline and decay, and its expansive promises of liberation.

Let me stress that this is not a simple view about the universality of cultural resistance. On the contrary, I think that people (myself included) find many ways to accommodate to power and domination. We align ourselves with it, we inhabit its spaces, bathe in its warmth, comply with its instructions and opt for its material and emotional rewards. Some of the time, it may not be possible to slide a thin blade between the identities inscribed by power and those adopted by its subjects. People do come when power calls – and to argue that domination is incomplete and unstable is not the same as saying that domination does not exist. But even where power becomes naturalized, becomes habituated – becomes, as Gramsci said, 'second nature' – its continued reproduction cannot be guaranteed. The dialogic view that I have advanced at various points during this book insists that we do not know what will happen when power calls.[3] People may recognize themselves in its hailing – but they may not. They may mishear it, they may not recognize themselves (thinking the call is for someone else altogether), or they may be too busy (or having too much fun) being someone else. They may decide that it's worth hearing the call this time, or decide reluctantly that they have nothing better to do. But they may also ignore it, refuse to listen, or tune in to alternative hailings that speak of different selves, imagined collectivities and futures. Dominant tendencies are only tendencies – and power's effects cannot be guaranteed. Nor, of course, can the triumph of progressive alternatives. But I do think it matters to understand this incompleteness – the problem of how to secure circuits of power – as a fundamental element of social analysis.

By fundamental element I mean something more substantial than a tagged-on last paragraph about 'resistance'. The 'last paragraph' version usually involves a rhetorical gesture (about resistance or other possibilities) at the end of a study which has told the compelling story of a totalizing system, strategy or force. Such conclusions are merely rhetorical (in the pejorative sense) and they leave the work of figuring out how to resist or create alternatives to the reader (or some other subject) who has just been told that they are confronted by a seamless, inevitable and irresistible force. I want, instead, to argue for analyses that begin from an attention to the contested, contradictory and unstable qualities of social formations. Such starting points are more likely to locate the possibilities of refusals, resistances and alternative possibilities within the analysis – rather than as a dislocated gesture at the end. This view of the potential significance of scepticism, critical distance and conditional compliance gives rise to some questions about how we address readers, users, students and citizens (the identities are, of course, multiple and variable). For example:

1 What can we add to the substantive and methodological repertoire of people's scepticism about dominant tendencies and strategies? How, so to speak, can we enrich and enlarge the sceptical capacity?

2 What can we say about the 'faults, fractures and fissures' of dominant systems and strategies? What are their characteristic contradictions, tensions and forms of instability?

---

3 Since I am writing this book in the year that British Sign Language became officially recognized as a language in the UK (2003), let me be clear that the imagery of call and response here is a metaphor: the summons of power can take a variety of symbolic forms. And, of course, the official certification of BSL is another mark left on the state by political-cultural struggles 'from below'. The deaf community/movement has been involved in a protracted struggle, first to release itself from lip-reading and subsequently to gain official status for signing.

3 What are the other voices and vocabularies that are in play but marginalized, subordinated or silenced in the present situation? How might we enlarge their capacity to articulate other imaginaries, other solidarities and other possible futures?

4 What are the emergent possibilities for rearticulating welfare, state and nation – and how can they be enhanced against the dominant and regressive formations?

These are modest conceptions of the politics of intellectual work. They are about what connections might be made between our ways of knowing things, the things that we know, and the forms of critical distance and scepticism to be found in 'common sense'. Such an approach is, in Stuart Hall's terms, 'without guarantees' in a number of ways (Gilroy, Grossberg and McRobbie, 2000). We cannot certify that what we know is true – though we may be able to say that we occupy a (relatively) privileged position that allows us the time and space to see more and differently than those denied such privileges. We cannot guarantee that anyone acting on what we claim to know will be successful – since knowledge, social life and politics are not 'law-like'. Most worryingly, we cannot even guarantee that anyone will bother to listen to us. Anti-intellectualism is both deeply rooted – and deepening – for both good and bad reasons. Academic work in general operates in a hostile environment; and critical academic work invites particular hostility. But doing critical work is a form of tax on academic privilege (however limited that privilege might be); it is the price to be paid for the possibility of collective progress (Commission on Taxation and Citizenship, 2000).

Let me end with a heartfelt plea. I know there are dangers in romanticizing resistance. I recognize that not all resistances are productive, progressive or transformative. I understand the risks of setting subordinated survival strategies against the dominant trends and tendencies of the day as though they are equivalent. But I also think that the world – and its dominant globalizations – are depressing enough without academic writers adding to our troubles. While people find ways of surviving, negotiating, accommodating, refusing and resisting, while they do not act like the automatons envisaged in the governmental plans and strategies of the powerful, may we please have academic work that acknowledges this? To the extent that strategies don't work as intended and people fail to come when they're called, domination is always fragile, always needs to be reproduced, always needs to search for better, more efficient and effective ways of securing its rule. In short, the non-total nature of domination and subjection 'makes a difference'. While people can still bother to be difficult, so should academic work.

References

Abbott, P. and Meerabeau, L. (eds) (1998) *The Sociology of the Caring Professions*. London: UCL Press.

Abdela, R. and Withorn, A. (eds) (2002) *Lost Ground*. Boston, MA: South End.

Abel, C. and Lewis, C. (2002) 'Exclusion and Engagement: A Diagnosis of Social Policy in Latin America in the Long Run'. In C. Abel and C. Lewis (eds) *Exclusion and Engagement: Social Policy in Latin America*. London: Institute of Latin American Studies.

Abramovici, G. (2003) 'The Social Protection in Europe'. *Eurostat Statistics in Focus Theme 3*. Luxembourg: Eurostat.

Ahmad, W. (ed.) (1993) *'Race' and Health in Contemporary Britain*. Buckingham: Open University Press.

Alcock, P. and Craig, G. (eds) (2001) *International Social Policy*. Basingstoke: Palgrave.

Allen, J. (2003) *Lost Geographies of Power*. Oxford: Blackwell.

Amenta, E. (1998) *Bold Relief: Institutional Politics and the Origins of Modern American Social Policy*. Princeton, NJ: Princeton University Press.

Andersen, J.G. and Jensen, P.H. (2002) 'Citizenship, Changing Labour Markets and Welfare Policies: An Introduction'. In J.G. Andersen and P.H. Jensen (eds) *Changing Labour Markets, Welfare Policies and Citizenship*. Bristol: Policy.

Appadurai, A. (ed.) (1996) *Modernity at Large: Cultural Dimensions of Globalization*. Minneapolis: University of Minnesota Press.

Appadurai, A. (2001) *Globalization*. Durham, NC: Duke University Press.

Aslama, M., Kantola, A., Kivikuru, U. and Valtonen, S. (2001) 'Politics Displaced, Politics Replaced: Elites' and Citizens' Talk on the Economic Crisis'. In J. Kalela, J. Kiander, U. Kivikuru, H. Loikkanen and J. Simpura (eds) *Down from the Heavens, Up from the Ashes: The Finnish Economic Crisis of the 1990s in the Light of Economic and Social Research*. Helsinki: Valtion Taloudellinen Tutkimuskeskus (Government Institute for Economic Research).

Baldock, J. (2003) 'On Being a Welfare Consumer in a Consumer Society'. *Social Policy and Society*, 2 (1), pp. 65–71.

Ball, S. (1998) 'Performativity and Fragmentation in "Postmodern Schooling"'. In J. Carter (ed.) *Postmodernity and the Fragmentation of Welfare*. London: Routledge.

Baritz, L. (1998) *Servants of Power*. Westport, CT: Greenwood.

Barnes, M. and Prior, D. (1995) 'Spoilt for Choice? How Consumerism Can Disempower Public Service Users'. *Public Money and Management*, July–September, pp. 53–9.

Barnes, M., Newman, J., Knops, A. and Sullivan, H. (2003) 'Constituting "the Public" in Public Participation'. *Public Administration*, 81 (2), pp. 379–99.

Barrett, L., Dunbar, R. and Lycett, J. (2001) *Human Evolutionary Psychology*. Basingstoke: Palgrave.

Barrett, M. and McIntosh, M. (1981) *The Anti-Social Family*. London: Verso.

Bartlett, W., Le Grand, J. and Roberts, J. (eds) (1998) *A Revolution in Social Policy: Quasi-Market Reforms in the 1990s*. Bristol: Policy.

Barton, L. (ed.) (1996) *Disability and Society: Emerging Issues and Insights*. London: Longman.

Batty, D. (2002) 'Draining the South'. *The Guardian*, 11 March 2003, p. 21.

Baubock, R., Heller, A. and Zolberg, A. (eds) (1996) *The Challenge of Diversity: Integration and Pluralism in Societies of Immigration*. Aldershot: Avebury.

Bauman, Z. (1998) *Work, Consumerism and the New Poor*. Buckingham: Open University Press.

Beck, U. (2000) *What is Globalization?* Cambridge: Polity.

Bennett, T., Grossberg, L. and Morris, M. (eds) (forthcoming) *New Keywords*. Oxford: Basil Blackwell.

Berger, P. and Luckmann, T. (1966) *The Social Construction of Reality*. London: Penguin.

Berlant, L. (1991) *The Anatomy of a National Fantasy: Hawthorne, Utopia and Everyday Life*. Chicago: University of Chicago Press.

Beyeler, M. (2003) 'Globalization, Europeanization, and Domestic Welfare State Reforms: New Institutionalist Concepts'. *Global Social Policy*, 3 (2), pp. 153–72.

Beynon, H., Grimshaw, D., Rubery, J. and Ward, K. (2002) *Managing Employment Change: The New Realities of Work*. Oxford: Oxford University Press.

Biersteker, T. and Weber, C. (eds) (1996) *State Sovereignty as Social Construct*. Cambridge: Cambridge University Press.

Blair, A. (1998) *The Third Way*. London: Fabian Society.

Boggs, C. (2000) *The End of Politics: Corporate Power and the Decline of the Public Sphere*. New York: Guilford.

Boris, E. (1998) 'When Work is Slavery'. *Social Justice*, 25 (1), pp. 28–46.

Bourdieu, P. (1999) *Acts of Resistance*. New York: New Press.

Boyne, G. (2003) 'What is Public Service Improvement?' *Public Administration*, 81 (2), pp. 211–27.

Brah, A. (1996) *Cartographies of Diaspora: Contesting Identities*. London: Routledge.

Breitenbach, E., Brown, A., Mackay, F. and Webb, J. (eds) (2002) *The Changing Politics of Gender Equality in Britain*. Basingstoke: Palgrave.

Briggs, A. (1961) 'The Welfare State in Historical Perspective'. *European Journal of Sociology*, 2, pp. 221–58.

Brodkin, K. (2001) 'Diversity in Anthropological Theory'. In I. Susser and T. Patterson (eds) *Cultural Diversity in the United States*. Malden, MA: Blackwell.

Brown, M. (1983) 'The Development of Social Administration'. In M. Loney, D. Boswell and J. Clarke (eds) *Social Policy and Social Welfare*. Buckingham: Open University Press.

Brown, W. (2001) *Politics out of History*. Princeton, NJ: Princeton University Press.

Burrows, R. and Loader, B. (eds) (1994) *Towards a Post-Fordist Welfare State?* London: Routledge.

Butcher, T. (1995) *Delivering Welfare Services*. Buckingham: Open University Press.

Campbell, J. and Oliver, M. (1996) *Disability Politics: Understanding Our Past, Changing Our Future*. London: Routledge.

Carabine, J. (1996) 'Heterosexuality and Social Policy'. In D. Richardson (ed.) *Theorizing Heterosexuality*. Buckingham: Open University Press.

Carabine, J. (2000) 'Constituting Welfare Subjects through Poverty and Sexuality'. In G. Lewis, S. Gewirtz and J. Clarke (eds) *Rethinking Social Policy*. London: Sage/Open University.

Carrier, J. (ed.) (1997) *Meanings of the Market: The Free Market in Western Culture*. Oxford: Berg.

Carter, J. (ed.) (1998) *Postmodernity and the Fragmentation of Welfare*. London: Routledge.

Castells, M. and Himenan, P. (2002) *The Information Society and the Welfare State: The Finnish Model*. Oxford: Oxford University Press.

Castles, S. (2000) *Ethnicity and Globalization*. London: Sage.

Castles, S. and Davidson, A. (2000) *Citizenship and Migration: Globalization and the Politics of Belonging*. Basingstoke: Macmillan.

CCCS (1982) *The Empire Strikes Back. Centre for Contemporary Cultural Studies*. London: Hutchinson.

Chaloupka, W. (2001) *Everybody Knows: Cynicism in America*. Minneapolis: University of Minnesota Press.

Chaney, D. (1994) *The Cultural Turn*. London: Routledge.

Ching, L. (2001) 'Globalizing the Regional, Regionalizing the Global: Mass Culture and Asianism in the Age of Late Capital'. In A. Appadurai (ed.) *Globalization*. Durham, NC: Duke University Press.

Christiansen, T., Jorgensen, K. and Wiener, A. (eds) (2001) *The Social Construction of Europe*. London: Sage.

Christie, N. (1996) 'Crime and Civilisation'. *New Internationalist*, no. 282, pp. 10–12.

Clarke, A. (1994) 'Leisure and the New Managerialism'. In J. Clarke, A. Cochrane and E. McLaughlin (eds) *Managing Social Policy.* London: Sage.

Clarke, A. (2000) 'Leisure: Managerialism and Public Space'. In J. Clarke, S. Gewirtz and E. McLaughlin (eds) *New Managerialism, New Welfare?* London: Sage/Open University.

Clarke, J. (1990) 'Pessimism and Populism: The Problematic Politics of Popular Culture'. In R. Butsch (ed.) *For Fun and Profit: The Transformation of Leisure into Consumption.* Philadephia: Temple University Press.

Clarke, J. (1991) *New Times and Old Enemies: Essays on Cultural Studies and America.* London: HarperCollins.

Clarke, J. (1996) 'The Problem of the State after the Welfare State'. In M. May, E. Brunsdon and G. Craig (eds) *Social Policy Review 8.* London: Social Policy Association.

Clarke, J. (1997) 'Capturing the Customer: Consumerism and Social Welfare'. *Self, Agency and Society,* 1 (1), pp. 55–73.

Clarke, J. (1998) 'Thriving on Chaos? Managerialisation and Social Welfare'. In J. Carter (ed.) *Postmodernity and the Fragmentation of Welfare.* London: Routledge.

Clarke, J. (1999a) 'Making a Difference? Markets and the Reform of Welfare States'. Paper presented to seminar on Anglo-German Public Sector Reform 'Learning from Experience', Humboldt University, Berlin, December.

Clarke, J. (1999b) 'Whose Business? Social Welfare and Managerial Calculation'. In M. Purdy and D. Banks (eds) *Health and Exclusion.* London: Routledge.

Clarke, J. (2000a) 'Putting People in Their Places: The Cultural Turn in Social Policy'. In I. Cook, D. Crouch, S. Naylor and J. Ryan (eds) *Cultural Turns, Geographical Turns.* London: Longman.

Clarke, J. (2000b) 'Unfinished Business? Struggles over the Social in Social Welfare'. In P. Gilroy, L. Grossberg and A. McRobbie (eds) *Without Guarantees: In Honour of Stuart Hall.* London: Verso.

Clarke, J. (2001a) 'US Welfare: Variations on the Liberal Regime.' In A. Cochrane, J. Clarke and S. Gewirtz (eds) *Comparing Welfare States, 2nd edn.* London: Sage/Open University.

Clarke, J. (2001b) 'The Production of Transparency: Audit, Inspection and Evaluation in the Governance of Public Services'. Paper presented to European Group on Public Administration (EGPA) Conference, Vaasa, September.

Clarke, J. (2001c) 'Unstable States: Globalisation, Neo-Liberalism and the Remaking of Welfare'. Paper presented to American Anthropological Association Conference, Washington, DC, November.

Clarke, J. (2002a) 'Inventing Independence: Audit and the Recomposition of the State'. Paper presented to Social Policy Association Annual Conference, Teesside, July.

Clarke, J. (2002b) 'Reinventing Community? Governing in Contested Spaces'. Paper presented to the 'Spacing Social Work – On the Territorialization of the Social' Conference, Bielefeld, November.

Clarke, J. (2002c) 'Social Policy and the Cultural Turn'. Paper presented to the ESPANET Conference, Tilburg, August.

Clarke, J. (2004) 'Dissolving the Public Realm? The Logics and Limits of Neo-Liberalism'. *Journal of Social Policy,* 33 (1), pp. 27–48.

Clarke, J. and Newman, J. (1997) *The Managerial State: Power, Politics and Ideology in the Remaking of Social Welfare.* London: Sage.

Clarke, J. and Newman, J. (1998) 'A Modern British People? New Labour and the Reconstruction of Social Welfare'. Paper presented to the Discourse Analysis and Social Research Conference, Ringsted, Denmark, September.

Clarke, J. and Newman, J. (forthcoming) 'Governing in the Modern World'. In D.L. Steinberg and R. Johnson (eds) *New Labour's Passive Revolution.* London: Lawrence and Wishart.

Clarke, J. and Piven, F. (2001) 'The USA: An American Welfare State?' In P. Alcock and G. Craig (eds) *International Social Policy.* Basingstoke: Palgrave.

Clarke, J., Cochrane, A. and Smart, C. (1987) *Ideologies of Welfare.* London: Hutchinson.

Clarke, J., Gewirtz, S. and McLaughlin, E. (2000a) 'Reinventing the Welfare State'. In J. Clarke, S. Gewirtz and E. McLaughlin (eds) *New Managerialism, New Welfare?* London: Sage/Open University.

Clarke, J., Gewirtz, S. and McLaughlin, E. (eds) (2000b) *New Managerialism, New Welfare?* London: Sage/Open University.

Clarke, J., Gewirtz, S., Hughes, G. and Humphrey, J. (2000c) 'Guarding the Public Interest? Auditing Public Services'. In J. Clarke, S. Gewirtz and E. McLaughlin (eds) *New Managerialism, New Welfare?* London: Sage/Open University.

Clarke, J., Langan, M. and Williams, F. (2001a) 'The Construction of the British Welfare State, 1945–1975'. In A. Cochrane, J. Clarke and S. Gewirtz (eds) *Comparing Welfare States, 2nd edn.* London: Sage/Open University.

Clarke, J., Langan, M. and Williams, F. (2001b) 'Remaking Welfare: The British Welfare Regime in the 1980s and 1990s'. In A. Cochrane, J. Clarke and S. Gewirtz (eds) *Comparing Welfare States, 2nd edn.* London: Sage/Open University.

Clasen, J. (ed.) (1999) *Comparative Social Policy: Concepts, Theories and Methods.* Oxford: Blackwell.

Clifton, J., Comin, F. and Fuentes, D. (eds) (2003) *Privatization in the European Union: Public Enterprises and Integration.* Amsterdam: Kluwer.

Cochrane, A., Clarke, J. and Gewirtz, S. (eds) (2001) *Comparing Welfare States, 2nd edn.* London: Sage/Open University.

Cohen, R. (1997) *Global Diasporas: An Introduction.* London: UCL Press.

Commission on Taxation and Citizenship (2000) *Paying for Progress.* London: Fabian Society.

Cooper, D. (1994) *Sexing the City: Lesbian and Gay Politics within the Activist State.* London: Rivers Oram.

Cooper, D. (1998) *Governing Out of Order: Space, Law and the Politics of Belonging.* London: Rivers Oram.

Cope, S. and Goodship, J. (1999) 'Regulating Collaborative Government: Towards Joined-Up Government?', *Public Policy and Administration*, 14 (2), pp. 3–16.

Corvellec, H. (1995) *Stories of Achievement: Narrative Features of Organizational Performance.* Malmo: Lund University Press.

Craig, G., Parks, T. and Taylor, M. (2002) 'In or Against the State: The Third Sector in the Policy Process'. Paper presented to Social Policy Association Conference, Middlesbrough, July.

Crouch, C. (2003) *Commercialization or Citizenship.* London: Fabian Society.

Cutler, T. and Waine, B. (1997) *Managing the Welfare State.* Oxford: Berg.

Daly, M. (1997) 'Welfare States under Pressure: Cash Benefits in European Welfare States over the Last Ten Years'. *Journal of European Social Policy*, 7 (2), pp. 129–46.

Daly, M. (2000) *The Gender Division of Welfare.* Cambridge: Cambridge University Press.

Daly, M. (2002) 'Governance and Social Policy'. *Journal of Social Policy*, 32 (1), pp. 113–28.

Daly, M. and Lewis, J. (2000) 'The Concept of Social Care and the Analysis of Contemporary Welfare States'. *British Journal of Sociology*, 51 (2), pp. 281–98.

Daly, M. and Rake, K. (2003) *Gender and the Welfare State.* Cambridge: Polity.

Davies, C. (2004) 'Regulating the Healthcare Workforce: Next Steps for Research', *Journal of Health Services Research and Policy*, January.

Davies, H., Nutley, S. and Smith, P. (eds) (2000) *What Works? Evidence-Based Policy and Practice in Public Services.* Bristol: Policy.

Davis, H., Downe, J. and Martin, S. (2001) *Inspection Regimes and Local Government: Driving Improvement or Drowning in Detail?* York: Joseph Rowntree Foundation.

Davis, H., Downe, J. and Martin, S. (2002) *External Inspection of Local Government: Driving Improvement or Drowning in Detail.* York: Joseph Rowntree Foundation and York Publishing Services.

Deacon, A. (2002) *Perspectives on Welfare.* Buckingham: Open University Press.

Deacon, B. (1997) *Global Social Policy* (with P. Hulse and M. Stubbs). London: Sage.

Deacon, B. (2001) 'International Organizations, the EU and Global Social Policy'. In R. Sykes, B. Palier and P. Prior (eds) *Globalization and European Welfare States: Challenges and Change.* Basingstoke: Palgrave.

Deacon, B., Holliday, I. and Wong, L. (2001) 'Conclusion'. In L. Wong and N. Flynn (eds) *The Market in Chinese Social Policy.* Basingstoke: Palgrave.

Dean, H. (forthcoming) 'The Third Way and Social Welfare: The Myth of Post-Emotionalism'. *Social Policy and Administration*, 37.

Dean, H. and Melrose, M. (1999) *Poverty, Riches and Social Citizenship.* Basingstoke: Macmillan.

Dean, M. (1999) *Governmentality: Power and Rule in Modern Society.* London: Sage.

Dench, G. (2003) 'Community Values'. *New Statesman*, 24 March 2003, pp. 29–32.

Dickson, M., Halpin, D., Gewirtz, S., Power, S. and Whitty, G. (forthcoming)'Education Action Zones: Model Partnerships?' In R. Franklin, M. Bloch and T. Popkewitz (eds) *Educational Partnerships: Democracy, Citizenship and Salvation in a Globalized World* New York: Palgrave.

Di Leonardo, M. (1998) *Exotics at Home: Anthropologies, Others, American Modernity.* Chicago: University of Chicago Press.

Donajgrodski, A.P. (ed.) (1977) *Social Control in Nineteenth Century Britain.* London: Croom Helm.

Dryzek, J. (2000) *Deliberative Democracy and Beyond: Liberals, Critics, Contestations.* Oxford: Oxford University Press.

Du Gay, P. (1999) *In Praise of Bureaucracy.* London: Sage.

Du Gay, P. and Pryke, M. (eds) (2001) *Cultural Economy.* London: Sage.

Duncombe, S. (ed.) (2002) *Cultural Resistance Reader.* London: Verso.

Dunleavy, P. (1991) *Democracy, Bureaucracy and Public Choice.* London: Harvester Wheatsheaf.

Dunleavy, P. (1995) 'Policy Disasters: Explaining the UK's Record'. *Public Policy and Administration,* 10 (2), pp. 52–70.

Dwyer, P. (1998) 'Conditional Citizens? Welfare Rights and Responsibilities in the Late 1990s'. *Critical Social Policy,* 18 (4), pp. 493–518.

Dwyer, P. (2000) *Welfare Rights and Responsibilities: Contesting Social Citizenship.* Bristol: Policy.

Eagleton, T. (2000) *The Idea of Culture.* Oxford: Blackwell.

Ehrenreich, B. (2002) *Nickeled and Dimed in America.* London: Granta.

Eley, G. and Suny, R. (eds) (1996) *Becoming National: A Reader.* Oxford: Oxford University Press.

Elson, D. (1994) 'Micro, Meso, Macro: Gender and Economic Analysis in the Context of Policy Reform'. In I. Bakker (ed.) *The Strategic Silence: Gender and Economic Policy.* London: Zed and North–South Institute.

Elson, D. (1995) 'Male Bias in Macro-Economics: The Case of Structural Adjustment'. In D. Elson (ed.) *Male Bias in the Development Process.* Manchester: Manchester University Press.

Esping-Andersen, G. (1990) *The Three Worlds of Welfare Capitalism.* Cambridge: Polity.

Esping-Andersen, G. (ed.) (1996) *Welfare States in Transition: National Adaptations in Global Economies.* London: Sage in association with UNRISD.

Esping-Andersen, G. (1999) *The Social Foundations of Post-Industrial Economies.* Oxford: Oxford University Press.

Eurostat (1991) *Basic Statistics of the Community.* Brussels: European Commission.

Fairclough, N. (2000) *New Labour, New Language.* London: Routledge.

Ferge, Z. (2001) 'Welfare and "Ill-Fare" Systems in Central–Eastern Europe'. In R. Sykes, B. Palier and P. Prior (eds) *Globalization and European Welfare States: Challenges and Change.* Basingstoke: Palgrave.

Ferguson, I., Lavalette, M. and Mooney, G. (2002) *Rethinking Welfare States.* London: Sage.

Ferguson, J. and Gupta, A. (2002) 'Spatializing States: Toward an Ethnography of Neoliberal Governmentality'. *American Ethnologist,* 29 (4), pp. 981–1002.

Ferlie, E., Ashburner, L., Fitzgerald, L. and Pettigrew A. (1996) *The New Public Management in Action.* Oxford: Oxford University Press.

Finch, J. and Mason, J. (1993) *Negotiating Family Responsibilities.* London: Routledge.

Fink, J. (2001) 'Silence, Absence and Elision in Analyses of "the Family" in European Social Policy'. In J. Fink, G. Lewis and J. Clarke (eds) (2001) *Rethinking European Welfare.* London: Sage/Open University.

Fink, J. (2002) 'Private Lives, Public Issues: Moral Panics and "the Family" in 20th-Century Britain'. *Journal for the Study of British Cultures,* 9 (2), pp. 135–48.

Fink, J., Lewis, G. and Clarke, J. (eds) (2001) *Rethinking European Welfare.* London: Sage/Open University.

Finlayson, A. (2003) *Making Sense of New Labour.* London: Lawrence and Wishart.

Finn, D. (2003) 'Employment Policy'. In N. Ellison and C. Pierson (eds) *Developments in British Social Policy 2.* Basingstoke: Palgrave.

Flynn, N. (2000) 'Managerialism and Public Services: Some International Trends'. In J. Clarke, S. Gewirtz and E. McLaughlin (eds) *New Managerialism, New Welfare?* London: Sage/Open University.

Foucault, M. (1979) *Discipline and Punish.* Harmondsworth: Peregrine.

Foucault, M. (1984) 'Nietzsche, Genealogy, History', trans. D.F. Bouchard and S. Simon. In P. Rabinow (ed.) *The Foucault Reader.* New York: Pantheon.

Frank, T. (2000) *One Market Under God: Extreme Capitalism, Market Populism and the End of Economic Democracy.* New York: Anchor.

Fraser, N. (1989) *Unruly Practices: Power, Discourse and Gender in Contemporary Social Theory.* Minneapolis: University of Minnesota Press.

Fraser, N. (1997) *Justice Interruptus: Critical Reflections on the 'Postsocialist' Condition.* New York: Routledge.

Friedman, M. and Freidman, R. (1984) *The Tyranny of the Status Quo.* Orlando, FL: Harcourt Brace Jovanovich.

Gabriel, Y. and Lang, T. (1995) *The Unmanageable Consumer: Contemporary Consumption and its Fragmentations.* London: Sage.

Garland, D. (2001) *The Culture of Control: Crime and Social Order in Contemporary Society.* Chicago: University of Chicago Press.

Gazeley, I. and Thane, P. (1998) 'Patterns of Visibility: Unemployment in Britain during the Nineteenth and Twentieth Centuries'. In G. Lewis (ed.) *Forming Nation, Framing Welfare.* London: Routledge/Open University.

George, V. and Wilding, P. (1976) *Ideology and Social Welfare.* London: Routledge and Kegan Paul.

Gewirtz, S. (2002) *The Managerial School: Post-Welfarism and Social Justice in Education.* London: Routledge.

Gewirtz, S., Ball, S. and Bowe, R. (1995) *Markets, Choice and Equity in Education.* Buckingham: Open University Press.

Gewirtz, S., Dickson, M. and Power, S. (forthcoming) 'Governance by Spin: the Case of New Labour and Education Action Zones in England'. In S. Lindblad and T. Popkewitz (eds) *Educational Restructuring: International Perspectives.* Greenwich, CT: Information Age Publishing.

Geyer, R. (2000) *Exploring European Social Policy.* London: Sage.

Giddens, A. (1990) *The Consequences of Modernity.* Cambridge: Polity.

Giddens, A. (1994) *Beyond Left and Right.* Cambridge: Polity.

Giddens, A. (1998) *The Third Way: The Renewal of Social Democracy.* Cambridge: Polity.

Gilbert, N. (2002) *Transformation of the Welfare State: The Silent Surrender of Public Responsibility.* Oxford: Oxford University Press.

Gilder, G. (1981) *Wealth and Poverty.* New York: Basic.

Gilens, M. (1999) *Why Americans Hate Welfare: Race, Media and the Politics of Antipoverty Policy.* Chicago: University of Chicago Press.

Gilling, D. and Hughes, G. (2002) 'The Community Safety "Profession": Towards a New Expertise in the Governance of Crime, Disorder and Safety in the UK?', *Community Safety Journal*, 1 (1), pp. 4–12.

Gilroy, P. (1987) *There Ain't No Black in the Union Jack.* London: Hutchinson.

Gilroy, P. (1993) *The Black Atlantic: Modernity and Double Consciousness.* London: Verso.

Gilroy, P. (2000) *Between Camps: Nations, Cultures and the Allure of Race.* London: Allen Lane: Penguin.

Gilroy, P., Grossberg, L. and McRobbie, A. (eds) (2000) *Without Guarantees: In Honour of Stuart Hall.* London: Verso.

Ginsburg, N. (1992) *Divisions of Welfare.* London: Sage.

Ginsburg, N. (2001) 'Globalization and the Liberal Welfare States'. In R. Sykes, B. Palier and P. Prior (eds) *Globalization and European Welfare States: Challenges and Change.* Basingstoke: Palgrave.

Giroux, H. (2001) *Public Space, Private Lives: Beyond the Culture of Cynicism.* New York: Rowman and Littlefield.

Gledhill, J. (2002) 'Some Conceptual and Substantive Limitations of Contemporary Western (Global) Discourses of Rights and Justice'. In C. Abel and C. Lewis (eds) *Exclusion and Engagement: Social Policy in Latin America.* London: Institute of Latin American Studies.

Glendinning, C., Powell, M. and Rummery, K. (eds) (2002) *Partnerships, New Labour and the Governance of Welfare.* Bristol: Policy.

Goode, J. and Maskovsky, J. (eds) (2001) *The New Poverty Studies: The Ethnography of Power, Politics and Impoverished People in the United States.* New York: New York University Press.

Gordon, L. (1988) *Heroes of Their Own Lives: The Politics and History of Family Violence.* New York: Viking.

Gordon, L. (1994) *Pitied But Not Entitled: Single Mothers and the History of Welfare.* Cambridge, MA: Harvard University Press.

Gordon, L. (1999) *The Great Arizona Orphan Abduction.* Cambridge, MA: Harvard University Press.

Gough, I. (1979) *The Political Economy of the Welfare State*. London: Macmillan.

Gough, I. (2000) *Global Capital, Human Needs and Social Policies*. Basingstoke: Palgrave.

Gramsci, A. (1971) *Selections from the Prison Notebooks*. London: Lawrence and Wishart.

Grossberg, L. (1996) 'On Postmodernism and Articulation: An Interview with Stuart Hall'. In D. Morley and K.-H. Chen (eds) *Stuart Hall: Critical Dialogues in Cultural Studies*. London: Routledge.

Grossberg, L. (forthcoming) *America's War Against Children*. New York: Palgrave.

Gupta, A. (1998) *Postcolonial Developments*. Durham, NC: Duke University Press.

Gupta, A. (2000) 'Rethinking the Conceptual Basis of State Welfare in the Era of Liberalization'. Paper presented to the International Crossroads in Cultural Studies Conference, Birmingham, June.

Gupta, A. and Ferguson, J. (1992) 'Beyond "Culture": Space, Identity and the Politics of Difference'. *Cultural Anthropology*, 7 (1), pp. 6–23.

Hackett, R. (2001) 'News Media and Civic Equality: Watch Dogs, Mad Dogs, or Lap Dogs?' In E. Broadbent (ed.) *Democratic Equality: What Went Wrong?* Toronto: University of Toronto Press.

Hall, C. (1998) 'A Family for Nation and Empire'. In G. Lewis (ed.) *Forming Nation, Framing Welfare*. London Sage/Open University.

Hall, C. (2002) *Civilising Subjects: Metropole and Colony in the English Imagination 1830–1867*. Chicago: University of Chicago Press.

Hall, S. (1992) 'The West and the Rest: Discourse and Power'. In S. Hall and B. Gieben (eds) *Formations of Modernity*. Cambridge: Polity.

Hall, S. (1996) 'Gramsci's Relevance for the Study of Race and Ethnicity'. In D. Morley and K.-H. Chen (eds) *Stuart Hall: Critical Dialogues in Cultural Studies*. London: Routledge.

Hall, S. (2001) 'The Multi-Cultural Question'. In B. Hesse (ed.) *Un/settled Multiculturalisms: Diasporas, Entanglements, Disruptions*. London: Zed.

Hall, S. and Jefferson, T. (eds) (1976) *Resistance Through Rituals*. London: Hutchinson.

Hall, S., Critcher, C., Clarke, J., Jefferson, Y. and Roberts, B. (1978) *Policing: The Crisis*. London: Macmillan.

Hansen, T.B. and Stepputat, F. (eds) (2001) *States of Imagination: Ethnographic Explorations of the Postcolonial State*. Durham, NC: Duke University Press.

Harden, I. (1992) *The Contracting State*. Buckingham: Open University Press.

Hardt, M. (2002) 'Folly of Our Masters of the Universe'. *The Guardian*, 18 December 2002, p. 18.

Hardt, M. and Negri, A. (2000) *Empire*. Cambridge, MA: Harvard University Press.

Harris, P. (1999) 'Public Welfare and Advanced Liberal Governance'. In A. Petersen, I. Barns, J. Dudley and P. Harris (1999) *Post-Structuralism, Citizenship and Social Policy*. London: Routledge.

Harrison, S. (2002) 'New Labour, Modernisation and the Medical Labour Process'. *Journal of Social Policy*, 31, pp. 465–85.

Harrison, S., Hunter, D., Marnoch, G. and Pollitt, C. (1992) *Just Managing: Power and Culture in the National Health Service*. Basingstoke: Macmillan.

Hebdige, D. (1988) *Hiding in the Light*. London: Comedia/Routledge.

Henkel, M. (1991) *Government, Evaluation and Change*. London: Jessica Kingsley.

Herrenstein, R. and Murray, C. (1996) *The Bell Curve: Intelligence and Class Structure in American Life*. New York: Simon and Schuster.

Hesse, B. (ed.) (2001a) *Un/Settled Multiculturalisms: Diasporas, Entanglements and Transruptions*. London: Zed.

Hesse, B. (2001b) 'Introduction: Un/Settled Multiculturalisms'. In B. Hesse (ed.) *Un/Settled Multiculturalisms: Diasporas, Entanglements and Transruptions*. London: Zed.

Hill, C. (1991) *The World Turned Upside Down*. London: Penguin.

Hillyard, P. and Watson, S. (1996) 'Postmodern Social Policy: A Contradiction in Terms?' *Journal of Social Policy*, 23 (3), pp. 321–46.

Hochschild, A. (2001) 'Global Care Chains and Emotional Surplus Value'. In W. Hutton and A. Giddens (eds) *On the Edge: Living with Global Capitalism*. London: Verso.

Hofstede, G. (1980) *Culture's Consequences: International Differences in Work-Related Values*. Beverly Hills, CA: Sage.

Hoggett, P. (1996) 'New Modes of Control in the Public Service'. *Public Administration*, 74, pp. 23–34.

Holland, D. and Lave, J. (2001a) 'History in Person: An Introduction'. In D. Holland and J. Lave (eds) *History in Person: Enduring Struggles, Contentious Practice, Intimate Identities*. Santa Fe, NM: School of American Research. Oxford: James Currey.

Holland, D. and Lave, J. (eds) (2001b) *History in Person: Enduring Struggles, Contentious Practices, Intimate Identities*. Santa Fe, NM: School of American Research. Oxford: James Currey.

Holquist, M. (1990) *Dialogism: Bakhtin and His World*. London: Routledge.

Home Office (2002) *Secure Borders, Safe Haven: Integration with Diversity in Modern Britain*. CM 5387. Norwich: Stationery Office.

Hondagneu-Soleto, P. (2000) 'The International Division of Caring and Cleaning Work'. In M.H. Meyer (ed.) *Care Work: Gender, Labor and the Welfare State*. New York: Routledge.

Hood, C., Scott, C., James, O., Jones, G. and Travers, T. (1998) *Regulation inside Government: Waste-Watchers, Quality Police and Sleaze Busters*. Oxford: Oxford University Press.

Huber, E. and Stephens, J.D. (2001) *Development and Crisis of the Welfare State: Parties and Policies in Global Markets*. Chicago: University of Chicago Press.

Hudson, R. and Williams, A.M. (eds) (1999a) *Divided Europe: Society and Territory*. London: Sage.

Hudson, R. and Williams, A.M. (1999b) 'Re-shaping Europe: The Challenge of New Divisions within a Homogenized Political-Economic Space'. In R. Hudson and A.M. Williams (eds) *Divided Europe: Society and Territory*. London: Sage.

Hughes, G. (ed.) (1998) *Imagining Welfare Futures*. London: Routledge/Open University.

Hughes, G. and Edwards, A. (eds) (2002) *Crime Control and Community: The New Politics of Public Safety*. Cullompton: Willan.

Hughes, G. and Lewis, G. (eds) (1998) *Unsettling Welfare: The Reconstruction of Social Policy*. London: Routledge/Open University.

Hughes, G., Mears, R. and Winch, C. (1996) 'An Inspector Calls? Regulation and Accountability in Three Public Services'. *Policy and Politics*, 25 (3), pp. 299–313.

Humphrey, J. (2002a) 'A Scientific Approach to Politics? On the Trail of the Audit Commission'. *Critical Perspectives on Accounting*, 13, pp. 39–62.

Humphrey, J. (2002b) 'Joint Reviews: Retracing the Trajectory, Decoding the Terms'. *British Journal of Social Work*, 32, pp. 463–76.

Humphrey, J., Clarke, J., Gewirtz, S. and Hughes, G. (1999) 'Audit and Inspection in the Public Sector'. Paper presented to the Social Policy Association Annual Conference, Roehampton, July.

Hyatt, S. (1995) 'Poverty and Difference: Ethnographic Representation of "Race" and the Crisis of "the Social"'. In D. Shenk (ed.) *Gender and Race through Education and Political Activism: The Legacy of Sylvia Helen Forman*. New York: American Anthropological Association/ Association for Feminist Anthropology.

Hyatt, S. (2001) 'From Citizen to Volunteer: Neo-Liberal Governance and the Erasure of Poverty'. In J. Goode and J. Maskovsky (eds) *The New Poverty Studies: The Ethnography of Power, Politics and Impoverished People in the United States*. New York: New York University Press.

Ignatieff, M. (1978) *A Just Measure of Pain?* London: Macmillan.

Jameson, F. (1997) *The Cultural Turn: Selected Writings on the Postmodern, 1983–1998*. London: Verso.

Jaworski, A. and Coupland, N. (eds) (1999) *The Discourse Reader*. London: Routledge.

Jessop, B. (2000a) 'From Keynesian Welfare National State to Schumpeterian Workfare Post-National Regime'. In G. Lewis, S. Gewirtz and J. Clarke (eds) *Rethinking Social Policy*. London: Sage.

Jessop, B. (2000b) 'Governance Failure'. In G. Stoker (ed.) *The New Politics of British Local Governance*. Basingstoke: Macmillan.

Jessop, B. (2002) *The Future of the Capitalist State*. Cambridge: Polity.

Johnson, R. and Steinberg, D. (eds) (forthcoming) *New Labour's Passive Revolution*. London: Lawrence and Wishart.

Johnson, T. (1973) *Professions and Power*. London: Macmillan.

Jones, C. and Novak, T. (1999) *Poverty, Welfare and the Disciplinary State*. London: Routledge.

Jonsson, C., Tagil, S. and Tornqvist, G. (2000) *Organizing European Space*. London: Routledge.

Katz, C. (2003) 'The Detritus of Neo-Liberalism and the Politics of Social Reproduction'. Paper presented to CASCA/SANA Conference, Halifax, Nova Scotia, May.

Katz, M. (1986) *In the Shadow of the Poorhouse: A Social History of Welfare in America*. New York: Basic.

Katz, M. (ed.) (1993) *The Underclass Debate*. Princeton, NJ: Princeton University Press.

Katz, M. (2001) *The Price of Citizenship: Redefining the American Welfare State*. New York: Henry Holt.

Keesbergen, K.v. (2000) 'The Declining Resistance of Welfare States to Change?' In S. Kuhnle (ed.) *Survival of the European Welfare State*. London: Routledge.

Kennet, P. (2001) *Comparative Social Policy*. Buckingham: Open University Press.

King, D. (1999) *In the Name of Liberalism: Illiberal Social Policy in the United States and Britain*. Oxford: Oxford University Press.

King, D. and Wickham-Jones, M. (1998) 'Bridging the Atlantic: The Democratic (Party) Origins of Welfare to Work'. In M. Powell (ed.) *New Labour, New Welfare State?* Bristol: Policy.

Kingfisher, C. (ed.) (2002) *Western Welfare in Decline: Globalization and Women's Poverty*. Philadelphia: University of Pennsylvania Press.

Kofman, E. and Sales, R. (1998) 'Migrant Women and Exclusion in Europe'. *European Journal of Women's Studies*, 5, pp. 381–98.

Kooiman, J. (ed.) (1993) *Modern Governance: New Government–Society Interactions*. London: Sage.

Kooiman, J. (2000) 'Societal Governance: Levels, Models and Orders of Social-Political Interaction'. In J. Pierre (ed.) *Debating Governance: Authority, Steering and Democracy*. Oxford: Oxford University Press.

Kosonen, P. (2001) 'Globalization and the Nordic Welfare States'. In R. Sykes, B. Palier and P. Prior (eds) *Globalization and European Welfare States: Challenges and Change*. Basingstoke: Palgrave.

Kuhnle, S. (ed.) (2000) *Survival of the European Welfare State*. London: Routledge.

Kuhnle, S. and Alestalo, M. (2000) 'Introduction: Growth, Adjustments and Survival of European Welfare States'. In S. Kuhnle (ed.) (2000) *Survival of the European Welfare State*. London: Routledge.

Kvist, J. and Jaeger, M. (forthcoming) 'Up for the Challenge: Western European Welfare States under Pressure'. *Social Policy and Administration*.

Labour Party (2001) *Ambitions for Britain: Labour's Manifesto 2001*. London: Labour Party.

Land, H. (1997) 'Families and the Law'. In J. Muncie, M. Wetherell, R. Dallos and A. Cochrane (eds) *Understanding the Family*. London: Sage/Open University.

Langan, M. and Ostner, I. (1991) 'Gender and Welfare'. In G. Room (ed.) *Towards a European Welfare State?* Bristol: School for Advanced Urban Studies.

Leach, B. (2003) 'Capitalism's Cutting Edge: How Homework Prefigured the Reconstitution of Work'. Paper presented to CASCA/SANA Conference, Halifax, Nova Scotia, May.

Leibfried, S. (2000) 'National Welfare States, European Integration and Globalization: A Perspective for the Next Century'. *Social Policy and Administration*, 34 (1), pp. 44–63.

Lem, W. and Leach, B. (eds) (2002) *Culture, Economy, Power: Anthropology as Critique, Anthropology as Praxis*. Albany, NY: State University of New York Press.

Leonard, P. (1997) *Postmodern Welfare*. London: Sage.

Leontidou, L. and Afouxenidis, A. (1999) 'Boundaries of Social Exclusion in Europe'. In R. Hudson and A.M. Williams (eds) *Divided Europe: Society and Territory*. London: Sage.

Levitas, R. (1998) *The Inclusive Society?* Basingstoke: Macmillan.

Levitas, R. (2001) 'Against Work: A Utopian Incursion into Social Policy'. *Critical Social Policy*, 21 (4), pp. 449–66.

Lewis, G. (ed.) (1998a) *Forming Nation, Framing Welfare*. London: Routledge/Open University.

Lewis, G. (1998b) 'Welfare and the Social Construction of "Race"'. In E. Saraga (ed.) *Embodying the Social: Constructions of Difference*. London: Routledge/Open University.

Lewis, G. (2000a) 'Introduction: Expanding the Social Policy Imaginary'. In G. Lewis, S. Gewirtz and J. Clarke (eds) *Rethinking Social Policy*. London: Sage/Open University.

Lewis, G. (2000b) 'Discursive Histories, the Pursuit of Multiculturalism and Social Policy.' In G. Lewis, S. Gewirtz and J. Clarke (eds) *Rethinking Social Policy*. London: Sage/Open University.

Lewis, G. (2000c) *'Race', Gender, Welfare: Encounters in a Postcolonial Society*. Cambridge: Polity.

Lewis, G. (2002a) 'Introduction: Expanding the Social Policy Imaginary'. In G. Lewis, S. Gewirtz and J. Clarke (eds) *Rethinking Social Policy*. London: Sage/Open University.

Lewis, G. (2002b) 'Culture as Practice, Culture as Sign: Postcolonial Anxiety in the Midst of Multiculturalism'. Paper presented to Crossroads in Cultural Studies Conference, Tampere, Finland, June.

Lewis, G. (2003) '"Difference" and Social Policy'. In N. Ellison and C. Pierson (eds) *Developments in British Social Policy 2*. Basingstoke: Palgrave.

Lewis, G., Gewirtz, S. and Clarke, J. (eds) (2000) *Rethinking Social Policy*. London: Sage/Open University.

Lewis, J. (1992) 'Gender and the Development of Welfare Regimes'. *Journal of European Social Policy*, 2 (3), pp. 159–73.

Lewis, J. (2000) 'Gender and Welfare Regimes'. In G. Lewis, S. Gewirtz and J. Clarke (eds) *Rethinking Social Policy*. London: Sage/Open University.

Li, T.M. (1996) 'Images of Community: Discourse and Strategy in Property Relations'. *Development and Change*, 27, pp. 501–27.

Li, T.M. (1999) 'Compromising Power: Development, Culture, and Rule in Indonesia'. *Cultural Anthropology*, 14 (3), pp. 295–322.

Li, T.M. (forthcoming) 'Situating Resource Struggles: Concepts for Empirical Analysis'. *Economic and Political Weekly*.

Lister, R. (1997) *Citizenship: Feminist Perspectives* (2nd edn 2003). Basingstoke: Macmillan.

Lister, R. (1998) 'From Equality to Social Inclusion: New Labour and the Welfare State'. *Critical Social Policy*, 18 (2), pp. 215–25.

Lister, R. (2002a) 'Towards a New Welfare Settlement?' In C. Hay (ed.) *British Politics Today*. Cambridge: Polity.

Lister, R. (2002b) 'The Responsible Citizen: Creating a New British Welfare Contract'. In C. Kingfisher (ed.) *Western Welfare in Decline*. Philadelphia: University of Pennsylvania Press.

Lloyd, D. and Thomas, P. (1998) *Culture and the State*. London: Routledge.

Loney, M., Bocock, R., Clarke, J., Cochrane, A., Graham, P. and Wilson, M. (eds) (1987) *The State or the Market: Politics and Welfare in Contemporary Britain*. London: Sage/Open University.

Lund, F. (2001) 'South Africa: Transition under Pressure'. In P. Alcock and G. Craig (eds) *International Social Policy*. Basingstoke: Palgrave.

Lury, C. (1996) *Consumer Culture*. Cambridge: Polity.

Lutz, H., Phoenix, A. and Yuval-Davis, N. (eds) (1995) *Crossfires: Nationalism, Racism and Gender in Europe*. London: Pluto.

Lyotard, J.-F. (1984) *The Postmodern Condition: A Report on Knowledge*. Manchester: Manchester University Press.

Malveaux, J. (1987) 'The Political Economy of Black Women'. In M. Davis (eds) *The Year Left 2: Towards a Rainbow Socialism*. London: Verso.

Mandelson, P. (2003) 'We Need to Rethink the Welfare State'. *The Guardian*, 25 April 2003, p. 24.

Mann, K. (1998) 'Lamppost-Modernism: Traditional and Critical Social Policy'. *Critical Social Policy*, 18 (1), pp. 77–102.

Manning, N. and Davidova, N. (2001) 'Russia: Revolution or Evolution?' In P. Alcock and G. Craig (eds) *International Social Policy*. Basingstoke: Palgrave.

Marfleet, P. (1999) 'Europe's Civilising Mission'. In P. Cohen (ed.) *New Ethnicities. Old Racisms*. London: Zed.

Marshall, T.H. (1950) *Citizenship and Social Class*. Cambridge: Cambridge University Press.

Martin, G. (2001) 'Social Movements, Welfare and Social Policy'. *Critical Social Policy*, 21 (2), pp. 361–83.

Marx, K. (1973) *The Grundrisse*. London: Penguin.

Massey, D. (1999) 'Imagining Globalisation: Power-Geometries of Time-Space'. In A. Brah, M.J. Hickman and M. Mac an Ghaill (eds) *Global Futures: Migration, Environment and Globalization*. Basingstoke: Macmillan.

Mayer, M.H. (ed.) (2000) *Care Work: Gender, Labor and the Welfare State*. New York: Routledge.

McSweeney, B. (1988) 'Accounting for the Audit Commission'. *The Political Quarterly*, 59 (1), pp. 28–43.

McSweeney, B. (2002) 'Hofstede's Model of National Cultural Differences and Their Consequences: A Triumph of Faith – A Failure of Analysis'. *Human Relations*, 55, pp. 89–117.

Mead, L. (1992) *The New Politics of Poverty: The Nonworking Poor in America*. New York: Basic.

Melossi, D. and Pavarini, F. (1980) *The Prison and the Factory*. London: Macmillan.

Miles, R. (1999) 'Analysing the Political Economy of Migration: The Airport as an "Effective" Institution of Control'. In A. Brah, M. Hickman and M. Mac an Ghaill (eds) *Global Futures: Migration, Environment and Globalization*. Basingstoke: Macmillan.

Miliband, D. (1999) 'This Is the Modern World'. *Fabian Review*, 111 (4), pp. 11–13.

Miller, D. (2003) 'What is Best "Value"?' Paper presented to Open University Workshop on 'Defending Bureaucracy', Oxford, March.

Mink, G. (1990) 'The Lady and the Tramp: Gender, Race and the Origins of the American Welfare State'. In L. Gordon (ed.) *Women, the State and Welfare*. Madison, WI: University of Wisconsin Press.

Mink, G. (1998) *Welfare's End* Ithaca, NY: Cornell University Press.

Mishra, R. (1990) *The Welfare State in Capitalist Society*. Hemel Hempstead: Harvester Wheatsheaf.

Mishra, R. (1999) *Globalization and the Welfare State*. Cheltenham: Elgar.

Mohan, J. (2002) *Planning, Markets and Hospitals*. London: Routledge.

Moody, K. (1987) 'Reagan, the Business Agenda and the Collapse of Labor'. In R. Miliband et al. (eds) *The Socialist Register 1987*. London: Merlin.

Mooney, G. (1998) 'Remoralising the Poor? Gender, Class and Philanthropy in Victorian Britain'. In G. Lewis (ed.) *Forming Nation, Framing Welfare*. London: Sage/Open University.

Mooney, G. (2000) 'Class and Social Policy'. In G. Lewis, S. Gewirtz and J. Clarke (eds) *Rethinking Social Policy*. London: Sage/Open University.

Mooney, G. (ed.) (2004) *Work: Personal Lives and Social Policy*. Bristol: Policy/Open University.

Morgen, S. and Maskovsky, J. (2003) 'The Anthropology of Welfare "Reform": New Perspectives on U.S. Urban Poverty in the Post-Welfare Era'. *Annual Review of Anthropology*, 32, pp. 315–38.

Morley, M. and Petras, J. (1998) 'Wealth and Poverty in the National Economy: The Domestic Foundations of Clinton's Global Policy'. In C. Lo and M. Schwartz (eds) *Social Policy and the Conservative Agenda*. Oxford: Blackwell.

Morris, L. (1994) *Dangerous Classes: The Underclass and Social Citizenship*. London: Routledge.

Morris, M. (1998) *Too Soon, Too Late: History in Popular Culture*. Bloomington and Indianapolis: Indiana University Press.

Muncie, J. (2000) 'Decriminalizing Criminology'. In G. Lewis, S. Gewirtz and J. Clarke (eds) *Rethinking Social Policy*. London: Sage/Open University.

Muncie, J. (2004) 'Youth Justice: Globalisation and Multi-Modal Governance'. In T. Newburn and R. Sparks (eds) *Criminal Justice and Political Cultures: National and International Dimensions of Crime Control*. Cullompton: Willan Publishing.

Murray, C. (1984) *Losing Ground: American Social Policy, 1950–1980*. New York: Basic.

National Deviancy Conference (1980) *Permissiveness and Control*. London: Macmillan.

Neal, S. (2002) 'Rural Landscapes, Representations and Racism: Examining Multicultural Citizenship and Policy-Making in the English Countryside'. *Ethnic and Racial Studies*, 25 (3), pp. 442–62.

Needham, C. (2003) *Citizen-Consumers: New Labour's Marketplace Democracy*. London: Catalyst Forum.

Neubeck, K. and Casenave, N. (2001) *Welfare Racism: Playing the Race Card against America's Poor*. New York: Routledge.

Newman, J. (2001) *Modernising Governance: New Labour, Policy and Society*. London: Sage.

Newman, J. (2002) 'New Labour, Social Policy and Cultural Change: Modernising Discourses and Leadership Narratives'. Paper presented to European Social Policy Research Network Conference, Tilburg, August.

Newman, J. and Mooney, G. (2004) 'Managing Personal Lives'. In G. Mooney (ed.) *Work: Personal Lives and Social Policy*. Bristol: Policy/Open University.

Newman, J. and Williams, F. (1995) 'Diversity and Change: Gender, Welfare and Organisational Relations'. In C. Itzin and J. Newman (eds) *Gender, Culture and Organisational Change: Putting Theory into Practice*. London: Routledge.

Newman, J., Barnes, M., Knops, A. and Sullivan, H. (2004) 'Power, Participation and Polical Renewal'. *Journal of Social Policy*.

Niskanen, W.A. (1971) *Bureaucracy and Representative Government*. New York: Aldine Atherton.

Nobles, M. (2000) *Shades of Citizenship: Race and the Census in Modern Politics*. Stanford, CA: Stanford University Press.

Nonini, D. (2003) 'American Neoliberalism, "Globalization" and Violence: Reflections from the United States and Southeast Asia'. In J. Friedman (ed.) *Globalization and Violence*. New York: Guggenheim Foundation.

Nugent, D. (2003) 'When States State, Who Listens?' Paper presented to CASCA/SANA Conference, Halifax, Nova Scotia, May.

O'Brien, M. and Penna, S. (1998) *Theorising Welfare: Enlightenment and Modern Society*. London: Sage.

O'Connor, J. (1973) *The Fiscal Crisis of the State*. New York: St Martin's.

O'Connor, J., Orloff, A. and Shaver, S. (1999) *States, Markets, Families: Gender, Liberalism and Social Policy in Australia, Canada, Great Britain and the United States*. Cambridge: Cambridge University Press.

O'Malley, P. (1996) 'Risk and Responsibility'. In A. Barry, T. Osborne and N. Rose (eds) *Foucault and Political Reason.* London: UCL Press.

Offe, C. (1984) *Contradictions of the Welfare State.* London: Hutchinson.

Office of Public Services Reform (2002) *Reforming Our Public Services.* London: Office of Public Services Reform.

Office of Public Services Reform (2003) *Inspecting for Improvement: Developing a Customer Focused Approach.* London: Office of Public Services Reform.

Omi, M. and Winant, H. (1986) *Racial Formation in the United States.* New York: Routledge.

Ong, A. (1999) *Flexible Citizenship: The Cultural Logics of Transnationality.* Durham, NC: Duke University Press.

Ong, A. and Nonini, D. (eds) (1997) *Ungrounded Empires: The Cultural Politics of Modern Chinese Transnationalism.* New York: Routledge.

Ooeschot, W.v. and Abrahamson, P. (2003) 'The Dutch and Danish Miracles Revisited: A Critical Discussion of Activation Policies in Two Small Welfare States'. *Social Policy and Administration,* 37 (3), pp. 288–304.

Orloff, A. (1993) 'Gender and the Social Rights of Citizenship: The Comparative Analysis of Welfare States'. *American Sociological Review,* 58 (3), pp. 303–28.

Parekh, B. (2000) *The Future of Multi-Ethnic Britain. Parekh Report from the Runnymede Trust Commission on the Future of Multi-Ethnic Britain.* London: Profile.

Paton, R. (2003) *Managing and Measuring Social Enterprises.* London: Sage.

Pawson, R. and Tilley, N. (1997) *Realistic Evaluation.* London: Sage.

Pearson, G. (1974) *The Deviant Imagination.* London: Macmillan.

Peck, J. (2001) *Workfare States.* New York: Guilford.

Peters, G. (2000) 'Governance and Comparative Politics'. In J. Pierre (ed.) *Debating Governance: Authority, Steering and Democracy.* Oxford: Oxford University Press.

Peters, G. (2003) 'Governance and the Welfare State'. In N. Ellison and C. Pierson (eds) *Developments in British Social Policy 2.* Basingstoke: Palgrave.

Petersen, A., Barns, I., Dudley, J. and Harris, P. (1999) *Post-Structuralism, Citizenship and Social Policy.* London: Routledge.

Picciotto, S. (2002) 'Introduction: Reconceptualizing Regulation in the Era of Globalization'. *Journal of Law and Society,* 29 (1), pp. 1–11.

Pierson, C. (1991) *Beyond the Welfare State?* Cambridge: Polity.

Pierson, P. (1994) *Dismantling the Welfare State? Reagan, Thatcher and the Politics of Retrenchment.* Cambridge: Cambridge University Press.

Piven, F.F. (1998a) 'Welfare and the Transformation of Electoral Politics'. In C. Lo and M. Schwartz (eds) *Social Policy and the Conservative Agenda.* Malden, MA and Oxford: Blackwell.

Piven, F.F. (1998b) 'Welfare and Work'. *Social Justice,* 25 (1), pp. 67–81.

Piven, F.F. and Cloward, R. (1993) *Regulating the Poor: The Functions of Public Welfare, 2nd edn.* New York: Vintage.

Pollitt, C. (1993) *Managerialism and the Public Services, 2nd edn.* Oxford: Blackwell.

Pollitt, C. (1995) 'Justification by Works or by Faith? Evaluating the New Public Management'. *Evaluation,* 1 (2), pp. 133–54.

Pollitt, C. and Bouckaert, G. (2000) *Public Management Reform: A Comparative Analysis.* Oxford: Oxford University Press.

Pollitt, C. and Summa, H. (1999) 'Performance Audit and Public Management Reform'. In C. Pollitt, X. Girre, J. Lonsdale, R. Mul, H. Summa and M. Waerness (eds) *Performance or Compliance? Performance Audit and Public Management in Five Countries.* Oxford: Oxford University Press.

Pollitt, C., Birchall, J. and Putnam, K. (1998) *Decentralising Public Service Management.* Basingstoke: Macmillan.

Pollitt, C., Girre, X., Lonsdale, J., Mul, R., Summa, H. and Waerness, M. (1999) *Performance or Compliance? Performance Audit and Public Management in Five Countries.* Oxford: Oxford University Press.

Poole, L. (2000a) 'New Approaches to Comparative Social Policy: The Changing Face of Central and Eastern European Welfare'. In G. Lewis, S. Gewirtz and J. Clarke (eds) *Rethinking Social Policy.* London: Sage/Open University.

Poole, L. (2000b) 'Health Care: New Labour's NHS'. In J. Clarke, S. Gewirtz and E. McLaughlin (eds) *New Managerialism, New Welfare?* London: Sage/Open University.

Power, M. (1997) *The Audit Society.* Oxford: Oxford University Press.

Prime Minister (1998) 'Foreword and Introduction'. In Secretary of State for Social Security and Minister for Welfare Reform, *New Ambitions for Our Country: A New Contract for Welfare.* Cm 3805. London: Stationery Office.

Prince, M. (2001) 'How Social Is Social Policy? Fiscal and Market Discourse in North American Welfare States'. *Social Policy and Administration*, 35 (1), pp. 2–13.

Probyn, E. (1998) 'Mc-Identities: Food and the Familial Citizen'. *Theory, Culture and Society*, 15 (2), pp. 155–73.

Quadagno, J. (1994) *The Color of Welfare: How Racism Undermined the War on Poverty.* New York: Oxford University Press.

Rao, N. (1996) *Towards Welfare Pluralism: Public Services in a Time of Change.* Aldershot: Dartmouth.

Ray, L. and Sayer, A. (1999) *Culture and Economy After the Cultural Turn.* London: Sage.

Rhodes, R. (1997) *Understanding Governance: Policy Networks, Governance, Reflexivity and Accountability.* Buckingham: Open University Press.

Rhodes, R. (1999) 'Foreword'. In G. Stoker (ed.) *The New Management of British Local Governance.* Basingstoke: Macmillan.

Riley, D. (1983) *The War in the Nursery: Theories of the Child and Mother.* London: Virago.

Rodger, J. (2003) 'Social Solidarity, Welfare and Post-Emotionalism'. *Journal of Social Policy*, 32 (3), pp. 403–22.

Rose, H. and Rose, S. (2001) *Alas Poor Darwin: Escaping Evolutionary Psychology.* London: Vintage.

Rose, N. (1996a) 'The Death of the Social? Re-figuring the Territory of Government'. *Economy and Society*, 25 (3), pp. 327–56.

Rose, N. (1996b) 'Governing "Advanced" Liberal Democracies'. In A. Barry, T. Osborne and N. Rose (eds) *Foucault and Political Reason.* London: UCL Press.

Rose, N. (1999) *Powers of Freedom.* Cambridge: Cambridge University Press.

Rose, N. (2000) 'Governing Cities, Governing Citizens'. In E. Isin (ed.) *Democracy, Citizenship and the Global City.* London: Routledge.

Roseneil, S. (2003) 'Re-imagining Care: Transformations of Intimacy, Sociability and Welfare in the 21st Century (or, Why We Should Care About Friends)'. Paper presented to Social Policy Association Conference, Middlesbrough, July.

Ross, A. (1998) *Real Love: In Pursuit of Cultural Justice.* London: Routledge.

Said, E. (1979) *Orientalism.* New York: Vintage.

Sainsbury, D. (ed.) (1994) *Gendering Welfare States.* London: Sage.

Saloma, J. (1984) *Ominous Politics: The New Conservative Labyrinth.* New York: Hill and Wang.

Saraga, E. (ed.) (1998) *Embodying the Social: Constructions of Difference.* London: Routledge/Open University.

Sassen, S. (2001) *The Global City, 2nd edn.* Chicago: University of Chicago Press.

Saville, J. (1977) 'The Welfare State: An Historical Introduction'. In M. Fitzgerald, P. Halmos, J. Muncie and D. Zeldin (eds) *Welfare in Action.* London: Routledge and Kegan Paul. (Originally published in *The New Reasoner*, 1957–8, vol. 3 (winter), pp. 5–24.)

Schmidt, V. (1999) 'Convergent Pressures, Divergent Responses: France, Great Britain and Germany between Globalization and Europeanization'. In D. Smith, D. Solinger and S.Topik (eds) *States and Sovereignty in the Global Economy.* London: Routledge.

Schram, S. (1995) *Words of Welfare.* Minneapolis: University of Minnesota Press.

Schram, S. (2000) *After Welfare: The Culture of Postindustrial Social Policy.* New York: New York University Press.

Schram, S. (2002) *Praxis for the Poor: Piven and Cloward and the Future of Social Science in Social Welfare.* New York: New York University Press.

Schram, S. and Soss, J. (2002) 'Success Stories: Welfare Reform, Policy Discourse and the Politics of Research'. In S. Schram (ed.) *Praxis for the Poor.* New York: New York University Press.

Service, R. (2002) *Russia: Experiment with a People.* London: Macmillan.

Shore, C. and Wright, S. (1997) 'Policy: A New Field of Anthropology'. In C. Shore and S. Wright (eds) *Anthropology of Policy: Critical Perspectives on Governance and Power.* London: Routledge.

Skelcher, C. (1998) *The Appointed State: Quasi-Governmental Organizations and Democracy.* Buckingham: Open University Press.

Skocpol, T. (1997) *Boomerang: Health Care Reform and the Turn against Government, 2nd edn.* New York: Norton.

Slack, J. (1996) 'The Theory and Method of Articulation in Cultural Studies'. In D. Morley and K.-H. Chen (eds) *Stuart Hall: Critical Dialogues in Cultural Studies.* London: Routledge.

Smart, A. (1998) 'Economic Transformation in China: Property Regimes and Social Relations'. In J. Pickles and A. Smith (eds) *Theorising Transition: The Political Economy of Post-Communist Transformations.* New York: Routledge.

Smart, A. (2001) 'Unruly Places: Urban Governance and the Persistence of Illegality in Hong Kong's Urban Squatter Areas'. *American Anthropologist,* 103 (1), pp. 30–44.

Smith, A. (1971) *Theories of Nationalism.* London: Duckworth.

Smith, N. (2003) *American Empire: Roosevelt's Geographer and the Prelude to Globalization.* Berkeley, CA: University of California Press.

Smith, N., Westmarland, L., Vidler, E., Newman, J. and Clarke, J. (2003) 'Creating Citizen-Consumers'. Paper presented to Social Policy Association Annual Conference, Middlesbrough, July.

Standing, G. (2002) *Beyond Paternalism.* London: Verso.

Stedman-Jones, G. (1971) *Outcast London.* Oxford: Clarendon.

Stein, J.G. (2001) *The Cult of Efficiency.* Toronto: House of Anansi.

Steinmetz, G. (ed.) (1999) *State/Culture: State-Formation after the Cultural Turn.* Ithaca, NY: Cornell University Press.

Stenson, K. (2000) 'Crime Control, Social Policy and Liberalism'. In G. Lewis, S. Gewirtz and J. Clarke (eds) *Rethinking Social Policy.* London: Sage/Open University.

Stiglitz, G. (2002) *Globalization and Its Discontents.* New York: Norton.

Stoker, G. (ed.) (1999) *The New Management of British Local Governance.* Basingstoke: Macmillan.

Stoker, G. (ed.) (2000) *The New Politics of British Local Governance.* Basingstoke: Macmillan.

Stone, D. (2000) 'Caring by the Book'. In M.H. Mayer (ed.) *Care Work: Gender, Labor and the Welfare State.* New York: Routledge.

Sum, N.-L. (1999) 'New Orientalisms, Global Capitalism, and the Politics of Synergetic Differences: Discursive Construction of Trade Relations between the USA, Japan and the East Asian NICs'. In A. Brah, M. Hickman and M. Mac an Ghaill (eds) *Global Futures: Migration, Environment and Globalization.* Basingstoke: Macmillan.

Sun Ge (2000) 'How Does Asia Mean? Part 1'. *Inter-Asian Cultural Studies,* 1 (1), pp. 13–48.

Susser, I. (2001a) 'Cultural Diversity in the United States'. In I. Susser and T. Patterson (eds) *Cultural Diversity in the United States.* Malden, MA: Blackwell.

Susser, I. (2001b) 'Poverty and Homelessness in US Cities'. In I. Susser and T. Patterson (eds) *Cultural Diversity in the United States.* Malden, MA: Blackwell.

Susser, I. and Patterson, T. (eds) (2001) *Cultural Diversity in the United States.* Malden, MA: Blackwell.

Swann, D. (1988) *The Retreat of the State: Deregulation and Privatization in the UK and the US.* New York and London: Harvester Wheatsheaf.

Sykes, R. (1998) 'Studying European Social Policy: Issues and Perspectives'. In R. Sykes and P. Alcock (eds) *Developments in European Social Policy: Convergence and Diversity.* Bristol: Policy.

Sykes, R., Palier, B. and Prior, P. (eds) (2001) *Globalization and European Welfare States: Challenges and Change.* Basingstoke: Palgrave.

Taylor, D. (ed.) (1997) *Critical Social Policy.* London: Sage.

Taylor, G. (1993) 'Challenges from the Margins'. In J. Clarke (ed.) *A Crisis in Care? Challenges to Social Work.* London: Sage/Open University.

Taylor, I., Walton, P. and Young, J. (1973) *The New Criminology.* London: Routledge.

Taylor-Gooby, P. (1996) 'In Defence of Second-Best Theory: State, Class and Capital in Social Policy'. *Journal of Social Policy,* 26 (3), pp. 171–92.

Taylor-Gooby, P. (ed.) (2001a) *Welfare States Under Pressure.* London: Sage.

Taylor-Gooby, P. (2001b) 'Welfare Reform in the UK'. In P. Taylor-Gooby (ed.) *Welfare States Under Pressure.* London: Sage.

Taylor-Gooby, P. (2001c) 'The Politics of Welfare in Europe'. In P. Taylor-Gooby (ed.) *Welfare States Under Pressure.* London: Sage.

Thompson, E.P. (1963) *The Making of the English Working Class.* London: Penguin.

Thompson, G., Frances, J., Levacic, R. and Mitchell, J. (eds) (1991) *Hierarchies, Markets and Networks: The Coordination of Social Life.* London: Sage.

Titmuss, R. (1963) 'The Welfare State: Images and Realities'. *Social Service Review*, 37 (1), pp. 1–11.

Trifiletti, R. (1999) 'Southern European Welfare Regimes and the Worsening Position of Women'. *Journal of European Social Policy*, 9 (4), pp. 210–30.

Trinder, L. and Reynolds, S. (eds) (2000) *Evidence-Based Practice: A Critical Appraisal*. Oxford: Blackwell.

Twigg, J. (2000) *Bathing, the Body and Community Care*. London: Routledge.

Veit-Wilson, J. (2000) 'States of Welfare: a Conceptual Challenge'. *Social Policy and Administration*, 34 (1), pp. 1–25.

Wacquant, L. (1999) 'How Penal Common Sense Comes to Europeans: Notes on the Transatlantic Diffusion of the Neoliberal Doxa'. *European Societies*, 1 (3), pp. 319–52.

Wallace, C. (1999) 'Crossing Borders: Mobility of Goods, Capital and People in the Central European Region'. In A. Brah, M. Hickman and M. Mac an Ghaill (eds) *Global Futures: Migration, Environment and Globalization*. Basingstoke: Macmillan.

Walsh, K. (1995) *Public Services and Market Mechanisms: Competition, Contracting and the New Public Management*. Basingstoke: Macmillan.

Wedel, J. (2001) *Collision and Collusion: The Strange Case of Western Aid to Eastern Europe*. New York: Palgrave.

White, G. (1998) 'Social Security Reform in China: Towards an East Asian Model?' In R. Goodman, G. White and H.J. Kwon (eds) *The East Asian Welfare Model*. London: Routledge.

Whitfield, D. (2000) *Corporate Welfare*. London: Pluto.

Williams, F. (1989) *Social Policy: A Critical Introduction*. Cambridge: Polity.

Williams, F. (1995) 'Race/Ethnicity, Gender and Class in Welfare States: A Framework for Comparative Analysis'. *Social Politics*, 2 (2), pp. 127–59.

Williams, F. (1996) 'Postmodernism, Feminism and the Question of Difference'. In N. Parton (ed.) *Social Theory, Social Change and Social Work*. London: Routledge.

Williams, F. (2000) 'Principles for Good-Enough Welfare'. In G. Lewis, S. Gewirtz and J. Clarke (eds) *Rethinking Social Policy*. London: Sage.

Williams, R. (1988) *Keywords: A Vocabulary of Culture and Society, revised and expanded edn*. London: Fontana.

Williams, R. (1989) *The Politics of Modernism: Against the New Conformists*. London: Verso.

Williamson, J. (1986) *Consuming Passions*. London: Marion Boyars.

Wilson, E. (1977) *Women and the Welfare State*. London: Tavistock.

Wincott, D. (2003) 'Slippery Concepts, Shifting Context: (National) States and Welfare in the Veit-Wilson/Atherton Debate'. *Social Policy and Administration*, 37 (3), pp. 305–15.

Winson, A. and Leach, B. (2002) *Contingent Work, Disrupted Lives: Labour and Community in the New Rural Economy*. Toronto: University of Toronto Press.

Withorn, A. (1998) 'Fulfilling Fears and Fantasies: The Role of Welfare in Right-Wing Social Thought and Strategy'. In A. Ansell (ed.) *Reweaving the Right*. Boston: Westview.

Wolfe, A. and Klausen, J. (2000) 'Other People'. *Prospect*, December.

Yeates, N. (2001) *Globalization and Social Policy*. London: Sage.

Yeates, N. (forthcoming) 'Nannies, Nurses and Nuns: Broadening the Scope of Global Care Chain Analysis'. *Feminist Review*.

Yuval-Davis, N. (1997) *Gender and Nation*. London: Sage.

Zeitlin, J. and Trubeck, D. (eds) (2003) *Governing Work and Welfare in a New Economy: European and American Experiments*. Oxford: Oxford University Press.

Index

Abel, C., 96
Abrahamson, P., 98
academic work, 157, 159
    politics and, 149–51, 157–9
    study of welfare states, 153–4
Africa, neo-liberalism in, 96–7
African-Americans, exclusion from social
    insurance programmes, 44
Aid to Dependent Children (ADC), 45
Aid to Families with Dependent Children
    (AFDC), 22, 23
alliances, in neo-liberalism, 94, 102, 103
Amenta, E., 44
Andersen, J.G., 53–4
anthropology, 34, 35, 37, 153
anti-elitism, 145–6
anti-welfarism, 61, 127
Appadurai, A., 83, 85
articulated ensembles, 37–8, 55–6, 148
articulation, 37–8, 39–40
Aslama, M., 90
assistance, 22, 23, 44, 45
asylum-seekers, 67, 68, 69
attachment, 154–5
audiences, for performance of states, 136,
    137, 142–3
audit, 131, 135, 137
autonomy, 110
    conditional, 119
    managerial, 124, 131

Bauman, Z., 69
Beck, U., 74
Beyeler, M., 75, 80
biology, 58
    difference and, 55–6, 63–4
Blair, Tony, 23–4, 132, 145

Blunkett, David, 145
borders, 34, 82
    permeability of, 81–2, 83
Bouckaert, G., 124
Bourdieu, P., 61
Brah, A., 60
breadwinner models, 78
bricolage, 39
Brodkin, K., 43
Brown, W., 150, 154

capital, 73, 75
    global, 73, 81, 86
    neo-liberalism and, 89
    state and, 76
    welfare, 26
capitalism, 81, 86
    Asian model, 97
    neo-liberalism and, 90–1
care work, 78, 79, 121–2
casualization of labour market, 121
centralism, 133, 144
Charity Organization Society, 49
children, 55, 56
Christian democracy, 97–8
citizenship, 29, 93, 152
    New Labour and, 67–8, 69
    transnational, 80
    welfare 129–30
civil rights, 45
class, 46, 49, 53
    culture and, 37
Cloward, R., 45
collaboration, 119, 139
collectivism, 93
collusion, 110
    in evaluation, 139–40

colonial governance, 114
commitments
    to nation, 29
    to welfare state, 146, 154
common sense, 38, 40, 135, 156, 157
    New Labour and, 145
Communist bloc, 86, 97
community empowerment, 124
comparative social policy, 6–7, 18, 20
competition, 74, 87, 119, 131, 138
conflict, 114–15
conjunctural analysis, 5, 25–6, 29, 146
Conservative Party 131, 132 see also public
    services; Thatcher, Margaret
constructivism, 135
consumerism, 129–30, 144
consumers of welfare services, 4, 90, 113,
    119, 129–30
contracting out, 109, 119, 121
control, 21, 49
Cooper, D., 114–15, 116, 121, 123
Corvellec, H., 138
criminal justice, 21
crises, 89–90, 128
cultural diversity, 57
cultural studies, 2, 5, 18, 29, 37, 50–1, 153
culture, 31, 32–3
    difference and, 32, 33–4, 64–5
    European, 85
    nation and, 32–3, 35–6, 41–3, 48–51
    as practice, 39–40
    as property, 34–5, 41
    relations between, 35
cynicism, 143, 145–6, 156

Daly, M., 20, 107, 111
Dean, H., 29
Dean, M., 113
decentralization, 117, 118
decision-making, 133
decommodification, 75, 122
deconstruction of welfare state, 19–21, 50
Dench, G., 68
development, normative model, 101–2
di Leonardi, M., 32
dialogism, 40
difference, 53, 60, 129
    biology and, 55–6, 63–4
    culture and, 32, 33–4, 57, 64–5
    economy and, 62–3
differentiation, 87
disability, 55, 59, 60
discursive practice, 39
dispersal of state, 116–20, 123–4, 128–9, 133
diversity of welfare states, 18
domination, 157–8

domination, cont.
    culture and, 35
doubt, 125, 134, 143–6
Dunleavy, P., 119

Eagleton, T., 32
East Asia, neo-liberalism in, 97
Eastern Europe, neo-liberalism in, 97
economics, 128
    and inequality, 62–3
    politics and, 72–4, 90, 105
education, targets and testing in, 140
efficiency, 90, 122, 128
Eley, G., 41, 42–3
employment effects, 17 see also labour mar-
    kets; work
English language, 103
Esping-Anderson, G., 26, 74, 75, 98
ethnicity, 155
Europe, 8, 85–6
    spending on social protection in EU, 16–17
evaluation, 131–40
    and production of success, 140–1, 144
evidence-based policy, 131, 132, 133
exclusion, 42, 60, 69

family, 42, 58–9, 77–9, 80 see also private realm
    neo-liberalism and, 91
    New Labour and, 66, 78
feminism, 48, 58, 76–7, 78
Ferguson, J., 35
fiscal crisis of the state, 128
flexibility, 80, 87, 92, 122
Flynn, N., 117
Foucault, M., 70, 154
Frank, T., 89, 90, 125, 143
freedom, 89
    of choice, 92

Garland, D., 103
gender differences, 55, 58, 63
gender relations, 77–8
genetics, and difference, 63
geography, 55, 64
Gilbert, N., 101
Gilens, M., 45–6
Gledhill, J., 96
globalization, 9, 72, 99, 127
    apocalyptic theories, 72–4
    as external force, 80–1
    institutional theories, 72, 74–5, 80
    nation-state and, 73–4, 80–6
    neo-liberal, 86–7, 88, 94, 98–100
    in USA, 102, 103
Gordon, L., 45
Gough, I., 73

governance, 107–11
    instability of, 123–5
    liberal, 112–14
    new, 117–20, 125
government, 108, 110 *see also* state/s
governmentalities, 70, 114–16
    poststructuralism and, 111–14
Gramsci, A., 25, 70, 89, 93, 154
Gupta, A., 8, 35, 83–4, 85

Hall, S., 5, 159
Hansen, T.B., 29, 136
Harris, P., 112
Harrison, S., 134
hegemony, 48, 70
    neo-liberal, 93, 102
Hesse, B., 33
hierarchies, 108, 109
history, 65, 153
Hochschild, A., 79
Holland, D., 39, 40, 70, 124
home-working, 92
homogenization, 87, 155
Hondagneu-Soleto, P., 79
households, 77, 78
    formation of, 53, 55, 80
Huber, E., 17, 24
Hudson, R., 87
Humphrey, J., 139

ideology, 48
imaginary, political-cultural, welfare state as,
    19–20, 97, 106, 148
immigration, 68, 69 *see also* migration
income transfer programmes, 20
individualism, 62–3
inequality
    economic, 62–3
    historicizing, 65
    social, 54–5, 60, 61
information, 133, 134
inspection, 131, 134
instability, 25–9, 123–5, 148
institutional racism, 57
institutions
    supranational, 81, 86, 136
    welfare, 56

Jenkin, Patrick, 58–9
Jensen, P.H., 53–4
Jessop, B., 110, 115
Joint Reviews, 139

Keesbergen, K. von, 15–16, 74
King, D., 103
Kingfisher, C., 91–2, 94, 99

Klausen, J., 68
Kofman, E., 79
Kooiman, J., 108

labour markets, 53–4, 55 *see also* work
Latin America, neo-liberalism in, 95–6
Lave, J., 39, 40, 70, 124
Leach, B., 92
Lewis, C., 96
Lewis, G., 41, 57, 61, 64, 69
Li, T., 70
liberalism, 112–13 *see also* neo-liberalism
lone mothers, 92
    attacks on, 46–7
Lund, F., 96–7

management, universalization of, 121
managerialism, 117, 128–9, 131 *see also* new
    public management
managers, 124, 131, 138
Mandelson, Peter, 68
market/s, 15, 73, 94, 108
    politics and, 90
    in public services, 109–10, 127–8, 137
    state and, 75–80
market liberalism, 96
market populism, 89, 90, 127–8
marriage, 55
Marshall, T.H., 5
Marx, K., 36
Marxism, 48, 49, 76
Massey, D., 101
Mayhew, H., 32
meanings, 37–8, 39
measurement, 134, 135
media, reporting of evaluation of public
    services, 142
Melrose, M., 29
meta-governance, 115
migrant workers, 54, 79, 82, 121
migration, 54, 64, 67–8, 69, 155
Miller, D., 134
Mink, G., 45
minority ethnic communities, 33, 64–5
mobility, transnational, 79–80, 82, 155, 156
modernization, 132–3, 145, 154
moral fitness, 22, 45
Morris, M., 93
multiculturalism, 33, 57, 68–9

nation/s, 27–8, 29, 40
    culture and, 41–3
    identity and, 42
    racialized, 155
    social policy, 42, 82–3, 84
    welfare states and, 148, 152, 153, 156

nation-states, 26, 27–8, 108, 148
    effect of globalization, 73–4, 80–6
    end of, 83–5
national culture, 35–6
national formations, 40–4
National Health Service, 29
    changes in work processes, 95, 120–1
    privatization of, 122–3
national popular, 27–8, 43, 47–8, 93, 94–8, 99
nationalism, 41
neo-liberalism, 9, 75–6, 88–94
    in alliances, 94
    in Anglophone countries, 94–5, 103–4
    and globalization, 88, 94, 86–7, 94, 98–100
    and individualism, 62–3
    and national popular, 94–8, 99
    and private realm, 70, 91–2
    social democratic view, 75
    and state reform, 117–20
    and transnational popular, 98–100
    in USA, 95, 100–5
    and welfare, 92–3, 127–8, 130
networks, 94, 108, 109–10
New Deal (UK), 67, 69, 95
New Deal (USA), 22, 44
New Labour, 24, 61, 95, 104, 144–6
    constant innovation, 145
    and family, 66, 78
    and public realm, 132
    and public services, 108–9, 119, 132–4
    and social, 65–71
    and work, 66–7, 95, 120
new public management, 117–20, 124, 125
New Right, 21–2, 45–6, 61
new social movements, 56–7, 59–60
Newman, J., 107, 111, 119, 120, 123

O'Malley, P., 113
Ong, A., 79–80, 101
Ooeschot, W. von, 98
organization studies, 34
organizations, 121, 122, 137
    evaluation of, 138–9, 142
'other', culture and, 32, 35, 64

partnership, 119
Paton, R., 138
Peck, J., 14, 15, 23, 46, 100–1, 103, 120
performance, 126–31
    evaluation of, 131–4, 135
    management of, 133–4, 138
    of states, 136–40
    success in, 140–1
Personal Responsibility and Work
    Opportunities Reconciliation Act (USA),
    21, 22–3, 46–7

Peters, G., 108, 124
Pierson, P., 98
Piven, F.F., 45
place, race and, 64
politics, 133
    academic work and, 149–51, 157–9
    market and, 90
    theory and, 150
politics of welfare, 155–6
    in United Kingdom, 23–4
    in United States of America, 21–3, 45–7
Pollitt, C., 124, 126–7
polysemy, 38
'poor people's movements', 45, 47
post-Fordism, 14, 76
postcolonialism, 48, 57, 67, 84, 86
poststructuralism, 48, 111–14
poverty, 55
    representations of, 45–6
power, 157–8
practice, 39–40
private realm, 67, 76–7, 87 see also family;
    public/private realms, blurring of boundaries
    neo-liberalism and, 70, 91–2
private sector, 17, 125
privatization, 67, 91, 117, 118, 121, 122–3, 137
professionalism, 60, 121
public choice theory, 127–8
public expenditure, on social protection, 16–17
public/private realms, blurring of boundaries,
    53, 67, 77, 91, 121–2, 125
public realm, 69–70, 91, 130, 132
public services, 122, 130
    changing work processes, 120–3
    evaluation of, 133, 137, 141–2
    horizontal relations, 119, 138
    marketization of, 109–10, 127–8, 137
    new public management and, 118–19
    vertical relations, 118–19, 137–8

Quadagno, J., 44–5

race, 155
    difference and, 63, 64
    place and, 64
racial formations, 44–7
radical deviancy, 49
redistribution, 55
reform of welfare states, 11, 23–4, 60–1
resistance, 157, 158–9
responsibility, 69
Rhodes, R., 108
Riley, D., 64
Rose, N., 111–12, 113
Ross, A., 33

Sales, R., 79
Sassen, S., 81, 84
scepticism, 133–4, 143, 145–6, 156–7
Schmidt, V., 85–6
Schram, S., 141, 142
scrutiny agencies, 131, 141
service sector, 122
sexuality, 59, 60
Shore, C., 37
signifying practice, 39
Smith, N., 102
social, 55, 111
    conceptions of, 55
    New Labour and, 65–71
social construction, 48, 135
    welfare state as, 19
social democracy, 75, 95, 97–8, 109, 155–6
social protection, 16
social security, 22, 23, 44
sociology, 2
solidarities, 29, 68, 93, 97–8, 155–6
Soss, J., 141, 142
South Africa, neo-liberalism in, 96–7
standards, 132
state/s, 9–10, 17–18, 21, 25, 27, 29 see also
    nation-states; welfare state/s
    changing, 106–7
    demands on, 136
    dispersal of, 116–20, 123–4, 128–9, 133
    governance and, 110–11, 115–16, 118
    performing like states, 136–40
    reform of, 117–20, 128–9
statework, 120–3
Stedman-Jones, G., 49
Stein, J.G., 128
Steinmetz, G., 48
Stephens, J.D., 17, 24
Stepputat, F., 29, 136
Stoker, G., 108
subordination, 60
success, 140–2
Summa, H., 126–7
Suny, R., 41, 42–3
supranational institutions, 81, 86, 136
Susser, I., 36, 54
Sykes, R., 20

targets, 140, 141
Taylor-Gooby, P., 74, 83, 87
testing, in education, 140
Thatcher, Margaret/Thatcherism, 62, 66,
    130, 132, 133
theory, 5, 150
'Third Way', 61, 95, 109, 129
Titmuss, R., 19
tolerance, 68
traditional societies, 34–5
transnationalism, 80, 86

underclass, 23, 46
unemployment, 38
United Kingdom, 52, 108 see also New Labour
    British culture, 35
    and Europe, 104
    as multinational nation, 82
    neo-liberalism in, 95, 103–5
    post-war social settlement, 54–62
    public service reform, 131–4, 137
    relations with United States, 103–4
    welfare discourse, 23–4, 42
United States of America
    exceptionalism, 100–5
    neo-liberalism in, 95, 100–5
    politics of welfare, 21–3, 44–7
    workfare, 95
universalism, 14, 57, 129
universities, 150–1

voluntary sector, 17, 122

Wacquant, L., 99, 104–5
Washington Consensus, 96
Wedel, J., 110, 139
welfare, 18–20, 26–7, 156
    deconstruction of, 19–21, 50
    end of, 21–5
welfare state/s, 26, 82, 152–3
    change in, 11, 12–15, 23–4, 83
    commitment to, 154–5
    crisis of, 52–3, 56, 60–1
    cultural turn, 47–51, 154
    end of, 15–18
    external pressure, internal adaptation
        model, 81, 83
    meaning of, 18, 19–21, 24, 27
    and nation-states, 26, 27
    nations and, 29, 42, 43
    neo-liberalism and, 92–3, 127–8, 130
    as political-cultural imaginary, 19–20, 106, 148
    settlements, 25, 29
    study of, 153–4
West, 8, 114
Williams, A.M., 87
Williams, F., 59
Williams, R., 20, 26, 29
Wolfe, A., 68
women, 92
    in labour market, 17, 78, 121
    work, 42, 120
    neo-liberalism and, 90–1
    New Labour and, 66–7, 95
    in public services, 60, 120–3
workfare, 14–15, 46, 95, 101
Wright, S., 37

Yeates, N., 73, 76, 82